T0194919

I Tell Ya—
It's All
but Lies

Shannon Paddy O'Malley

Illustrated by: Ange-Lyne Patenaude

authorHOUSE®

AuthorHouse™
1663 Liberty Drive
Bloomington, IN 47403
www.authorhouse.com
Phone: 1 (800) 839-8640

© *2019 Shannon Paddy O'Malley. All rights reserved.*

*No part of this book may be reproduced, stored in a retrieval system, or
transmitted by any means without the written permission of the author.*

Published by AuthorHouse 08/02/2019

ISBN: 978-1-7283-2014-4 (sc)
ISBN: 978-1-7283-2013-7 (e)

Print information available on the last page.

*Any people depicted in stock imagery provided by Getty Images are models,
and such images are being used for illustrative purposes only.
Certain stock imagery* © *Getty Images.*

This book is printed on acid-free paper.

*Because of the dynamic nature of the Internet, any web addresses or
links contained in this book may have changed since publication and
may no longer be valid. The views expressed in this work are solely those
of the author and do not necessarily reflect the views of the publisher,
and the publisher hereby disclaims any responsibility for them.*

So... This Is the Gist of Things

Right from the very beginning, I always said, "I'm going to write a book someday because there is no way in hell that anybody is ever going to believe the fucking shit that we got away with." When I first started thinking about writing this memoir, chronicle, or biography, I wanted to be as truthful as possible. But that went out the window as each chapter developed. It wasn't that I wanted to write a tell-all; I just wanted everyone to know some of the funny shit that had happened over the years—whether it was considered, calculated, planned, or just fell into place. Most of the time, you just had to painstakingly set the wheels in motion. I want to show how people can be Tricked, Influenced, or Manipulated—TIM for short. Or as I say, sometimes all you needed was an idea, a good plan, or a planted seed and, of course, a great poker face.

I wasn't sure how I was going to start it or finish it. Most, if not all, of the stories consisted of a lot of drinking; I mean heavy drinking. See, I'm an alcoholic. Hell, we were all alcoholics back then. I have probably forgotten or can't remember most everything that we pulled off. Funny thing—as each one of the chapters was written, something new would be remembered or revealed, and so on. The problem is, as I said, these things all happened a very long time ago. So, as each story was written, as I remembered it; I found that some of the stories intertwined with the next. Or worse, sometimes I would even get the characters all mixed up. Remember, you can't write down what you can't remember. I tried to be as truthful and as accurate as possible. However, as I wrote; I would get more distracted and sidetracked with my imagination and all of my fantasies. Sometimes I would have to check with the person I was writing about just to help fill in some of the blanks. It was amazing how they could fill in almost every detail and aspect that had transpired. How could they remember every little *fucking* detail?

The other thing that became apparent as each story was written; was that twenty years ago, we were not all that politically correct. It's not that we were racists, it's just that we seemed to make a lot of jokes about minorities back then. We did a lot of name-calling back then towards *"those people."* Were we all that prejudiced against anyone? No, I don't think we were, but that was back then. Hopefully I think we have all learned to be smarter.

It was amazing, with all the stuff that was done, pulled, or planned, that no one really got hurt, or let's say seriously, besides Buddy. And after saying the above statement, it was also amazing that no one went to jail; well, besides Buddy. You will learn more about Buddy and the rest of the crew as you read these stories. See, Buddy was his own worst enemy, but I'm getting a little ahead of myself here.

You'll find out more as the stories unfold. Or as some would say, *"I tell ya, it's all but lies."*

CHAPTER 1

The Redneckishest Three

It was the three of us to start. There was me; my twin brother, Johnny; and of course, Buddy. Johnny and I weren't really twins, but with the way we acted when we got together, you would think that we were just that. As I say, we were the original three. We were the Three Amigos, the Three Musketeers, or, as I liked to call us, the Redneckishest Three. If any one of us—or, for that matter, anyone else—was ever down and out or needed help, we were there for one another. But only after we had embarrassed, ridiculed, made fun of, and of course stomped all over their sorry ass. We all knew it, we all expected it, so we all accepted it.

My name is Shannon. That's right. I have a girl's name. It could have been worse. Mom could have named me George. See, I have two brothers who were named George. But that will be another story for a later time.

Before I was born, Mom was convinced that I was going to be a girl. She did all the old wives' tale gimmicks and methods that could tell the sex of the baby, from hanging low and craving sweets to having a larger left breast and the old tried-and-true method of a pendant swinging in a circle. Back then, how could you argue with such science? I was to be born a girl; everything pointed toward me being a girl. There should have been no argument. So, looking back, I guess that was my first big prank, and I didn't even know it. She named me Shannon anyways. Thinking about it now, was the joke on me? See, Mom had a great sense of humor. That is where I got it from. Or, I should say, that is where me and all my siblings got it from.

Besides having a girl's name, I was born on St. Patrick's Day, a real drunk's birthday. It's like Santa Claus being born on Christmas, the Easter Bunny being born on Easter, or Don Juan being born on Valentine's Day.

I remember one time when I phoned Mom up to see if she could sew my pants. They were my lucky pants. I told her that the club championship was the following Saturday. I was in the final group and four strokes down. If I had a chance on winning that year, I would need to wear my lucky pants. And maybe play some great golf. See, my lucky pants had holes inside the two front pockets. I told her; I had been losing a lot of money from them. I'm not sure how much money I lost, but I lost balls, tees, ball markers—you name it. I think I might have lost a few phone numbers as well—wink, wink, nod, nod! I did say that they were my lucky pants. (Hey, Jennifer, if you are reading this, phone me. I do love you.) They were not only my lucky pants but also my favorite. They were my go-to pants.

Anyways, Mom said, "Drop them off, and I will have them ready for Saturday." Earlier in the week, I phoned her every day to see if my pants were ready. She always said that she had gotten busy each day but not to worry because they would be done by Saturday morning. She already had looked at them and knew it was not going to be a big job.

One thing led to another, and I had forgotten all about the pants until I was getting dressed on Saturday morning. I gave her a quick call to see if she had finished my pants. She had, so I told her that I was running a little late and would be right over to make a quick change. In my mind, I couldn't lose because I would have my lucky pants on.

When I arrived at the course, I saw my three combatants heading over towards the first tee. Over the years, I had never gone to the driving range or putting green to practice. Today was no different, even if this was an important match. I grabbed a couple of beers and rushed over to the first tee just in time to not get disqualified for missing the tee time. They were worried now. It was windy, it was cold, it was raining, and they saw that I had my lucky pants on. It was just the way I liked it. I was a mudder; I loved to play in the rain, the mud, and anything else that Mother Nature could throw at me. They didn't call me a mudderfucker for nothing.

See, I had shot some of my best rounds in the pouring rain. When it was going to be nasty outside, like a beautiful, blistery, cold day in Scotland—rain coming down sideways with forty-mile-per-hour winds—I not only would put my lucky pants on but would also put on my heavy long johns for warmth. But the secret was I not only had long johns on but also wore my pair of sheer pantyhose for extra protection. It not only made me feel all fuzzy and warm but was so silky smooth that it made me feel all *sexy* and aroused. I always played my best when I was aroused. Doesn't everyone?

It's funny when you are on the first tee and your golfing buddies are all wondering if you are wearing your secret, sexy weapon. They finally would realize that they just wouldn't have a chance today; when you lift your pant leg to reveal their downfall.

"It's not fair!" someone would always scream in front of the puzzled starter. "It's not wet or cold enough for you to be wearing your secret weapon! Not today!"

On one particular round, I was dressed to win. It was just above freezing, with a two-club wind, and about every other hole, the sky opened up and we had a torrential downpour. Most greens couldn't handle that much water, so portions of the greens were underwater.

I had just birdied the sixteenth, so all I had to do was par out for a sixty-nine. I had shot a sixty-nine before, so this would tie my best round ever at the Thousand Islands Golf Club. My buddies had all quit playing around hole fourteen. I wouldn't let them go into the clubhouse to get dry because I wanted to finish this round, no matter what. I bribed them into staying by saying they could drink all my beer.

To make a long story short, I birdied seventeen. Now I got to thinking, *I can shoot my best round ever. And in these conditions. Wow!* Hole eighteen was a long par five, with a pond in front, guarding the green. And it was playing against the wind. That hole always played against the wind.

I had to hit three perfect three-woods to get to the green today, just to have a chance of saving par. She was playing long and tough. My three-wood approach landed about three feet short of the green. I didn't make the green, but at least I was over the water. I just had to chip it close and one-putt, and then I would have my sixty-eight.

I was looking for a safe spot to chip it to, but there were puddles around the pin. I picked a spot, and as soon as the ball hit the green, water started to rooster-tail up from behind the ball. I knew it was going to be short; a puddle about ten feet from the cup devoured my ball. I tried to take relief from the casual water. But there was no dry route to the hole. I decided to chip it over the puddles. That was my best bet.

The chip was almost perfect as it lipped out. I got my bogey six for a sixty-nine. A great bogey, if there is such a thing. I would take it any day of the week.

One time I talked Buddy into wearing his wife's pantyhose. He just wanted to see what all the fuss was about and if it could help his own game out. We were on the first tee and had our shirts pulled up to reveal our pantyhose. The thing is—women must be built differently, because it seemed that they had a higher waistline than most men. I have yet to find a pair that I don't use as a control top. We had never felt so slim as we all compared the sheerness and sexiness of the hosiery. "What's with this one-size-fits-all bullshit?" we asked as we raised Buddy's shirt even more to reveal that his wife's control top reached up to under his armpits. He never looked so good.

But Buddy was way too busy rubbing all that silky goodness from Marilyn's control top all day long to notice. I had to keep yelling at him, "Will you quit playing with it? You are going to go blind."

What did he do? He shot a pretty good score that day. As Buddy explained, "I wasn't thinking about my round. All I wanted to do was get the round over with so I could get home to my Marilyn."

He never did wear another pair of her pantyhose—not that I know of. Anyway, as Buddy said, "When she found out that I had worn her best pair and had ruined them, she called me everything but a white man. She basically ripped me a new asshole—not only a new asshole but an asshole that was massive."

I could see it all now: Marilyn giving Buddy complete shit. "What in *fuck* were you thinking?"

"But—"

"But nothing. You stretched them all out. Look at them. You shouldn't have to wear suspenders to hold them up. I'll never be able to wear them again, I tell you."

"But Shannon made …"

"But Shannon nothing. You have ruined them. Look at them. Are you going fucking queer on me?"

"Noooooooo … Neverrrrrrrrrr."

"Then why in fuck are you wearing fucking girlie clothes?"

"I wore them to keep warm. He told me that they make him feel all warm and fuzzy."

"Warm and fuzzy. And is this a skid mark? You've got to be kidding me."

"Skid mark? I didn't do that."

"Ohhhhhh, are you saying that I did that?"

"Noooooooo … That fucking Shannon, I'm going to kill him."

"Why are you blaming Shannon?"

"Okay, I guess maybe it must have been me."

"And look at this hole you fucking put in them. I suppose Shannon did that also?"

"No, that was all me. When I was slipping them on, I accidentally put my big toe through the end of them. I guess I should have cut my toenails before …"

"Toenails? They're not toenails. They're fucking hooks. You could poke someone's eye out with those curled-up fuckers."

"But Shannon suggests that maybe next time I should just borrow your stockings, because he believes that your control top was cutting off my circulation."

"Cutting offffffff? Are you fucking kidding me? I'll fucking cut something off."

"He was thinking about that good pair of fishnet stockings you have."

"Like fuck. Look into my eyes. Now focus. You are not to touch my stuff again. I don't care what he says."

"But he told me that it would improve my golf game."

"Improve your game? When are you not going to be so stupid? If he told you to jump off a bridge, would you?"

"No. He would never tell me to …"

"When, in the fuck are you going to start thinking for yourself?"

"Uh, honey, I'm so sorry. I'll never, ever …"

"That's right. You'll never …"

Then, I'm sure, Buddy would apologize and ask for forgiveness, something like this: "I'm so sorry. Will you ever forgive me? How could I have been so wrong? Please, please forgive me. How could I have been so stupid? You are right, and I am wrong. It will never, ever happen again. And I love you to the moon and back." It was always a great day when Buddy was asking for forgiveness.

So, to get back to my story of Mom and my lucky pants. We were all standing there on the first tee waiting for the group ahead to clear. We were complaining about the weather, talking about the new *sexy* bartender, and of course, making a few bets. To see who was going to hit first, we usually threw a tee up in the air; and when it landed on the ground, whoever it was pointing at would have the honors. I went to reach into my pocket for a tee to throw in the air like I had done a thousand times before. But I couldn't; I had no front pockets. Mom had sewn the tops of my pockets shut. Both of them! "What the fuck?" I told myself. I smiled and thought, *she got me good, real good*. I told my story to the rest of my foursome about my lucky pants having holes in the front pockets, losing money, and Mom sewing them up tight. They all had a good laugh.

That day I remember I got soaked and covered in mud from head to toe, but my competition did also. The only difference was they all shot in the eighties and nineties, whereas I shot a seventy-six and won the club championship by four. Besides the bragging rights, I also got a trophy. Now you have to understand, this was no little trophy. This was huge! It was a life-size replica of a Canada goose. It was almost two and a half feet long by over two feet tall. The original trophy from the early 1900s went missing a long time ago. I'm thinking that a champion had forgotten to return it one year, just as I did. It was heavy; it weighed almost twenty pounds. I think it was carved out of oak instead of the usual pine. My good friend Dicky Small, who was also a member, had carved it for the club. When he was close to being finished, I joked that he should hollow it out somewhat to bring the weight down; as I told him, I didn't think I was strong enough to carry it around over my head. All he answered with was, "It's for display on a mantel." And then he added, "First you have to win it." You have to understand that he was also shooting for the club championship that day. Now I couldn't let him win his own trophy that day, could I? He came in a close second.

That afternoon on my way home, I stopped by Mom's to show her the trophy that I had won and to give her bloody hell. I told her that she had ruined my lucky pants. What good were they now if they didn't have any front pockets? I also asked her why in hell she had sewn the front pockets closed.

She answered with, "I don't see the problem here; you told me to fix them. Did you win? Did you win some money? Hmm. I guess you won't be losing any more money out of those front pockets of yours ever again."

I told her that she was right and that everyone had a real good chuckle over it at the clubhouse. I gave her the trophy, as she was the one who deserved it. She displayed it proudly right up on her mantel, right behind one of Johnny's runner-up ribbons for lawn bowling. She called it her bragging shelf. So when all of her lady friends would come over to play cards, she was sure to let them all know how good a golfer she was. But first, I'm sure she let them all know that lawn bowling was her favorite sport since she was a little girl.

My twin brother Johnny was the oldest in the family. Well, not really, we really weren't twins, but the way we acted and carried on, you sure would think we were. He was better looking and the smarter one of us, so he told me and everyone else for that matter, but I'm not quite sure of that. He even had Mom on his side. I think only because he was her favorite. "The day I was born was Mom's best day of her life," he would brag.

"No, Johnny, it was the longest day of her life," I'd shoot back. See, she was in labor for more than twelve hours, and he was born on the longest day of the year, the summer solstice, June 21. He was her firstborn. You know, you just got to love your firstborn. He had twenty-two more years to work at it than me. But I was the bigger one of us, and everyone could see it. After all, I was the biggest O'Malley. We were twins, as we would tell everyone. He was only born a few minutes before me. I think it was more like a few million minutes. You do the math.

I was always trying to keep up with him, trying to fill his shoes. He would always say, "Hey, Kid; don't worry, you're still in training." When it came to pranks, we were inseparable. When one of us would come up with something, then the other would push it to the limit. See, we were brothers, and we were twins; we would do anything for each other.

Then there was Buddy; he was a living version of an animated cartoon caricature. Buddy was a short little man, five foot two, I think. He must have been of Mexican descent; because right from the very beginning, we called him our little Mexican, or Pedro for short. Buddy was probably one of the funniest guys that I knew; he always had a joke to tell, especially if there was a nationality or minority to make fun of. He could butcher any drawl and any accent with the best of them. Let's put it this way: he was the one who wasn't very politically correct most of the time. But back then, we did not know what that meant. Let's say he was a little rough around the edges, especially in the early years. But if you really knew him deep down, he was one of the nicest, kindest, sincerest, and maybe one of the tallest, persons you would ever meet. Not really; he was still short. Johnny and I liked to keep Buddy around; that way we ganged up on him and not each other. He was our little safety net. Most days he just didn't have a chance. It was always two against one. He was always fair game, almost open season if you will. Although Johnny and I played many a trick on each other, we always had each other's back. Buddy was the one always looking over his shoulder. He never knew when it was coming or what was coming. He was like that big two-bit prizefighter who was getting clobbered with all those left hooks; he would be begging for some rights. He would keep an eye on one of us O'Malley's, and *bam*; the other O'Malley would swoop in. Sometimes for days, Buddy would expect something was coming, something big. And when it didn't come, he would feel neglected, rejected, or just left out; it was like he had missed out on something. You add beer and rum to this mix, and we could do anything. That was the three of us. We were the Three Musketeers, the ones who didn't give a fuck.

CHAPTER 2

The Three Amigos and the Rest of the Crew

The other thing that you should know about me is that I was a sex maniac, or as some would say, a perv. I believe those words are little harsh and are not needed. Why do we have to put a label on everything? Just because I love sex, why do you have to call me a perv? I love alcohol; does that make me an alcoholic? I guess it does in a way. But if you can control your addictions, I would argue that you are not an alcoholic or a perv. So I will let you decide after you have read my book of lies.

Over the years, I wasn't sure what it was, and I sure as hell didn't want it to end either. Was it a form of ESPN (extrasensory sexual perception needed) or what? It seemed that every time I was going to get lucky, loud music would start to play in my head. Although on a few occasions, it was simply the music playing in the background that would either change or simply just get louder. That was an indication for me to get ready; I was going to get laid, whether I wanted to or not. One song that played in my head on more than one occasion was Kim Mitchell's "Lager & Ale," with its chorus of "ready, willing, and able." That could be the soundtrack for my life. You may ask, was I a sex maniac? No, I say; I just loved sex. Didn't everyone?

Most of the time, it was rock and roll that would start to play, but on occasion, other types of music started to creep in. Nothing wrong with a different beat or rhythm, I say. Basically, the sexual encounter would match the song or vice versa. So in a way, I'm sure I did have some kind of ESPN. I was sure as hell not going to turn down sex because I didn't like the music playing in my head. But after thinking about it, if Lawrence Welk was playing, would I, or even could I, walk away? "Cissy and Bobby, take it away … and ah one, and ah two" Can you have sex to the polka? Sure you can. It's not like I can change the channel on the radio station; even if I could, would I? Would it change the outlook of my sexual encounter? Did I really want to take the chance of losing out on one of my most favorite things to do in life?

Maybe the first time that I recognized that I might have a problem was when I was in an elevator going down. I was on about the twelfth floor, and the worst elevator music was playing in the background. Abruptly, the music stopped playing, and it sounded like someone was searching for the next great radio station. Suddenly the dial stopped on one of my longtime favorites, "Going Down/Love in an Elevator" by Aerosmith. The music not only changed, but it became very loud. Over time, I became aware that the louder the music, the more intense the sexual encounter was going to be. It brought a big smile to my face—not only because I loved Steven Tyler; but I knew what was about to happen next. I was a bit confused, though; how was I ever going to have sex in such a short period of time? It was like my sixth sense kicked in, and it was going to take control of me. In the past, I had on occasion tried to fight it, but I always found out that it was a losing battle. So, I just stopped fighting it.

Sometimes when I heard the music, sex didn't always happen right away. I could be listening to the music in my head, and suddenly, the music would abruptly end. That just meant that the sex would happen in the future—the near future, I hoped. I just might have to wait a little longer to get off.

A lot of times I would walk into a bar, and suddenly, a song would start screaming in my head. I would turn my head slightly—just to maybe get a glance of the new lucky combatant? Abruptly the song would change to another song. And when I would change my focus back to the original candidate, the music would also change back. I have seen me walk over to a table of five girls, and as I made small talk with each one of them, I would have five different songs all jumping back and forth, matching the ladies whom I was talking to. Some would say that would be a little confusing, trying to keep everyone straight. Not me! That was the way that my sixth sense would organize them all. The rock and roll girls right up front of me, country over there, and the younger pop over there. And so on, till everyone was itemized and categorized. You might ask, "Did you ever have multiple songs playing at the same time?" Of course I did, but that will be some more stories for later on.

Unlike my other senses, I didn't have to actually see it, taste it, or even touch it. But lately, sometimes when the music starts to play, I have been starting to smell it. Are my senses evolving and taking control? Maybe, but I do not know, because as I say, I am not going to fight it. "What does sex smell like?" you may ask. Well, it's unexplainable; it's a combination of vanilla and chocolate chip cookies. That, my friends, is what an orgasm smells like—heaven.

Back to the elevator. I had a big old smile on my face, and the blood started pumping to other parts of my extremities, which in turn triggered a bigger smile on my face. Like I said, I was going down in this elevator; and the bad music in the elevator had changed to loud rock and roll. Thank God! The lights dimmed, so I knew before I got to the bottom floor, there was going to be a female who had to get on sooner or later. And from the loudness of the music, I had to think she was going to be beautiful and that the sex was going to be intense and passionate.

By the time I got down to the second floor, I was starting to feel a little dejected, when suddenly, the elevator stopped, and the door slid open to reveal a young, beautiful girl about to step in. Her daring, new, pageboy haircut suited her to the max. I just loved her bright-red hair color. It was almost too vivid and glossy to be real. But I was thinking I had to find out if the carpet matched the drapes. She was a mere five foot four inches tall. Weight was about 110 pounds, almost too skinny for my liking. But remember she was the one who was stepping into my fantasy, or was I stepping into hers? She was wearing a short, tight-fitting dress, which was white with a circular pattern of brightly colored flowers. At the time I was thinking, how did she ever get that little size-four dress on that size-six body of hers? I just hoped that it was not going to be that difficult to remove.

"Going down?" I said to her as we made first eye contact.

"Oh no, I'm sorry; I'm going up to the seventeenth floor," she said with a smile as she stepped in, all the while trying to locate her floor's button.

"Wow, me too," I answered quickly, as I reached over to help her find her floor that she was looking for.

"Thanks. Oh, is that right?" she said, trying to start a conversation. "Wow, is this ever-great music? I just love Steven Tyler and Joe Perry."

"You can hear this?" I asked. I was still trying to figure out if she had the same ESPN addiction that I did.

"Yes, can't you? Aerosmith is just the greatest band ever," she added as she gave me a discerning look. "I know it's only rock and roll, but I just love it. It's what gets me off." There would be many musical elevator rides before it dawned on me what she actually meant by that statement.

The next thing I knew, we were still going up, and she was going down. Wow! The elevator must have been moving too quickly for her liking because, without missing a stroke, she reached over and pushed the off button to the elevator. It was like she knew exactly where that off button was without even looking. I was figuring she might have done this a few times before. What skill. A few moments later, we were getting dressed and readjusting our apparel when the emergency alarm went off.

"Don't worry. The elevator will start to move again after the alarm goes off for the second time," she mumbled as she reached over and skillfully turned it off.

"I see you have done this a few times before?"

"Yes, yes, I have," she answered quickly as the alarm went off for the second time. "Haven't you?"

Just as she said would happen, the elevator jerked forward as it started to move toward her selected floor. By this time, I must have been really weak at the knees, because the elevator's floor seemed to be swaying back and forth, and it also seemed to be moving a lot faster than before. As we got to the seventeenth floor, the elevator came to a screeching halt.

As the doors slid opened, she said, "Aren't you coming?"

Looking up I noticed a sign on the wall, just outside the elevator, which stated:

SEX ADDICTION CLINICS
SAA MEETING
ROOM #173
TUESDAY at 6:30PM

Looking at my watch, I realized that it was indeed Tuesday and that it was close to six thirty. I was just about to ask her what SAA stood for when I finally realized that it stood for Sex Addicts Anonymous. "Noooooooooooooo."

"Are you sure you don't want to join me?" she begged as she tried to talk me in to following her.

"Hell no," I cried. I was thinking that it hadn't worked for her, so why would she think it would work for me? "Why would I want to ruin a good thing?"

"You are right. But if you want to meet me here next Tuesday at this time, maybe you can talk me into not going?" she begged again as she stood holding the elevator door open, waiting for an answer.

"Okay, sounds like a date," I approved as I gave her a passionate kiss goodbye. "See you next week."

"Maybe I could introduce you to some of my fellow alumni who haven't been able to control their urges either?" she asked me. I wasn't sure if she was still trying to entice me into joining her or was trying to talk herself out of going.

"Urges … wow, that sounds like a lot of fun. Well, then, we will see you next Tuesday," I accepted as I pushed a floor button, any floor button, just to get out of there before I changed my mind. "Six-thirty p.m., right?"

"Yeah, but make sure you come a few minutes before, if you know what I mean," she stated as she let go of the door.

I met Cindy, and we played musical elevators every Tuesday for almost a year. I'm sure we must have almost worn out that Aerosmith album *Pump.* The wife and kids thought I was playing pool at the Tuesday-night pool league. If they only knew … She finally did talk me into joining SAA, but just like AA, it didn't last long. There were way too many steps for me to grasp, and I just could not get by that first step. What were the chances of me meeting a girl who was the spitting image of me at an SAA meeting? Come to find out most everyone there was just like us. Some didn't have music on the brain, but most did have some sort of their five senses controlling their lives.

So back to my lies. It was going to be the ultimate road trip, the road trip to end all road trips. It all started some twenty plus years ago; it was going to be our first golf vacation. The three of us had just quit smoking, and our loving wives suggested as a reward that we all go on a golf vacation. All the money we would save from not smoking in a year, we could spend on this golf trip. They thought it was a reward to get all that smoke out of our lungs, but I still don't think our livers will ever recover from all that beer that we would consume. To this day, I don't think our wives knew what they had started.

So, I'm blaming our wives: Sandy, Patricia, and Marilyn.

My wife's name was Sandy, but everyone called her Saint Sandy for putting up with all my shenanigans. In the end, it finally did catch up with me and cost me my marriage. But that will be a bunch more stories for another time. When I remember and get them all written down.

Patricia, Johnny's wife, she was the boss. She wore the pants, the underwear, and everything else in the family. I'm not sure if Johnny knew it, but he liked it that way. He liked it; he liked it a lot. Pattie, she liked to throw her weight around. Because she was a fairly big girl, she had quite a bit to throw. Over the years, she got to be known as an island girl—Wellesley Island, that is. Although Pat was a little rough around the edges, she had one of the biggest hearts of gold. She could not stop giving and giving and giving. When she was happy on the golf course, everyone would know it because everyone could hear her. She was a cackler from way back; especially her renditions of Woody Woodpecker's cackling laugh … ha-ha-ha-*ha*-ha.

Buddy's wife, Marilyn; we called Marilyn Wonders! Wonders; why she put up with Buddy all these years. But they loved each other very much. Over the years, she helped him mellow out somewhat. She looked after him because she had to look after him. If it wasn't for Marilyn, I'm sure that Buddy would have hurt himself by now. Or even worse, hurt Johnny or me.

Our first trip south was to Shady Hills, South Carolina. This little town was trying to compete with Myrtle Beach for golfing dollars. Though on a much smaller scale than

Myrtle Beach, it sure was a whole lot cheaper and a whole lot friendlier.

The town of Shady Hills was on this huge lake, which is world-famous for their large catfish. I mean a hundred pounds plus. Someone has to look this up. They are gigantic. It might even be the Catfish Capital of South Carolina, if maybe not the world.

I believe it was around the middle or maybe near the end of January. Dallas and Buffalo might have been playing in the Super Bowl that year. It was going to be six days of gambling, booze, nightlife, and with a little luck with the weather, we would be playing some great golf.

The cost of the package for the trip was $124.50 Canadian. It was for six nights of shared accommodations at the local Happy Holiday Hotel, breakfast in the morning, and seven rounds of golf with a cart. How could you go wrong in the middle of winter? So all we had to have was a little money for food and a lot of money for beer, gambling, and nightlife. The only thing that we did more than drink beer was gamble. We gambled on everything. From golf to sports teams to downright stupid things, like what color of car would be the next to pass us. I remember once when I was driving, a red car was about to pass, and Buddy had the color red. For about twenty miles, I think I was going at least a hundred miles per hour. There was no way in hell that I was ever going to let that red car pass, no matter what, even if I had to cut that fucking speeder off. Buddy was none the wiser. I would rather have paid a $400 speeding ticket than pay Buddy $20. We even had a $20 pool on when we would arrive in Shady Hills. Maybe that was why Buddy wanted to keep such a tight schedule. Winner would take half, and the rest would go towards the gas. The other thing about our O'Malley's wagers was, when you won, you lost. Basically, what it meant was that when you won a bet, you were obligated to spend all your winnings on drinks or whatever for everyone till it was all gone … so basically, when you won, you lost.

There were about ten or twelve golf courses in the area, that we could pick or choose from. I believe we had picked seven different courses for the week; so we did not have to replay any of them. We have always tried to stay away from Country Clubs. Nothing worse than, snooty members looking down on us O'Malleys; and don't get me started on dress codes. We just didn't like to be told that we couldn't wear our jeans, especially my lucky jeans. Dress code, what dress code? You were lucky we got dressed. Or what do you mean we can't take our own cooler? "But it's my lucky cooler, and besides, I have to keep my medicine cold." Rednecks should just stay away from Country Clubs. Just saying. But after saying all that, the golf courses in Shady Hills were just perfect for our first trip. There were no dress codes, so we could wear just about anything that we had passed out in the night before. And the best thing of all was we could bring our own coolers to all the courses that we played that week. The first day we played at Wyboo Golf Course. One of us forgot their cooler back at the room. I won't mention any names. Oh yes, I will. They not only lent Paulie a cooler, but they threw in a couple of free beers and filled it with ice. We were in heaven. As I said, there is nothing wrong with a blue-collar golf course.

There were going to be seven golfers and a designated driver for the week. The designated driver's name was

Theodore Babcock; we called him Teddy for short. Teddy was a farmer and was supposed to be our DD for the week, but he turned out to be our designated drunk for the week. As I said, he was supposed to be our designated driver for the week; all we had to do was keep him sober. Theo wanted to come because he had never been anywhere before. He worked sixteen-hour days, from sunup to sundown, seven days a week, 365 days a year. He was a farmer, plain and simple. Theodore was in his fifties and looked like he was in his seventies. I remember one night out for dinner, the waitress thought that he was our grand-dad, Johnny was the dad, and I was the son. But we would find out later that Johnny was actually older than Theodore by years. Babcock had worked hard all his life, and life had taken its toll on him. He had never taken a vacation, so he thought this would be an opportune time for a little R and R. His vacation plan was to drive us to the golf course, take a tour of the countryside, and if he didn't get lost, pick us all up about four and a half hours later. When he picked us all up, he would have our coolers full of beer and fresh ice, and of course, he would get Johnny's daily allowance of pork rinds. On occasion, Theodore would stumble across a local farmer to discuss—what else? The weather. What do farmers talk about other than weather? Well, maybe hard work, taxes, and government. I think he told us that he had stopped at a farm or two, and you know what they have: guns, big guns. They do not like trespassers. But after all the introductions and apologies, they would invite him in for a drink or two or three or … Most days; when Theodore did come to pick us up, one of us would jump behind the wheel. That way, it was a much safer drive home.

The seven golfers going were Albert, Stewart, Kevin, Paulie, and of course, us Three Amigos.

Albert Groper, he was a big, burly guy, just like a big ole teddy bear, whom we called Pudden. We called him Pudden because he was so soft and jiggly. The other thing about Pudden was that he was a very hairy man; maybe we should have called him Chewbacca. The funny thing is, I had warned him on many occasions that one of these days I was going to shave him from head to toe and then polish him up nice and shiny. So he would look smooth and slippery, like a newborn, three-hundred-pound piglet. I could at the very least just shave his back bare, or maybe just shave my initials into his hairy mounds. To date I have not, but that's not to say that it won't happen. I've just got to get him to pass out long enough to do the job. Pudden was by far the smartest one of the group. I have to say that because he was also my boss; he was the General Manager at the resort. He also had just quit smoking, so his wife said, "Sure, take him too; please take him." But to be honest, we really had to take him so we could get the eight-passenger van from work.

Stewart Weirdon was my best friend. He was just married and really could not afford to go, but I offered to pay for him if he painted my house when we got home. He promised. The house never did get painted. But to be honest, every time he showed up with a paintbrush, wouldn't you know it, the sun was shining. And you know when the sun is shining, you've just got to go golfing. Why he never learned to paint in the rain, I'll never know. How come you can't paint in the rain, anyways? I'm sure I could have convinced Buddy to hold the umbrella for him. See, Stewart also worked for Buddy, he was his right-hand man. So you would think he would have to be nice to him, but not so. It was like Buddy had to keep an eye out for that third O'Malley.

Kevin Cowell was related to Pudden; maybe his brother-in-law? He was a very low-key guy. It was almost like he was not there, or maybe he was just smart enough to avoid us at any cost. He just kept slipping under the radar, but he sure could hit a golf ball. Although I think that Kevin had fun on the trip, I don't believe he ever made another golf trip with us. I think Johnny must have scared him away.

Paulie Groper was Pudden's first cousin; he was down in his luck and in life in general. He had health problems, a bad back, and was on a disability pension of some kind. We call that a fixed income, so he really didn't have much money to spare. Paulie had just turned forty something but acted most of the time like he was eight years old. This kid was the most gullible and naive person alive. He was the one guy who Buddy could take full advantage of. Well, to be honest, we all did. He deserved it; he was Paulie. Buddy picked on him constantly. It was like the more we picked on Buddy; the more Buddy picked on poor Paulie. But to be honest, Buddy also looked after him; he was Paulie's safeguard against us O'Malleys.

CHAPTER 3

Come and Knock on Our Door

I remember the day that we picked Paulie up for the trip. He came rushing out of the house, all excited to go. It was like he had to come out first to make sure that this was not all a dream. He was actually going on a golf trip with his best friends. He had forgotten almost everything that he had packed inside, so it took him several trips to get himself fully loaded and positioned in the van.

As he climbed back into the van for the umpteenth time, we could see that he indeed needed glasses, or should I say his left eye needed them. "Paulie, where are your glasses?" I asked. "You know you are blind as a bat."

"Oh, right; I almost forgot them. Thanks. I don't know what I would have done without them," Paulie answered before he rushed back inside to retrieve his Coke-bottle glasses. The thing was, he was only blind in the one eye. So when he had his glasses on, his left eye was magnified by a hundred, while the other eye seemed somewhat normal.

"I'm not sure how you made it this far without them," Buddy reported as he laughed out loud. "You didn't even run into anything." See, his glasses were always taped up with white medical tape at the bridge of his nose. And they always looked like they had been taped up on more than one occasion.

"Are you sure you don't have contacts in?" I joked. "Did you get that new laser surgery done? You know, where they fry your eyelids open?"

"You guys know I can't afford that. And besides, there is no way in hell I would ever let someone fry my eyelids open. That would have to hurt, wouldn't it?" Paulie informed us. "And besides, I would look stupid, wouldn't I?"

"Paulie, that's why I asked. It's just that it looked like your eyelids were fried." I insulted him again. "Did you go out drinking last night?"

"Huhhhhh?" Paulie asked for clarification. "Oh no, Mummy would never let me drink on a weeknight."

Now you must understand that each time he went in for something he had forgotten, he had to unload his antiquated golf bag and dig out his keys. Then each time he would put the keys back for safekeeping, reload his bag, and climb back into the van, where we would remind him of something else that he had forgotten.

I think I could have kept this going for hours, but Buddy being impatient; finally screamed, "Paulie, will you finally sit the fuck down? I don't care what you have forgotten; you are not going back in. You hear?"

"Paulie, did you pee?" I teased him once again. "You know, it's going to be a very long sixteen hours before we get there."

"Sixteen hours? I won't make sixteen minutes. I'll be right back," Paulie retorted as he jumped out of his seat to go pee.

"Fuck him … I'm leaving him," Buddy bellowed as he started to drive away, leaving poor Paulie standing behind the van, having a leak. It was kind of funny watching poor Paulie trying to put his member back in his pants and run after us. "I'm going to kill him. He's already getting on my nerves. You guys will thank me in the end."

"Hurry, Paulie. You can make it. I know you can," someone screamed as we watched poor Paulie hurrying after the van. "Runnnnnn."

"Buddy stop already. We can't leave him," I cried as Buddy slowly stopped the van. "Look, now he is going to have to change his pants."

"We have wasted enough time," Buddy yelled. "Paulie get in the fucking van, now. We've got to go."

Scurrying toward the van, Paulie had to stop midway to catch his breath and wheezed, "Don't do that. Where's my puffer?"

"Buddy, you are going to kill him. Back up," Pudden warned.

"If I wanted him dead, I would have run over him by now," Buddy added as he only backed the van up about two feet closer to him. "He will be all right. Look at him. He needs the exercise. The fat fuck."

Climbing into the van once more, Paulie tried to settle into his seat, cried, "Can I at least change? This is going to be very uncomfortable … You know."

"No, now fuck-off," Buddy yelled as he climbed out of the driver's seat. "I can't take this anymore. Pudden, you drive."

Suddenly, for some reason, the *Three's Company* soundtrack started to play in my head; "Come and Knock on Our Door." I started to smile as I was thinking that any minute now, a young Chrissy or Janet was going to come bouncing out of the house. It didn't make any sense at the time, because I knew Paulie didn't have any sisters. But it wasn't the young girls who come running out; it was Paulie's mother that came running out, screaming. "Pookie, Pookie."

She was waving a bright orange pillow of sorts around in the air. She was wearing a short, pink, fuzzy bathrobe, with matching slippers. Her light-brown hair was done up haphazardly in day curlers. She had a lit "Export A" dangling out from the side of her mouth. The matching ash was almost as long as her protruding cigarette. The hair on the side of her head, where her cigarette dangled, was a nicotine-stained smudge that surely was caused by many years of smoking. As she screamed out the other side of her mouth, I wondered at the time how she could yell so loudly and keep that ash attached to the cigarette butt for so long. "Pookie, Pookie, you have forgotten your knee pillow. You know you can't sleep with your large scrotum resting on the inside of ... You know how your inner thighs like to chafe."

"Mummy be quiet. You promised, you promised me you wouldn't come out and embarrass me like ... like this," Paulie interrupted as he climbed out of the van to retrieve his much-loved member-alignment-equalizer.

"But Pookie," Mummy cried. "I just didn't want chafing to ruin your trip; like the last time we went away, to Nan's. Remember?"

"Mommm … Mom, I was eleven."

"Pookie … scrotum, large … knee pillow … Mummy … Nan's?" Then, like clockwork, around the van everyone started to laugh as they watched Mummy giving Paulie a loving hug and kiss goodbye.

Noticing that she had smeared her bright lipstick all over Paulie's cheek, she tried to wipe the smudge from his face with her thumb. "Be good now and have fun … And you make sure you change your underwear often. Just in case you have to go to the hospital down there."

"Mummmmmm … Go inside," Paulie cried with embarrassment as he pointed up toward the house.

"Oh, Pookie; don't be like that," Mummy warned as she hugged him tightly one more time, still trying to wipe the smudge of lipstick off his face. "You guys make sure you look after him. You know he has never been away from home before."

"Oh, we will, Mumm … Err, Mrs. Groper, I will look after him," Buddy agreed. "I promise."

"I know you will, Buddy. You are one of his very dearest and closest friends. He talks about you all the time." She redirected her attention toward Buddy.

"Hey, Mrs. G, how are you doing today?" I yelled out the back of the van, trying to get her attention.

"Shannon, is that you?" She seemed somewhat surprised that I was going on this trip as she looked inside the van, trying to spot me.

"Yeah, this is going to be the best trip ever," I responded as I climbed out of the van so I could go over and give her a big hug hello and a bigger hug goodbye. "So how are you doing?"

"Oh, I'm doing just great. I sure am going to miss my Lil-Pookie … my Lil-Man," she responded as she embraced me tightly with a kissy on the cheek. "You know, everyone calls me Gertrude. But you can call me Gertie."

"Okay, Mrs. Groper … err, Mrs. G … err, Gertie … You sure are looking quite fine this morning. Have you done something with that hair of yours?" I answered as it finally dawned on me why the soundtrack of *Three's Company* was playing in my mind. Did I want this to happen? Did I have a choice? I would just have to see where this led to, or I might have to check this out when I got home.

"Oh, this ole do?" she came back with as she grabbed some of the curlers from her hair and put them in her housecoat's pockets, all the while batting her eyelashes. "Oh, you sure know what to say to us old gals."

"Hey, why don't you come?" I asked, as I was sure this would upset Buddy a little more. "I'm sure you would have a great time."

"Oh you guys don't want some old lady coming and spoiling all your fun … or do you?" she came back with as she tried to flirt back with me. "Do you have room for me?"

"Buddy, we've got room, don't we?" I said as I held my arm wrapped tightly around her waist.

"Nooooo, O'Malley. I'm sorry, Mrs. Groper, the van is full. You can see that there is no room." Buddy tried to be polite as he shook his head in disbelief at me. "Maybe next time."

"Full, are you sure?" she disappointedly answered. It sounded like she really wanted to come, as she stuck her head in the van to take a look to see who was actually going. "I see a couple empty seats back there, don't I? I won't take up much space. It won't take me long to pack."

"No, we are full. Sorry; we still have to pick up a few more guys," Buddy disclosed, still shaking his head at me.

"Buddy, I'm sure we could find room," I snickered as I gave her another big hug. But this time I could feel Mrs. Groper rubbing her big bosoms all over me through her tight-fitting bathrobe. "She could sit on my …"

"Shanneeeeee, that's my *mum*," Paulie interrupted me as he wrestled her from my clenched arms so he could give her one last hug goodbye. "Let go of her."

"Sorry Pookie, I must have lost my head there," I apologized as I thought I saw some tears in each one of their eyes. Paulie's tears from going to miss his mummy; Mrs. G's tears of not being able to come.

"Come on Pookie. Give your mummy one more kiss goodbye. We've got to get going," I joked as I could see that he was beginning to get more upset. "You guys are going to make me cry."

"Okay, okay," Paulie cried out as he hugged her, which seemed to take forever. It was like he was not going to let her go. "Mummy, maybe you can go next time."

"Pookie, get in the fucking van, or we're going to leave you behind," Buddy vowed. "Drive Pudden, drive. Leave him."

"Don't call me Pookie," Paulie demanded.

"You better go, Poooo, err, Paulie. Have fun. I'll miss you. I love you," Mummy said. "Hey, Shannon, you will have to come over for breakfast when you get home. Paulie will make some of his world-famous pancakes. I'll let him bring out the good syrup."

"It's a date, Mrs. Roper, err, I mean Mrs. Groper," I answered, as I still could not get the music to stop playing in my mind. "I can't wait."

Just then I faintly overheard someone in the van say, "That doesn't mean going over the night before. Is there anybody he won't do? It's pretty bad when we had to protect our sisters from him. Now we have to lock up our mothers."

At her age, I was hoping that her hearing aid was turned off, so she did not hear all the sarcastic mumbling coming from within the van.

"I love you, too." Paulie finished saying goodbye as he finally climbed back up into the van. "Don't forget to feed Fluffy."

"I'll feed him, but he is always pecking at me," Mummy said. "That stupid bird doesn't like me, I tell you."

As we started to drive away, we all screamed out the windows of the van, "Bye, Mummy. I love you. Make sure you look after my Fluffy."

Someone asked Paulie, "Where did you get the name Pookie from?"

"Never mind about that. Tell us about your Fluffy the Bird. Or better yet, tell us about your scrotum-alignment-pillow." I asked for clarification. "Oh, by the way, how old is your mummy? Do you think someday you could call me Daddy?"

"O'Malley, will you leave him fucking alone? Can you not see that he is sad and upset for leaving his mummy?" Buddy joked. "So how old is your mother? I bet you she was quite the looker back in her day. What was that, fifty years ago?"

"Will you guys just leave me alone?" Paulie wept as he looked back toward his mummy, who was still waving goodbye. He held his scrotum pillow up against his face with one hand for comfort, and he laid his other hand flat up against the window of the van to say his goodbye. After a while he looked around the van, as he was looking for some kind of comfort that was not going to come from us.

When Paulie first loaded up, he had his little blue gym bag; it was loaded full of everything he would need for the week. It looked like it was bursting at the seams. I'm sure he must have brought his silky with him, as he had his favorite pillow strapped securely to the top of his bag. He had an old black leather golf bag that must have been thirty to forty years old. The old golf bag had seen better days; it was loaded with some of the oldest, rustiest golf clubs that you could have ever found. He was wearing a green-and-white fifties beer hat. It was made of a mesh-type material that had been stained over the years. The cap looked like an old fishing cap that was worn by good old boys.

"Is that your lucky hat?" Buddy asked as Paulie repositioned himself in his seat in the back of the van.

"No, no, it's my 50's fishing cap. You know, like the '50's-Fishing-Cap' in that new song by the Tragically Hip. I know all the lyrics. Aren't they just the greatest band ever? They're local, eh? They are all from Kingston, you know." Paulie tried to explain his stupidity.

"Paulie, you're just a fucking idiot. It's not a fishing cap in the song. It's a fifty-mission-cap," Buddy tried to correct him.

"Buddy, you're wrong. That doesn't make sense. It's a green-and-white, 50's beer-cap just like this one. It's a fishing cap, just like the one my dad wore all his life. And it was Bill Barilko who went on a fishing trip, not on a mission. That doesn't make any sense. I should know. I've got Barilko's hockey card, and he played for the Leaf's. That's my team. I just love the Leaf's," Paulie argued as he took the hat off to show how he had contoured the brim to look like that.

"Do you have their album?" I asked.

"No, I can't afford it. But I had someone make me a copy, till my sweet little Fluffy pecked away at the cassette till it was ruined. So now I just do a lot of requesting on the radio," Paulie replied.

"Paulie, the song is called 'Fifty Mission Cap.' Not some 'Fifty Fishing Cap,'" Buddy informed Paulie as he shook his head in disbelief. "Is there anything that you are not stupid about?"

"You're wrong. You're totally wrong. I should know; I'm their biggest fan. I know the song by heart. Here, I will sing it for you," Paulie argued, and before we knew what was happening, Paulie broke out in a chorus in which he only had to hum a few of the lines out of key.

> Bill Barilko disappeared one summer.
> He went on a fishing trip.
> He kept a card under his hat.
> It was his fifties fishing cap.
> He won the cup that year;
> I believe he worked it in to look like that.

"Paulie, shut the fuck up. That's not how it goes. And don't you ever dare sing or hum again on this trip," Buddy warned him, "or I will fucking kill you."

"Hey, Paulie, that wasn't that bad considering you were off-key, a little slow, and you definitely don't know the words." I tried to compliment his effort and effort only. "Hey, can you play an instrument?"

"Actually, I do. I play the harmonica," Paulie bragged as he reached into his duffel bag and pulled out a small purple-felt Crown Royal bag. He anxiously tried to unwrap his harmonica so he could show everyone his prize possession. When he finally did get it out of the wrapping, he put it right up to his mouth and blew a few off-key notes into his mouth organ. You could tell that he could not play it very well either.

"What about that fishing cap song? Can you play it? I wonder what it sounds like on a harmonica." I tried to persuade him to play a few more notes, as I knew this would surely upset Buddy a little further.

"O'Malley, what the fuck are you thinking?" Buddy warned me. "Will you quit it? Don't encourage him."

Putting the harmonica up to his mouth, Paulie started to play loudly, proudly, and off-key.

The next thing I knew, Buddy was looking at him, severely upset; he grabbed the organ and yelled, "You are not to ever bring this out on this trip again. You hear? If I hear that cat-in-heat-screech while I'm on vacation, I will throw it away. I will throw you away. I'll just punch you in the throat. You hear me?"

"But, Buddy, I have to play it. I usually play a few songs before I go to bed at night. It helps me sleep. It's like my sleeping pill." Paulie tried to plead his case with Buddy.

"You won't need a sleeping pill. I'll knock you out if you play that screech you call music. You are not going to be my roommate, you hear?" Buddy informed him. "You can go sleep with those fucking O'Malleys."

"But, Buddy, you told me you were going to keep me safe. You were going to protect me. Remember? You were going to protect me from those O'Malleys. Remember?" Paulie pleaded. "You told Mummy that you were going to look after me."

"Oh, just fuck off," Buddy yelled.

"That's my Little Buddy; I know you will look after me." Paulie tried to convince himself that he would be safe.

"Aren't you guys glad that he didn't bring his juice harp?" His cousin Pudden suggested.

"Juice harp? What the fuck is that? Is that a drink? I don't think that I have ever had that before," a few questioned.

"Isn't that made by Guinness? You know, the people who make that dark, muddy, god-awful beer? Tastes worse than molasses," Stewart added.

"Oh, I don't mind Guinness. Actually, I kind of like it. It's a nice change from that watered-down shit that you guys call beer." Pudden reported his preference of beer types. "Yeah, Coors Light. It is as close to water as you can get. Did anybody bring some of that dark Harp beer? Pass one up if you did."

"Here, take a fucking Coors Light, and shut the fuck up," Buddy scolded everyone as he passed a beer up to the front of the van.

"You can't drink; you're driving," Paulie stated. "I'll take that."

"You are not going to start drinking already," Buddy informed Paulie as he passed the beer up to Pudden. "He has a free hand; that's why he has two."

"I'm not driving right now. I'm waiting for you to get situated in your seat, and then I will be driving, and besides, it's gone now. Gulp, gulp," Pudden reported as he handed back the empty bottle of beer.

"Paulie, have you got everything? Did you pack all of your medication? What about your puffers; you know you need them when you get all excited. And you know that's what going on vacation is all about," I stated so we could all get going on our much-needed vacation.

Paulie, thinking in his own mind that he probably would have to get to a hospital sometime on the trip, responded with, "Yes, I've been packed for weeks. I even brought an extra puffer or two, just so you guys don't have to take me to the hospital more than once or twice."

"Hospital? Like fuck we will," Buddy screamed at Paulie. "I might put you in a cab, maybe."

"See? You do love me," Paulie exclaimed. "I love you, too, my little Buddy."

"Paulie, will you just fuck off, already," Buddy swore.

"Come on, Buddy. Tell me you love me," Paulie begged. "Come on. You can do it."

"Paulie, will you just fuck off already?" Buddy cried.

"Buddy, you know you want to. Tell me you love me. Come on. Tell meeeee, please," Paulie pleaded in a little child's voice. "I'm not going to stop till you tell me you love me."

"Paulie, you can stop right now; I'm not telling you that I love you." Rethinking what he had just said, Buddy decided that he would tell Paulie he loved him, so we could all get going. "Elephant shoes, elephant-shoes."

"I elephant shoes you too," Paulie cried out proudly.

"Hey, Buddy, can you elephant shoes me too?" I asked for some love also.

"Fuck off."

This was going to be the best trip ever. Paulie had Buddy all upset, and we hadn't even left Canada yet. So all I would have to do was get Paulie to bring out his harmonica every once in a while, and Buddy would go ballistic.

Looking at Paulie, I noticed that he had a couple of large spoons sticking out from his breast pocket, right beside his eyeglass pouch. So I asked him, "What are the spoons for?"

"Oh, I play the spoons when I get bored. It helps the time pass," Paulie answered as he took the spoons out and positioned them between his fingers to play. He must have thought that they seemed a bit sticky, as he stuck each one of them in his mouth for a taste. "Ummm, I just love maple syrup. I guess I must have used these spoons at breakfast."

"Maple syrup? Breakfast? Why do you use a spoon? You can't eat pancakes with a spoon," Buddy asked. "Can you?"

"Well, I do, because I want to get every last drop of syrup," Paulie explained as he took another lick from the spoon.

"So what kind of music can you play with the spoons?" I inquired. "Can you play that fifty-fishing hat song?"

"Of course I can," Paulie bragged as he started tapping the spoons together in an unfamiliar rhythm.

"That's fucking it. I warned you for the last time," Buddy growled as he snatched the sticky spoons from Paulie's grasp and promptly threw them out the side window. "O'Malley, will you quit teasing him?"

"Buddy, noooooooo," Paulie cried out as he watched the spoons bounce down the highway. "That's my mummy's best silverware."

"I don't fucking care," Buddy warned.

"Are you still sleeping on your mom's couch?" someone asked.

"Yes. Why?" Paulie retorted. "All I know is Mum is going to be fit to be tied. She's not going to be very happy with you, Buddy."

"I don't fucking care. You just sit there and be quiet. And don't you dare bring out anything else that makes a noise. You hear?" Buddy howled, which led Paulie to sit and pout for many miles.

"Pookie, don't worry about your mother's spoons. I will make it up to her, I'm sure." I joked as I winked at Paulie. "I will replace them."

So as the week went on, at every eating establishment, I would steal two spoons, hoping to find a match for Mrs. Groper's silverware. Thinking I just needed an in, if you know what I mean.

"Thanks, Shannon. She's very attached to her silverware, you know," Paulie cried. "I think she spends all her extra time at night polishing them, because I keep hearing her motorized polisher all night long. Mum has been so lonely since Dad died."

Just as soon as I heard this, it was like an alarm went off in my head. That soundtrack for *Three's Company* started to play again. Why was it playing? Was this another sign? Whether I liked it or not, it looked like I was being attracted to Mrs. Groper.

"Is that so?" I asked, as it seemed everyone started to laugh out loud. "I don't think that I have ever called it that before. Is it an electric one, or is it one of those battery-operated ones?"

"What's so funny?" Paulie cried out. "I'm sure it is an electric one. It sounds really powerful."

"So what's her polisher sound like, Paulie?" I asked so I could pinpoint what kind of polisher she actually had.

"I don't know. It's like a low humming sound. Like ummmmmmmmmm," Paulie tried to explain. "Sometimes that low humming sound puts me to sleep. It's so soothing to hear."

"It doesn't have different speeds?" I inquired.

"Oh yes, it does. She must change the gears or something because she always works her way up to this higher-pitched squeal," Paulie tried to explain.

"Wow, so are there more than two speeds?" I asked. "Do you know what it looks like? Like how big is it?"

"O'Malleyyyyyy, will you leave him alone?" As Buddy scolded me; I could see that he had even broken into a smile, thinking about what I was up to.

"Buddy, it's okay. I need a new polisher at home. My forks and knives are all pretty tarnished. So I'm trying to find out if I need the multispeed one, or if the smaller ones would suffice or not," I claimed, as I could see that everyone in the van was either listening intently or chuckling to themselves. "Do you think I could borrow it, or do you think I could come over and maybe your mother could help me polish …?"

"Shannoneeeee," Buddy interrupted me.

"No, I don't think so. Mum's very protective of her stuff. She won't even let me use it," Paulie informed us. "I think there are maybe five speeds. I think each speed is a little more intense than the one before. The highest speed must be the best, because I think that she uses that speed the most. I bet we probably have the shiniest silverware on the block."

"So how big is it?" I asked again. "Have you seen it? What color is it? Does it light up or do anything else?"

"O'Malleyyyyyyyy," Buddy cried again.

"It's okay, Buddy," Paulie interrupted. "No, I have never seen it before, I have just heard it. And besides, I'm not allowed to touch Mummy's stuff."

"Well, if you haven't seen it before, how do you know that she is polishing forks and knives?" I asked.

"Because I asked her one night what the noise was, and that's what she told me she was doing." Paulie tried to justify his answer, as it got kind of quiet in the van for a few minutes. "What else would she be doing?"

"I'm sure that's what she was doing. Your silverware can never be too shiny," I agreed, as I didn't want to tell Paulie that it wasn't a polisher she was using—not just yet anyways.

"I remember when that polisher first arrived. The postman delivered it right to our front door. It came in a plain brown wrapper and was discreetly lettered. I wasn't sure what it was till I asked. Mummy told me it was a polisher, a silverware polisher. She was so excited when it arrived. It was just like Christmas that night. That was a special night; I remember the stack of waffles she made me," Paulie anxiously answered as he tried to show us all with his fingers how thick the stack of waffles was.

"You're not drooling, are you?" I asked, as I still wanted to know more about her new toy. "Okay, what about her new package that she got?"

"I'll get to that in a minute. The fresh fruit and real whipped cream. It was to die for. Oh, it was so good. Then she brought out the real maple syrup; it really was Christmas. She knows that I fall to sleep as soon as I eat that much maple syrup. The next thing I knew, she was shooing me off to bed. Then without any hesitation, she grabbed her new packaged polisher and the black box of her best silverware and headed toward her bedroom. She said that she was going to polish all of her silverware, even if it took all night to do it," Paulie informed us all.

"Then what?"

"She must have polished for hours. Mummy must have really enjoyed it a little, because occasionally I would hear a little shriek," Paulie said. "The next thing I knew, that humming sound must have put me to sleep, because I don't remember a thing till the next morning. And it must have been Christmas again. You guessed it; I had pancakes and syrup again. Mummy was in such a great mood. But come to think about it. Mummy is always in a good mood after a night of polishing."

"She is?"

"Yep. Like I said, since Dad died, she's been really lonely as of late. She has no hobbies and really doesn't have many friends out there. So when she polishes up her silverware at night, it's like she has found a new hobby. She enjoys doing it; well, it sounds like she enjoys doing it. She's got to be a pro at it by now," Paulie claimed as he looked around the van and saw that everyone was listening intently. "I wish she would just find someone."

"Find someone?"

"Yes, find someone. I could move out, then. So I would not have to do all the manly things around the house?"

"Manly things?"

"Yeah, you guys all know, those nightly chores us men have to do on a daily basis?" Paulie complained. "The womenfolk expect us to do it all. You guys know. Every, every night."

"No, I don't. What are you talking about, Paulie?"

"You know. Take the garbage out," Paulie griped.

"Well, I have never called it that before."

So after Paulie's amazing sad story, the van got awfully quiet. We didn't hear anything from Paulie for about two hours, when he finally broke his silence to scream, "I got to pee, cousin; pull her over."

CHAPTER 4

I Can't Believe the Price of Chicken in Pennsylvania

We all could not wait to tee it up. The original plan was we would leave at six in the evening, drive all night, and get there about noonish. We would settle in or just maybe find nine holes of golf to finish out the day in style. If anything, it was going to be our free day.

The weather report on the way down was not good. It was snowing when we left, turned into freezing rain in the mountains of Pennsylvania, and then rain all the way to South Carolina. The van was packed to the hilt. If you can imagine six sets of clubs, seven bags of luggage, and we still had to pick up Johnny in Syracuse. Buddy had suggested, that we divide up into partners. While one was driving, the other would make sure that he had plenty to eat and drink. The partner was also responsible for navigation. You must remember this was pre-GPS. So you didn't have some voice squawking, "Recalculating" when you inadvertently made a wrong turn. Buddy also let all the drivers and navigators know not to get lost, as do-overs, roundabouts, or turnarounds were unacceptable; and for each violation, they would be fined twenty dollars.

Pudden and Kevin were going to get us through New York and into Pennsylvania. Buddy and Theodore would get us through the mountains of Pennsylvania and into part of Virginia. Then Stewart and I would run it to the end, getting everyone to our destination safely. We would reverse the order on the way home. The plan was that everyone would drive for two to three hours each. We decided that Johnny and Paulie would not need to drive. Johnny was an American, and the van had Canadian insurance on it, so we thought it best if Johnny just sat in the back seat all night and drank beer and ate his pork rinds. He was more than happy about doing just that. And Paulie, it was just better not to let Paulie do anything. I'm not even sure, that he even had a driver's license.

I think someone suggested, "We should let Paulie drive through Maryland, to make him feel like part of the team. It's not very far and maybe only a couple miles through the state."

Buddy yelled—Buddy was always yelling— "Like fuck we will. It's only a couple fucking miles to hell also. Make him feel like part of the team? What fucking team? What the fuck are you guys thinking? That's just fucking stupid. If he gets behind the wheel, I'm sure as hell not going to ride in this death trap."

"Buddy, you know, he is sitting right here," I informed him. "You shouldn't talk about him like that. He has feelings, you know."

"Fuck you. The only feeling he has is that feeling he has between his legs, and he hasn't used it in years," Buddy alleged. "And you know what? He probably has never used it and never will."

"What are you talking about?" Paulie asked.

"Nothing."

"Buddy quit picking on him," I interrupted.

"Okay, but you know he is blind in one eye and can't see out of the other one," Buddy tried to inform the group.

"Oh, he is not that bad," I argued.

"Yes, he is," Buddy disagreed. "Do you not remember the last time you let him behind a wheel?"

"Yes, but that was different. Everything worked out in the end," I reasoned. "It was on your insurance."

"All I can say is it's a good thing that they never found out that he was driving," Buddy bickered.

"No, not that time. I'm talking about the other last time. You know, remember?" I goaded Buddy.

"Last time? What last time?" Buddy screamed. "There was no other time, O'Malley."

"Oh, that's right. There was no other time," I lied, as I tried to antagonize Buddy a little more. "Paulie, I guess we got away with another one."

"Got away with what?" Buddy demanded. "Paulie, I know you can't lie."

"What?" Paulie answered.

"Do you know anything?" Buddy asked.

"About what?" Paulie retorted.

"What he is talking about?" Buddy questioned him.

"Talking about what?" Paulie answered again.

"Oh, never mind. It's like talking with an eight-year-old," Buddy continued. "Just fuck off."

It was going to be a great trip. We'd gotten Buddy all riled up for the second time, and we hadn't even left Canada yet. We stopped in Syracuse along Route 81 to pick up my twin. There he was on the side of the road in the middle of a snowstorm, wearing his bestest pair of Levi's, his blue, old, worn-out Buffalo Bills jacket, standing beside his golf bag. Right beside him sat his red, beat-up, Old Milwaukee Beer cooler. As Johnny stood there, you could see that he was not much bigger than his golf bag; they were almost the same size. But there he was, eager to go; he probably had been there for hours, waiting for us to pick him up, or at least waiting for the best offer to drive by.

Pudden pulled up alongside him, rolled down the window, and joked, "Hey, cutie, are you going our way? How much for a blow job?"

"Where have you been? I'm almost out of beer," Johnny eagerly stated as he took the last swallow from his can and threw it into the ditch. He hurried around to the other side of the van to climb aboard.

"Where's your luggage?" I asked him.

He came back, "Kid, you told me to pack light. Everything that I need or want is in this old cooler of mine. You got any beer?"

I told him that I had set him up in the back seat with a cooler of his favorite beer, Old Milwaukee, and a bag of his favorite pork rinds. I also told him about some of the pools and wagers that we had going on, and I let him know that he was down about fifty dollars already.

All he said was, "Kid, you got me covered, right?"

"You are looked after. It's a good thing you didn't bring any luggage. You would have had to hold it on your lap the whole way. Just to let you know, Buddy has informed us that we can only stop once in each state, whether it is to pee, to eat, or to buy more beer. He says that way we will arrive on some sort of schedule," I informed him.

"Well, we better stop for more beer soon. This six-pack you brought me is not going to get me out of New York State. And, Buddy, when did you become my Liquor Control Board?" He inquired, all while rooting through the cooler looking for more beer.

"Don't worry; we gotcha covered. There's more Old Milwaukee in my cooler," Buddy revealed.

So on the way down, about every two hours, Paulie would start crying, "I gotta pee, I gotta pee, I gotta pee." He was worse than an old woman. Later he told us that one of his health problems was that he had an extraordinarily small bladder. And if he didn't piss when he had to go, he would develop a bladder infection and more than likely would have to go to the hospital to get treated.

I think Buddy told him, "Too bad. Looks like you are going to have a fucking infection the rest of the week. What do they call that? A urinary tract infection?"

"Paulie, do you get yeast infections too?" I asked him.

"What about your knee pillow? Did you bring that also?" Johnny inquired.

Everyone just broke out laughing as someone said, "Hey, Johnny. He doesn't call it a knee pillow in his household. It's called a scrotum-alignment tool."

"A what?"

"Fuck off, guys. And, Johnny, just so you know; I did bring my knee pillow. I've got it right here" Paulie cried, gritting his teeth in anger as he held it up to prove that he had indeed brought it.

Everyone broke out laughing again.

When we left Canada, we had decided that we would stop the van at every state line and take a picture of the states' welcoming signs. In the beginning, it wasn't going to be just a picture of the sign, but it was all of us posing in front of the sign. We had brought a camera and a tripod, so we could all get in the picture. It was all fun in the beginning but having to get out of the van in the dark, in the snow and rain, and pose in front of this towering sign was just getting stupid. Most of the time, the flash wouldn't work anyways. Some just used it as a way to stretch their legs, while others like Paulie used it for a much-needed pee break. Everyone had lost their enthusiasm for the picture at the last couple of states. Or maybe it was we were just getting drunk.

We had just stopped for a picture in front of the sign "WELCOME TO THE KEYSTONE STATE." So we knew it was time to stop for more chips, mix, beer, and of course, I was sure Paulie needed to pee again. We pulled into this Wegmans grocery store, where we all piled out of the van. Buddy and I had a shopping list, and everyone else ran to the washroom. We got almost everything on the list that was needed. As we got back to the van and were about to pull away, I noticed Paulie was missing. "Where's Paulie?"

Buddy barked, "Fuck him; let's go."

"Buddy, we are only four hours into the trip; we don't want to lose anybody this early, do we? I'll run in and try to find him," I urged as I climbed down out of the van.

I think I heard Buddy saying something toward me like, "That stupid-bastard probably pissed himself again. And if you both are not out here in three minutes; you both are going to be walking."

I ran back into the grocery store, and you won't believe this. There was Paulie; he had his shopping cart pushed right up into the express line, twelve items or less. It was like he was shopping at home, doing his weekly grocery shopping. He had his cart half full of groceries. From what I could see, there was coffee, sugar, flour, a few bottles of maple syrup, a few fresh vegetables, a jug of milk, a couple dozen eggs, some ground hamburger, and at least six packages of fresh chicken.

I got up behind him as I tried not to startle him. "Do you happen to see a problem with all of this?"

"What? Oh, it's you," Paulie answered as he started to place his groceries on the moving conveyor.

"Paulie, what in fuck are you doing?" I screamed at him. "You have way too many items for this line."

"It's all right. I do it all the time back home. I'm only over by a couple items," Paulie said. "They won't even notice."

"Paulie, this is the States. Their cash registers shut down at twelve items," I lied. "There is no way around it."

"Really? *Wow.*" Paulie listened in disbelief as he grabbed a couple of items and placed them in the gum rack to hide. "I'm just picking up a few things. They have some great prices here. Look. They have real maple syrup from Canada for only seventy-nine cents."

"Seventy-nine cents? Christ, we can't even buy it in Canada for that. Maybe I should get some. What aisle is it in?" I asked as I looked up and around for a hint from all the hanging ceiling signs.

Paulie, looking up, said, "Oh, it's over in aisle four, I think."

"I don't fucking care," I scolded him as I tried to get him back out to the van, before it left. "What the fuck do you think you are doing? Buddy is going to kill you."

He got a shitty grin on his face and energetically informed me, "Shannon, you won't believe the prices." He eagerly grabbed one of the packages of chicken and handed it to me as he took a big inhale from his puffer. "Look. It's only sixty-nine cents a pound."

"Wow, sixty-nine cents a pound. Maybe I should get some at that price." I was trying not to laugh; I was trying not to be mad. But I knew Buddy was going to fucking kill him. So I asked him, "You really didn't put too much thought into this, did ya?"

"What do you mean?" he worried out loud as he threw the packages of chicken up onto the counter. "Should I get some for Buddy? Oh yeah, and I got Mummy some Tarn-X; it was on sale for three eighty-nine."

"Paulie, we are on holiday for the next seven days. What do you suppose we are going to do with all this food?" I came back with. "Do you not think that it will spoil by the time we get home?"

"Not if we put it in a freezer." He got a real worried look on his face as he took a bigger inhale from his puffer; then he begged, "Ohhhhh, you won't tell on me, will you? You can't. Oh, please, please don't tell Buddy; he'll kill me."

"Don't worry." I tried to comfort him as the saleslady at the cash register started to listen with a smile on her face. "I will just tell him that you pissed yourself again, and it just took a little longer to clean up."

Paulie said in relief, "Okay, would you?

"Sure I will, Paulie," I said as I gave him a reassuring glance.

Just as Paulie started to reach to put back some of the items, the saleslady informed him of the total. "Fourteen dollars and eighty-three cents."

"Leave it. We've got to go now, or we will be walking," I threatened him as I tried to drag him toward the exit.

"But, Shannon …"

"Sorry. He's got to go," I apologized to the saleslady as I tried to get Paulie moving. Thinking that I needed the Tarn-X for his mother, I grabbed it and threw down a five-dollar bill to cover it. "Keep the change," I said, hoping that this would be the best five dollars that I would ever spend, if you know what I mean.

Just as we got outside, we saw that the van had started to slowly pull away. "Run Paulie, run."

"Wait, wait, Buddy; don't leave us," Paulie screamed as he scampered quickly toward the moving van, all the while fumbling to get his puffer out of his pocket.

We were relieved to see the brake lights come on as we got closer to the back of the van. As the van came to a stop, the side door opened up, and Johnny yelled, "Get in here, Kid. I tried to get him to wait. He wouldn't listen to me."

"I warned you; I told you I would leave you," Buddy said as I hurriedly climbed in, with Paulie quickly following from behind.

We didn't even get seated before Buddy started yelling at Paulie, "Where the fuck have you been? How come it took you so fucking long? Blah, blah, blah, blah, fuck, fuck, fuck …" Buddy just kept yelling at him.

This was great. Only four hours in, and Buddy was about to explode, and me and Johnny had nothing to do with it. When Buddy gets mad, his one eye starts to water, then it starts to twitch, he turns very red, and these veins pop out of his neck and forehead. His Mexican side starts to shine through. This was going to be the trip of a lifetime.

Paulie was trying to get a word in to give Buddy the answer that he was looking for, but Buddy would have none of it. I finally looked at Paulie and said, "Everything's going to be just fine. Why don't you tell Buddy how much fresh chicken was?"

Buddy started laughing uncontrollably and said. "You fucking idiot. You fucking pissed yourself again, didn't you?"

"Nooooo, I'm not a baby," Paulie cried out as everyone started to laugh out loud.

To change the subject somewhat, I pulled the bottle of Tarn-X out of my pocket and handed it to Paulie. "That sure was a good price on Tarn-X, wasn't it? You make sure you give that to your mummy."

"Oh, I sure will. She will be so happy," Paulie agreed. "And I will make sure I tell her it's from you, Shannon."

"Make sure."

We didn't hear from Paulie for at least another two hours. You guessed it; he had to pee. After that I think Buddy's heart doubled in size, or maybe he thought he was picking on Paulie too much? Maybe, just maybe, he was a Canadian and not a Mexican as everyone thought? Nah, he was a Mexican. Because out of the blue, Buddy changed the piss rule to every two hours for Paulie and for Paulie only. He boldly told everyone, "Do not think for a fucking minute any one of you are getting out of this van to share that extra piss break with Paulie. Paulie doesn't need his hand held or anything else for that matter. Get it? If we don't keep going, we are never going to get there. You guys have to stop wasting time like this."

So anytime we needed to change a mood or a delicate subject down South, someone would blurt out, "Can you believe the price of chicken in Pennsylvania?"

We had not gotten out of the state, Paulie was sitting in the back seat, and you could tell he was getting a little antsy; downright fidgety, some would say. I was thinking he had to have a piss break or something, and I knew Buddy wouldn't pull over without a little coaxing. There had to be another twenty minutes or so before Paulie's next scheduled stop. Paulie was not going to ask because he did not want to upset Buddy any more than he had already.

I made my way back toward Paulie and said, "Hey, Paulie, so how long have you played the harmonica for? Is it hard to play? Or learn to play? Did your parents play? Or should I say, how well does your mummy blow?"

"O'Malley, what are you doing?" Buddy quizzed me as he looked back through the rearview mirror at me. He was trying to figure out what I was up to.

"Nothing. Do you mind? I'm just talking to my good friend Paulie; I'm trying to figure out if Gertie blows or not," I tried to explain as I glared back at him.

"Shannon, that's my mummy," Paulie embarrassedly cried.

"Okay, can she play?" I said.

"No, she's not very musically inclined, if you know what I mean. Luckily, I got it all," Paulie answered as he dug around in his knapsack looking for his instrument.

"I've played it for it seems like forever. At least a couple of years, I think. And it really is not that hard to learn to play. Here it is."

"Are there different brands, or who makes the best ones?" I asked as Paulie handed over his harmonica for me to examine. "Where can you buy one? Are they expensive?"

"The best ones are really expensive. The Hohner or Oskar brands are the best. I would think they would be upward of the twenty-dollar mark. Suzuki even makes them. I think people think that they are only famous for making motorcycles. But if it wasn't for the harmonica, I'm sure Suzuki would still be making trikes. I picked this one up on sale at the five and dime. I want to save up for the headrest piece, so I don't have to hold onto it when I play," Paulie informed me as I blew into the opening, making an unforgettable screech.

"Paulierrrrrr, what did I warn you about blowing into that fucking awful-sounding …" Buddy screamed as he glared back through the mirror at us again.

"It wasn't me. It wasn't me," Paulie claimed as he looked up, frightened, toward the annoyed Buddy.

"I don't care who it was. Don't make me come back there," Buddy warned. "I don't want to hear that fucking sound again. You hear me?"

"Buddy, Buddy, it's okay. It was me. I'm the one. I accidentally blew into it. I didn't mean to," I promised as I tried to reason with him.

"Accidentally, my ass. You want me to come back there and punch you in the throat too? I will," Buddy screamed at me as he gave me a threatening look from the rearview mirror.

"Okay, okay. Paulie, if you are going to teach me to play this throat organ, we will have to be quiet. Okay?" I whispered as I peered up toward the front of the van.

"I'm not sure if I can teach you without being able to blow into it," Paulie confessed, as he too glanced up toward Buddy. "You can't blow into this quietly, you know."

"Well, let's try, because I would think it would be quite the accomplishment to be able to play one of these properly. Because us O'Malleys have no abilities toward music at all," I quietly lied as I reached up and turned on a set of lights above our heads.

"Okay, this is how you hold it. See these holes? These are the ones you blow in to, and these holes on the backside are where the air comes out as beautiful musical notes." Paulie tried to quietly explain as he put the instrument up to his mouth to blow.

"So you want to hold it like you are eating a clubhouse sandwich?" I asked as I tried to mimic, putting the harmonica up to my mouth.

"No, no, more like a cheese sandwich," Paulie tried to explain. "You know, less filling."

"That's good to know; I was thinking that I was eating a sub there for a minute," I answered.

"It's more like a delicate grilled cheese sandwich with extra cheese." Paulie tried to enlighten me with his wealth of knowledge. "You know, when you pick up that grilled sandwich with both hands, and all that extra cheese seeps out? You are trying to keep as much cheese in the sandwich as possible, so be gentle."

I was gently holding the mouth organ up to my mouth, and for some reason; it just didn't feel right and probably looked worse, and all I wanted to do was blow into the instrument and piss Buddy off. "I feel my lips are too fat. These lips are for kissing, not for playing some mouth organ."

All the while as Buddy was trying to maneuver around all the traffic, he glared back toward us through the rearview mirror and demanded, "What are you guys up to back there?"

"Nothing, nothing at all. You don't hear anything, do you? You're driving, so just keep your eyes on the road." Paulie glared back toward Buddy. "Okay, your lips are a little puffy. But that's okay. It'll make you a better player in the long run. You will just have to adjust how you blow through them."

"I don't know. When I pull the harp to my bottom lip, it seems to push it up and forward, causing my upper lip to touch the bottom of my nose. I'm fighting to keep it in my mouth. I can see that my face and neck muscles would start to hurt after playing a while. Does yours hurt after a while?" I tried to explain with the harp up to my mouth, trying not to blow into it.

"Jesus, Kid, you are not sucking a cock here. Just blow it already, will ya?" Johnny started to laugh as he snatched the harp from my hands. "You are not the only one that has to piss." Johnny put the harp up to his mouth, took a great big breath, blew—and made a god-awful sound.

"That's it, Paulie. You're dead. I've warned you for the last time," Buddy screamed as he pulled the van over to the side of the thruway and slid to a stop on the slippery shoulder. He climbed out of the van and came around to the side doors. Just as he got to the side doors, there were already four out the door for a piss. "I'm going to fucking kill you."

Buddy got to the back of the van and seized the harmonica from Johnny's grasp.

Paulie spoke up. "See? It wasn't me."

"It doesn't matter," Buddy screamed as he headed back toward the front. "Anybody needs a piss, do it now." Just as Buddy got back to the side door, he realized that he had been taken. As he stepped out of the van, he whipped that harmonica deep into the woods. "That'll fix that."

"Noooooooooooooooooooooo. Say it ain't soooooooooooooo," Paulie cried in agony as he hurried out of the van to look for his harmonica. "How will I ever get to sleep at night?"

"It's all right, Paulie. He'll replace it. I know he will," I lied as I tried to comfort Paulie.

"Like fuck I will," Buddy yelled from outside the van.

"Don't worry. He will. If he doesn't, I'm sure he will sing you a lullaby to get you to sleep. Won't you, Buddy?" I joked.

"Will you fuck off, O'Malley? I can't believe you keep on teasing him like that," Buddy cried as he tried to get everyone back in the van. "Hurry up Paulie. Piss break is over. Everyone back in the van now."

"I'm not done yet," Paulie said as he fumbled around trying to do up his pants and take an inhale from his puffer all at the same time. "I can't believe you threw my harmonica away like that. What will I ever do?"

"I don't fucking care. I warned you. Now get in the van," Buddy exclaimed. "Now maybe we can have some peace and quiet."

The rest of the drive through Pennsylvania and Virginia was uneventful, except for some freezing rain in the mountains and skidding sideways around a twelve-vehicle pileup. A few lost their beer, a few lost their cards, and a whole lot of money hit the floor. I'm sure glad Buddy was at the wheel. Anyone else, and we would have been the thirteenth vehicle on its side. Not a good way to start a vacation.

When Teddy took over the wheel, all he did was miss the turnoff to get off Route 81 by a quarter mile. I blamed Buddy, as he was the map reader. Teddy slammed on the brakes and started to back up.

We were all screaming, "That's got to be a twenty-dollar fine."

"I don't think so, ladies and gents. That's what I call a back-me-up, and no one said anything about back-me-ups. That's why they put reverse in vehicles," Theodore argued as he backed up for nearly a quarter mile as truckers whizzed by, just laying on their air horns. Not really a good idea on an interstate in freezing rain. But he did it and was quite successful. The rest of night, I don't think any one of us got any sleep. We just drank beer, played cards, and occasionally, someone had to bring up the price of chicken in Pennsylvania to save Paulie from Buddy. But if it ever got really serious with Buddy and Paulie, we always could bring up about Mrs. Groper's nightly game of polishing-silverware that we could discuss at length.

CHAPTER 5

Motorboating in the State of North Carolina

Stewart took over the wheel sometime before the North Carolina border. By this time, it was awfully quiet in the back; as I think there must have been a few sleeping. Just south of Rocky Mount, North Carolina, off Interstate 95, there is a little town that is famous for the best breakfast in North Carolina. There is a truck stop there, where they serve an all-day breakfast twenty-four hours a day seven days a week. Besides the best breakfast in North Carolina, it serves up some of the best service you will ever see, among other things. So I told Stewart that I was hungry and pointed to the next ramp for him to take.

Stewart asked, "What gives? All these years that I have known you, I have never seen you eat breakfast."

"You will see, you will see. They must serve a great breakfast. It's 10:00 a.m., and the parking lot is full of transports." There must have been close to a hundred transports parked, and before I had a chance to say that it was a pee break and a quick breakfast, Paulie was out of the van on the run. Only five of us went in; as Buddy, Pudden, and Kevin decided that they would rather sleep than eat. Boy, were they ever going to be pissed?

As we opened the door to walk into the very dimly lit restaurant, the song "Sugar, Sugar" was playing. I'm not too sure if it was in my mind or if it was just background music. I was thinking at the time that it was the most appropriate song to play, with the lyrics "Sugar, Sugar … my candy girl … you've got me wanting you." The music was not playing very loudly, so I had myself convinced that it would be a prelim to some great sex that would happen in the future … the near future, I hoped.

As we moved in closer, there standing stupidly at the entrance was Paulie. I don't think he had moved once he had gotten in the doorway. There he stood with his mouth open. He had his puffer in hand, about to administer an inhale, when he muddled something to the effect, "Can you guys smell the maple syrup?" He took a huge puff from his inhaler and almost choked. "Hufffff … oooooooooooo … Oh, and by the way, there are boobies everywhere, and look: they come in all different sizes and colors."

"Paulie, that doesn't matter. Don't look at all those gorgeous perky boobies. We are here for breakfast," I argued.

"We are?" Although at first Paulie sounded very sad that we weren't there for the boobies, his attitude changed somewhat when he realized that he could have some breakfast. "Okay, let's have some pancakes."

"I'm only kidding. Of course, we are here for the boobies. And besides, they have the best flapjacks and grits in town. They not only serve them with a smile but serve them topless." Looking around I saw about a hundred truckers and five topless girls working. The place was full. I saw big girls, little girls, young and old; there were big boobies, small boobies, and I saw a pair of brand-new boughten boobies. There were round ones, perky ones, and even a set of hangers. It was a very impressive selection. If I remember right, there were five girls working: Felicity, Samantha, Patricia, Karen, and Jennifer. There could have been more, but I'm sure I only focused on ten breasts. I was only being polite when I asked them for their names because they really had no place to hang a name tag on. The great thing about this place was that you would have one of the girls seat you, another would look after the beverages, one would take your order, they all would help deliver your food, and then one would clear. It was like a tag team event of topless waitresses. They all interacted and flirted with each and every one of us and each other. They were women, we were men, and they knew what buttons to push. They all worked for their tips. What a great concept. As I looked around the room a little more, I saw a couple of brass poles strategically located. But I got to thinking that they must be there for show and show only. How would the waitresses climb a pole sexily with their hands full of dishes?

And I can't forget about the bouncer; his name was Winston. Winston was a big black guy, almost seven feet tall, about three hundred pounds. He collected all the money at the till for the girls. No credit cards, no interact, and especially no checks; just cash and cash only. What a business! But his main job was to look after the girls, and I'm sure the girls looked after him. Wink, wink, nod, nod!

Patricia escorted us to our table. It was the last table for four in the dimly lit room, but we were able to squeeze the five of us around it. I grabbed the only empty chair from an adjacent table and stated something to the effect, "I don't really need a place setting, as I usually don't eat breakfast."

Patricia informed me, "You might want to rethink that. The special of the day is steak and eggs. It's pretty good. And it comes with a motorboat with any one of the girls working."

"Wow, in that case, you might as well make it simple. Why don't you just bring five of those specials to us? I guess I could force myself to eat it. Who knows? This might become my favorite meal of the day." As Patricia started to walk away, I added, "Might as well make them all over easy and medium rare."

"But, Shannon, steak for breakfast? I don't know if I can eat steak medium-rare; I like it well-done, almost burned," Paulie cried as he picked up a menu to read.

"Guys, you will all be lucky if they don't all come out burned. This is no Ponderosa, and if that's what you came in here for, I would suggest the steakhouse down the road, but they are closed this time of day. And you sure as hell won't get the service that you are going to get here," Patricia added as she stopped and turned around to set him straight, giving us all a little wink.

"Don't listen to them. I'm sure whatever you bring us will be just perfect," Johnny stated as he settled into his seat looking around at all the eye candy. Or maybe he was looking for his Candy Girl… Sugar, Sugar.

"Shannon, what's a motorboat? I know, I know what a motorboat is. But what is a motorboat?" Paulie wondered.

Just then an older trucker, I think he must have been a regular, because Patricia called him by name. He was sitting next to us, so he must have overheard Paulie, and he mumbled, "You've got to be kidding me," as he grabbed Patricia walking by and sank his grey bearded face between her large, plump breasts, and then he spewed out this beautiful rhythmic motorboat sound. "Bubububububu." By the sound of things, it sounded like he had done this a few times before. But what made it even sexier was Patricia skillfully cupping her breasts around his face. She knew exactly what she was doing. You could see the skill and experience coming through with all of her gestures. The other thing that I noticed was that she really enjoyed doing her job and doing it well. What's the old saying? "A job is not worth doing unless you do it right."

She giggled as she pushed him away. "Cooter, that tickles. One of these days, you are going to have to cut that thing off."

"I only keep it on for you; you know that. See you tomorrow." As Cooter threw a twenty down on his table for a tip, he gave Paulie a gaze and said, "And, folks, that is what a motorboat is. You make sure you look after all the girls. And don't forget about Lil-Pammy in the back. She is an up-and-comer. You know, in training."

"Shannon, I usually only have pancakes and syrup for breakfast. But on special occasions, sometimes I'll do French toast; and on real, real special occasions, I might splurge for waffles. I got to have my syrup fix, and syrup doesn't go with steak," Paulie tried to explain.

Just then, Patricia, walking toward the kitchen, yelled, "Five more over-easy motorboats. Make them all medium rare. Oh yeah, make one of them a virgin, and he needs a side of maple syrup for dipping!"

"Paulie, think about it. I don't think that tree sauce you call maple syrup would go with motorboating either. Can you imagine how sticky all these girls' breasts would get?" Johnny concluded as he mimicked cupping his hands around breasts and driving his face into his fake valley of love. All you heard was him trying to imitate the sound of a 9.9 Evinrude.

"I don't know about that, Johnny. Paulie might have something here. Sticky nipples that taste like maple syrup. Ummm. I think sticky nipples would go with just about everything," I argued as I was already licking my lips with anticipation.

"Look, Paulie, if you don't want to eat steak, go the fuck out to the van and you can motorboat your cousin," Johnny surmised.

"Yeah, Pudden's got breasts. He's got bigguns," I agreed with Johnny.

"Okay, okay, I understand, but …" Paulie was looking at the menu; he leaned over and whispered, "Wow, it's kind of pricey in here. Also, it says that you only have two hours to eat your breakfast. Anything longer, and it is a dollar a minute. Who would take more than two hours to eat breakfast?"

"Holy fuck! A dollar a minute; that's sixty dollars an hour," Stewart added; he was astounded by the price. "For breakfast?"

"I told you those night courses for math would pay off," I teased him.

"Oh, will you fuck off?"

"Paulie, look around. Is this not worth it? When's the last time you had a boner on while you ate breakfast? Oh, that's right. I forgot that you live with your mother; you do that every morning. Okay, when's the last time you played with titties at breakfast? Probably never, so shut the fuck up and eat your breakfast. If it is too expensive for you, just go out in the van. You have two choices. You can motorboat your cousin or spoon with Buddy," I offered up. "And remember, you are only gay if you are on the bottom."

"Shannoneeee …"

"Hey, Paulie, does your mother really let you eat breakfast with a boner?" Johnny laughed.

"Johnny, I don't have a boner every morning. Well, not every morning. Well, okay, I do," Paulie said, thinking out loud.

Patricia finally delivered our breakfast. She was carrying all five. She had two in one hand, and the other three were balanced on her other arm, with the edge of the plate resting on her breast. She said, "More coffee?"

"What talent!" I stated, and I went on to say, "I would rather have beer. Can we get five beers?"

She said, "We are not licensed, but if you want to bring them in, all you have to do is pour them into these take-me-out-cups to conceal them."

I pulled five Old Milwaukees out from the left inside pocket of my jacket.

"Now, that is talent," Patricia concluded.

I came back with, "No, this is talent," as I pulled five more Old Milwaukees from the right inside pocket of my jacket. Trying to impress her even more, I pulled out two Mickeys of rum from my back pockets.

"I could be in love if you only drank something other than Old Milwaukee. Even Coors Light would be a better choice," she said as she grabbed the beer by one of the plastic rings. "Here, I will put these in the fridge to keep them cold for you."

"Coors Light, that's my favorite. I only carry the Old Milwaukees for my twin, Johnny," I told her as I pointed toward Johnny.

"Twins? Oh, I have never done twins before," she said with a mischievous grin and giggled. "Are you sure you are twins?" She was good, she was damn good, and she knew it. She was going to get every bit of tip money and then some from all of us.

"Oh, yeah. Can you not see the resemblance?" I tilted my face over toward Johnny's for her to compare. "I think Mom is the only one who can tell us apart. Right, Johnny?"

"Yep, Kid. And the only reason she can tell us apart is because I'm her favorite," Johnny bragged as he opened his beer and took a sip, dripping beer down his mustache as he finished.

"Noooo. I still don't see it. Are you really twins?" Patricia questioned us. "Am I missing something here?"

"By the time we leave, I'm sure you will see it," I warned her. "Patricia, just out of curiosity, who are we concealing it from? Is it the law, is it the owners, or is it Winston? I hope it is not Winston. That is the last thing that I would want to happen is to get thrown out of here."

"Not to worry. It is a Southern thing. They call it the brown-paper-bag law." She went on to explain, "It is nobody's business what you have in there."

Occasionally, you would hear a motorboat happening. The first time it happened, Paulie glanced over and shyly said, "I can't believe that I'm going to be able to do that."

"Have you picked out your boobies yet?" I whispered.

"I got it narrowed down to four," Paulie admitted.

"Four what? Boobies or girls?" I asked.

Paulie came back with, "Girls, of course. I just can't decide. They are all so beautiful. Look at them all. I might have to flip a coin."

"Well, look at it like this. You could have bought two breakfasts and got two girls. And they could have, even been different colors," I suggested with a chuckle.

"Oh, I couldn't have done that; that would have been too self-indulgent and frivolous. And besides, I can't afford that," Paulie informed us. You will come to find out as the story unfolds that the statement that he had just uttered was just plain bullshit. Remember, Paulie was like a little eight-year-old kid; he had no restraints.

The food was better than expected. Our two hours was almost up, and we only had one thing left to do—a round of motorboats to go. We had chosen all five girls, so not to leave anyone out. The five girls lined up, and then we lined ourselves up in front of the girls whom we had selected.

Paulie was going to go first, as he had his puffer in hand, just in case of an emergency. That had to be one of the sickest motorboats that I had ever heard. There was a lot of spitting and sputtering going on. It had to be the quickest motorboat on record. I'm sure he came in his pants as he rushed off to the washroom.

Then it was Theodore's turn. He had picked out this young, big-breasted black girl. I'm sure he didn't know what to do. The closest thing he had ever come to a black girl would have been watching Oprah every day at four o'clock before milking. He got scared and just politely shook both her hands and winked.

Stewart was to go next; he dove right in to those brand-new boughten boobies. She was probably one of the first Orientals that I had ever seen with perfectly round molded mounds. I think I had to remind him to come up for air. I'm sure that he had gone over his allotted time, because the next thing I knew, she was pushing him away.

Johnny went next, with Patricia, and once she had him in her grasp, it was hard for him to wriggle away. However, I'm sure that he wasn't trying very hard to get away. He sure was doing a lot of spitting and sputtering.

Then it was my turn. I said to Patricia, "Instead of me doing it, would it be all right if Felicity just took my turn with you?"

She said, "Sure, but only if you will join her."

It was perfect. I got a whole lot of tit and a whole lot of tongue. "I sure do love the South."

With tip, the bill was close to $200. Money well spent. We promised that we would stop on the way home. Maybe next time, Johnny and I could give Patricia that little twin action she was looking for and so deserved.

I think Johnny took a hankering to Patricia. Not sure if it was that she was a little on the big side or because she had the largest breasts, or maybe it was because his wife's name was Patricia. Nah, I think it was because she let him drink beer for breakfast.

We were walking back toward the van, and I told everyone, "Let's not mention this to the other guys. It would just make them mad. And Buddy has been mad and excited all the trip." Everyone agreed. We got back in the van, and the boys were just waking up.

Buddy looked at his watch and said with puzzlement, "Where have you fucking been, the last two hours?"

Trying to keep a straight face, I replied, "Oh, we were just eating some breakfast. Service was just awful. You just wouldn't have enjoyed it."

"It doesn't take no fucking two hours to eat breakfast. And you don't even eat breakfast," Buddy barked.

"Buddy, do you not know that breakfast is the most important meal of the day?" I affirmed as I tried to ease Buddy's mind-set.

We had just made it back on to Route 95, and Paulie could not hold it in any longer. He impatiently reported without taking a breath, "We had breasts for breakfast. That's why breakfast took that long, cause there was topless women in there; there were five of them. They were all different sizes; that's ten breasts. I had a boner the whole time. We ate steak and eggs, and that was the special, and we drank beer from a sippy cup. I learned the motorboat with Samantha, and I'm never going to wash my face ever again. I'm in love. It cost me forty dollars, and it was worth every dime, and I only had to use my puffer five times. Did I tell you that the whole place smelled like, like maple syrup? Did I tell you all of the waitresses' names? There was Samantha. Uhhh, there was … Shannon, what were the rest of the girls' names? Oh, it doesn't matter. Did I tell you about all the different-size boobies there were? And, and of course, there were different colors also, and, and you missed out. Ha-ha."

Buddy really looked puzzled by now. "What? You guys went to a topless breakfast place, and you didn't wake us up? What were you thinking?"

"Buddy, they were full, and we had to squeeze five seats around a table for four. There just would not have been enough room for you," I teased him.

Buddy countered, "Fuck you. You don't even eat breakfast, O'Malley, and you know I would have stood if I had to."

"Buddy, I have never seen you stand at a titty bar before. Ever. You've always been seated at the front. Right down there on pervert row." I argued.

"I know, but that's the only place where you can get all their sweat and sparkles on you." And then he thought for a moment on something that Paulie had said earlier. "And what the fuck is a motorboat?"

Paulie chimed in, "You don't know what a motorboat is? Well, my Little-Buddy, let me tell you what a motorboat is."

It was funny how Paulie was explaining everything to Buddy. He was explaining every little detail. Like he was the racing champ of motorboating. Buddy just got madder and madder with every little detail that Paulie spit and sputtered out.

CHAPTER 6

Pedro's Hometown

I had never been down south before, so I was not sure what I expected from Pedro's. We only had a little over a hundred miles left, to get there. All I can say is, they must have spent millions, on moving Mexico to South Carolina or at least on road signs. On Interstate 95, the road signs started about six hundred miles away. They were everywhere. For the last two hundred miles, they were at least every mile. We could not wait to see the next sign.

I was driving the van by then, so you knew I was going to stop. It was a twenty-four-hour tourist trap. They had a Pedro's Miniature Golf, a Pedro's Motel, a Pedro's Campground, Pedro's Amusement Rides, a Pedro's Reptile Zoo, and how about a Pedro's Observation Tower that overlooked the complex? They say that on real clear days, you can see Florida. There was no way in hell that I was going to climb all the way up to the top of that alien welcoming center. They had multiple restaurants, souvenir shops, and of course, a gas station. They even had a Pedro's Dirty Old Man's Sex Shop hidden in the back. We might have to stop on the way home to see Florida or "something." Wink, wink. Nod, nod.

I think I asked Buddy if he still had relatives working there. He told me to fuck off. Other years, Buddy had been there, so when we stopped and got out of the van, he was like our own personal tour guide. All he needed was a sombrero, and he could have looked like all the other Pedro's there. He was directing us to all the various places, restaurants, souvenir shops, and of course, a washroom for Paulie.

About five minutes into Buddy's tour, a family of four approached us and asked where the miniature golf course was.

"Does it look like I fucking work here?" Buddy snarled.

The family basically apologized and said, "It was just that you seemed to know where everything was."

"Well, I don't, so fuck off," Buddy yelled.

As the father ushered his family away, I apologized for Buddy for being such an asshole. "Buddy's father was one of the original guides here in the early sixties, and he just passed away some weeks ago. Buddy is very sensitive to the subject and not quite himself."

"O'Malley, where in fuck do you come up with this?" Buddy came back with, as the father safely directly his family away.

I told him, "I can't make this shit up. And you're just pissed because you do look like you work here, Pedro."

We were making our way around the Border of the South, and Buddy piped up, "I almost forgot. I've got to go to the Tall Man Shop."

"Tall Man Shop? You are kidding, right?" Johnny sarcastically asked. "What are you buying? A stepladder?"

"Nooooo. They have a Tall Man Shop for Little People here at the Border," Buddy stated. "You have heard of those Big and Tall stores? Well, they have a store here that specializes in little people like us."

"Speak for yourself. Did you not know that I'm the biggest O'Malley?" I said as we all tagged in behind Buddy.

"Yes, yes, you have told me and everyone else. Many, many times before," Buddy explained. "Even being the biggest O'Malley, you might find something here."

"I don't know; I'm pretty particular on what I wear," I concluded. "I'm not like you guys."

"They not only sell clothes that fit, but they give you a vision; you know, a new attitude. When you leave the store, you will feel much, much taller," Buddy assured us as we rounded the corner and headed toward the storefront.

"I don't know if I need anything. Patty and I have this sweet deal going on with Sears. I don't think too many people know about it," Johnny tried to explain. "I have jeans for life."

"Sweet deal! Jeans for life?" I asked. "What's that all about?"

"Well, Sears has this policy that your kids will never wear out their jeans. This is only for shopping in the Kids' aisle. So if you can fit into a kids' size fourteen, like me, you're all set. If you rip them or get a hole in them, or just wear them out, they will replace them with a new pair the same size. No questions asked. Look at these. I believe these jeans have been replaced probably thirty times in the last thirty years. Patty just goes in and cries that her teenage sons are hard on clothes," Johnny explained.

"Wow, that is good. But I can't believe that those salespeople think Pat has had that many teenage boys all those years," I joked.

"Oh, she can be quite convincing when she wants to be. And think about it; who is going to argue with Patty anyways?" Johnny asked. "I learned the hard way. I sure don't want to argue with her."

"But you have put on a few pounds over the years. How are you still getting them on?" I asked.

"I've got one of those newfangled extend-a-buttons at the waist. It can add about three inches to your waist size," Johnny informed us as he showed his waist button that extended his waist size by quite a bit. "And I know that I'm getting shorter all the time, so all I have to do is keep rolling up the pants legs."

As we walked up to the storefront, there were signs everywhere; and the neat thing was that most, if not all, the signs were at eye level or below for short people. Even the main store sign, which said "Tall Man Shop," came across below the top of the doorway. It had a little sign on it that said, "If you bump your head coming in, then more than likely, you will bump your head going out, so you are in the wrong store. Just keep walking; nothing to see here." Funny thing, if you were over five feet four inches tall, you didn't belong there. Buddy led the way into the store, under the low-clearance sign. We were like the Seven Dwarfs waddling in behind the even shorter Buddy. Three of us had to duck under the signage to get in, so we must have been classified as giants. I could see this was not like any other clothing store that I had ever been in before. Everything was built around, not just short people, but short, short little people, if you know what I mean.

"Where do you think they found all these short mannequins?" Johnny inquired as he walked around the store.

"Stupid, they just cut the legs off at the knees. Where else do you think?" I retorted.

"I'm not sure if that would bring them down under the height restriction," Johnny added.

"It's got to be close, I would think," I told him.

As we walked in, I noticed something real strange. The store's ceiling was not the normal eight feet or higher. It was closer to six feet, I would think. You might not notice if you were only three feet ten inches, but it was almost making me claustrophobic. A salesman hurried over to greet us. Later we would find out that he was the owner. As he got closer, I noticed that he wasn't just short; he was one of those little people. He made everyone in our group look large, even Buddy.

Paulie leaned over to me and whispered, "This store sells clothes to those little people; you know, midgets." The thought of it made Paulie break out in a chuckle as he finally met his first wee person.

"Yes, Paulie, we know. Now shut the fuck up," I scolded Paulie.

"But …" Paulie, all anxious; wanted to know more.

"Okay then, Paulie, go ahead and ask how tall he is," I interrupted.

"No, that's not …" Paulie lied.

"It's okay. I'm four feet five and a half inches tall. And proud of every inch I've got," he said proudly.

"Nooooo. What I wanted to know is, I got to pee. Is there a washroom I can use?" Paulie cried as he got all antsy in his pants.

"Over there to the right," the salesman said, pointing toward the washroom in the back.

"Thanks," Paulie said as he ran toward the back.

The salesman's name was Mario, and he said, "Wow, Mr. Parker, welcome back. I see you have brought some of your tall friends with you."

"Hey, Mario, how are things going? How's your wife, Mildred? Is she here?" Buddy asked.

"Yes, yes, she's here somewhere. Hey, Millie, look who's here. Mr. Parker, he's back. Millie?" Mario put his hand out to shake Buddy's. "Millie, where are you?"

"I told you I would be back. Did that special order come in?" Buddy asked.

"Yes, it came in. You are gonna love it. It's in the back. I'll go get it for you," Mario stated as headed toward the back of the store. "Millie, where are you? Mr. Parker is here, and he brought some short, err, shorter customers. I could use some help out here."

We were all looking around, and even the dummies were all dressed to look tall. They all had short-man syndrome. They all wore short pants, and all stood straight up. None of them slouched over. And all of them wore platform shoes to make them look taller. Someone should tell them that platform shoes have been out of style for at least fifteen years or so. And the real clincher for short-man syndrome is spiking your hair. It's got to add a couple of inches to your height. And don't get me started on the mirrors. I believe that they were all out of a circus or carnival. The distorted reflection made everyone look taller, much taller.

Mario came out from the back with a box for Buddy and said, "I'm not sure where Millie has gotten off to. She is very good at hiding. Look at this. They're going to make you look and feel bigger."

As he opened the box, Buddy said, "This will be perfect."

"What is it? What are they?" someone asked.

"Oh, these little things? They are going to add inches," Buddy said as he held up a long plastic …

"You didn't, Buddy! Did you? That isn't one of those cock extenders, is it?" Johnny said.

"Nooooo, it's lifts for my shoes," Buddy retorted.

"Buddy, I don't know. I would have gotten the cock extension. At least, Marilyn would have been happier," I said.

Johnny butted in. "Oh, it doesn't matter; she'll be happier. She won't have to pretend that she is shorter than you."

"Oh, fuck off. She doesn't care that she is taller than me," Buddy growled as he looked in a full-length mirror.

"Next time you are standing beside her, check it out. She slouches over or moves to the other side of the room," I informed him.

"No, she doesn't," Buddy argued as he took another look into a different mirror. "Does she?"

"Now that you mention it, I've seen that," Johnny added. "She does move around the room a lot."

"Just check it out next time," I stammered.

"Fuck off, both of you," Buddy cried. "I bet you they will fit in my golf shoes also."

"But, Buddy, why in hell do you want to be taller on the golf course?" I blurted out.

"I know, I know. It's so he can reach down into the well and get his own beer from the beverage cart." Johnny laughed.

"Will you fuck off for once?" Buddy warned as he slipped the new insoles into his shoes. "What do you think? They sure do feel good."

"They not only make you taller, but they really do make you stand up straighter," Mario informed him as he forced Buddy to look into the funhouse mirror.

"You think? I sort of feel it," Buddy agreed as he moved about in front of the mirror. "Wow, I got to get some new jeans. These seem to be too short now."

"But wearing them short like that, doesn't that make people think that you are taller than you are?" Johnny asked.

"Yeah, you're taller. Come on, Stretch. Grab what you want. We have to get going," I snickered.

Just then Paulie came running out of the washroom and anxiously said, "They have a dwarf…."

"Paulieeeeeee." Buddy interrupted him. "Mario, I've got to apologize for my friend here. He's an idiot. Just ask anybody."

"It's okay," Mario said. "We've just got to get him to start thinking smaller."

"Okay, okay. I'm so sorry, Mario," Paulie apologized as he wiped his hands clean. "It's just I have never seen such a small shitter before."

"Paulieeeee …"

"Well, you guys won't believe it. You should see the small toilet in there. I sat down, and I still pissed all over myself," Paulie cried. "Do I look taller or something? I don't feel taller. I still had to bend over to look in the mirror."

"No, Paulie. Will you just fuck off?"

The whole time that we were in the store, the song "Short People" would start to play in my mind, only to fade off into the distance and then, without warning, would start to play again. So I was going to make the assumption that Millie was, in fact, a wee person. The funny thing, though, was as quick as that song started to play, it would abruptly fade away. I'm not sure why, and I guess I will never know, because as far as I can remember, I never did meet Millie. I think I would have remembered her if I did. Over the years, though, we had on many occasions stopped there for Buddy to feel taller; but we never did run in to her. I know you are expecting me to give you this unbelievable sexual fantasy about Millie, the Midget. But I got nothing. It's probably the first time in my life that I lost a sexual fantasy with a female that I had just met. Maybe it was because I didn't meet her, and to be honest, I do not know if she was a small person or a big person. Ummmm, I should have gotten Stewart to ask. I know Paulie would have. I know I sure would have enjoyed meeting her. Maybe I will just have to plan a golf vacation for next week, so I can finish that song.

So by the time we got out of there, Mario had sold something to almost all of us. He had done his work, as everyone left either feeling taller or at least standing up straighter. Everyone walked out of there with confidence. As we were walking out to leave, you won't believe it, but Buddy bumped his head on the low-clearance sign at the front door. Maybe he was taller? No, he was not. Mario had lowered the sign somehow. I think that was how Mario influenced everyone with the illusion that when you left his store, you were actually taller.

We grabbed more beer, refueled, and were on our way. We only had half a state left, which would translate to two pee breaks for Paulie.

CHAPTER 7

Valet Parking Is Not Only for the Rich and Famous

We arrived alive. Shady Hills was just a sleep stop along Interstate 95. It had three or four motels, a couple of fast-food places, and a couple of gas stations. Not the big touristy area that I had expected. By the way, I did win the one hundred sixty bucks for the arrival-time pool, by about two hours. I guess taking two hours to eat breakfast and taking that quick motorboat ride had a plus side. Who would have thunk it?

I pulled into the Happy Holiday Hotel, right up to the front door, right under the big green Happy Holiday Hotel awning.

"We can't fit under there. We don't need to be that close?" someone screamed from the back.

"Watch me," I claimed as the van roof barely kissed under the flaps of the bottom of the awning. "This is where you get valet parking, isn't it?

"Fuck, you're an idiot," Buddy screamed.

"Wait for it. Wait for it. He will come," I stated.

"Who will come?" Paulie wanted to know.

"You can wait as long as you want; no one is coming to park this beast." Buddy interrupted Paulie as he started to climb down out of the van.

"Are you sure, Buddy? You wouldn't lie to me, would you?" I wondered out loud. "I'm sure I read somewhere that all Happy Holiday Hotels in the United States have some sort of valet parking. I got ten bucks says they will park this beast."

"Make it twenty. Now get the fuck out of the van and let's go check in," Buddy ranted.

"You're on." As we all climbed out of the van, all you could hear was about ten to fifteen empty beer cans hitting the pavement. Actually, I think you heard that sound anytime you opened any of the van doors that week. We must have been quite the sight, eight drunks falling out of the van, empty beer cans everywhere, and most of us having had no sleep for over twenty-four hours. Basically, everyone grabbed as many cans off the ground as they could, and we staggered in the front door. With no trash can in sight, we tried to line them all up on the front desk. We were all trying to be helpful, but with some of the cans being knocked over and some just being spilled, all you could smell was old, skanky beer.

Buddy rushed right up to the front desk and demanded, "Will you tell this fucking drunken idiot that you do not have valet parking?"

"Sweet Jesus. Look at y'all. Which one of these drunken idiots are you referring to, sir?" the clerk asked in a Southern drawl as she pointed around the room at the group of wobbly drunks before her.

Buddy started to point at me and said, "What the fuck; tell them all."

"But, sir, we do. Let me call Zackery down," she boasted as she reached for her walkie-talkie. "It might be safer that way."

"Whattttttt? Unbelievable. I just don't know how you pull this off all the time," Buddy said to me.

"Planning, a whole lot of planning," I admitted. I really did not want Buddy to know that I had called down and talked with Sally Sue earlier in the month. I did not want him to know that I had arranged to have a few pranks set up at Buddy's expense. When I had talked to Sally Sue originally about some of the shenanigans, I was not sure if she understood or not. Because each time I got off the phone with her, I was the one in the dark. I just could not understand her Southern drawl. So I was very happy when the valet parking went off without a hitch and found out that Sally Sue did, in fact, have a sense of humor, among other things.

"You must be the O'Malley and Parker golf group? It sure looks like y'all are going to have fun this week. Your golf group is the last one that has to check in today," she said with a sly smile.

The night manager's name was Sally Sue. She had the largest, roundest, blue eyes that I had ever come across. Although she was a bigger, older black lady, she was still very confident and beautiful and really didn't show her age. She was regimented and very militaristic; I did not think that I would want to be on the wrong side of her. I was giving her that once-over, and just then the song "Mustang Sally" started to play.

Sally Sue had a very heavy Southern accent. So heavy that, at times, it was hard to understand her, so we were all having her repeat herself a lot. She had been manager there for some time and was accustomed to putting up with a lot of drunken golfers over the years. But she was the one in charge and did not take any shit off nobody. I mean nobody.

Stewart and I gave each other that little smirk and a little wink we gave each other every once in a while, that meant, "I'd do her … No, I would do her first!" So in Stewart's mind, he was probably envisioning himself making mad, passionate love with Sally Sue. Boring. In my mind, I had her role-playing a dominatrix. "Ride, Sally, ride." I had her dressed in leather, with thigh-high, come-over-here-and-fuck-me boots, snapping her whip, all awhile riding around on my backside yelling out dirty commands. You got to love being scolded and yelled at, especially being scolded in a Southern accent.

While we were all filling out our registration cards, Sally Sue went through all the dos and don'ts at the motel. She looked us all in the eyes and said, "Now read my lips. I expect each and every one of you to conform to these rules. Right?" She repeated herself, as no one had answered. "Right?"

"Right!" we all bellowed together.

We all paid cash. Canadian cash! At the time, I think the US dollar was over a 30 percent premium.

She handed everyone their breakfast tickets for the week and said, "Now do not lose these. I repeat, do not lose these. They will not be replaced."

Paulie piped up, "Don't you wish they would serve breakfast like we just had?"

"Maybe they do, Paulie, maybe they do," I suggested.

She confirmed the golf courses and tee times that we were playing for the week and asked if someone in the group would drop by sometime after supper to pick up the golf vouchers that we needed to hand in at each course each day to play. She stated that she had not had enough time to fill them out earlier in the day. She also told us that she needed a credit card on file for each room to cover any thievery or damages that "would happen." Yes, she said, "would happen." She also went on to say that it was just a precaution and she thought that we looked like gentlemen and that we would not need the deposit, but management made her do it. Boy, did we ever have her fooled, I was thinking to myself. As she was handing out the eight keys, she said that she was going to run a twenty-dollar deposit on the credit cards for each key. Which meant what? When we checked out and handed back the key, we would receive the deposit back. All of us who had credit cards handed them over to Sally Sue.

Pudden and Kevin were going to share a room, as were Johnny and Theodore. Stewart and I would have a room together, and that left Buddy and Paulie to share the room right next to ours, and the great thing about that was that it had an adjoining door. When I had called down about the valet parking, I had also mentioned that it would be great if my room was beside Buddy's, and if it had an adjoining door, that would be great in the grand scheme of things.

Buddy handed her his credit card for their room since Paulie did not have such a thing. Buddy glared at Paulie and told him, "Now, you be careful. Don't steal any towels, and don't you dare lose that key."

Paulie, quickly grabbing his key; dropped it in the change pocket of his wallet and zipped it closed for safekeeping; quite confidently said. "Not to worry, Little Buddy, what could go wrong?"

"Paulie, what could go wrong? I want you to look over your shoulder. See those two fucking O'Malleys over there? They are going to eat you alive. They will devour you alive," Buddy warned him.

"Buddy don't be like that. We won't do it together. We will take our turns at him," Johnny informed him.

"See, Paulie? They are already preparing their attack." Buddy tried to enlighten Paulie. "You just be ready."

We were given directions to our rooms, the vending machines, and the ice machines. Sally Sue had also stated that the motel's ice machines were for in-house use and not for filling beer coolers. As we went outside, the van was already gone. Zackery had pulled the van down to the stairway that was out front of our rooms. He was already hard at work digging out our luggage and some of our golf clubs.

As we approached the van, there stood Zackery wearing his green Happy Holiday Hotel work shirt and a pair of blue jeans. He had a black Dale Earnhardt #3 hat on, tilted to one side. He was an older man, in his fifties. Zackery was head of maintenance at the motel and had done this for the last twenty years or so. He knew where every screw and nail was at the motel. He probably could fix anything and everything. He reminded me a lot of our Mac, back at the resort. Mac was our head of maintenance. If you needed something done, you called Mac to fix it. He was famous for Mac-a-sizing the job. So I'm sure Zackery could Zac-a-size a job also.

I looked at Buddy and mentioned, "No valet parking, eh? Just give Zackery the twenty dollars; he's the one who deserves it."

Buddy reluctantly gave Zackery the twenty dollars and said, "Thanks for nothing."

"Why, thank you, sir. Is there anything else you need?" Zackery eagerly volunteered.

"Can you top up our beer coolers with ice every day? I think Buddy will have at least a ten-dollar bill for you," I interrupted.

"No, I won't. And besides, they have ice machines here at the hotel. So, fuck off, O'Malley," Buddy countered.

"Buddy, did you not just hear Sally Sue? Does she not scare you? You want to get on the bad side of her already? What are you thinking?" I said. "Zackery don't worry; you keep us full of ice, and someone will have money for you. And more than likely, it will be Buddy."

The motel was over a hundred rooms, U-shaped, with the outdoor pool in the center. They had a restaurant and a bar. What else would we need? We were all on the second floor, all close together, so we had a great view of the pool. I'm not sure why that was great; it was going to be too cold all week for the honeys to be in the pool.

CHAPTER 8

Buddy's Room Needs to Be Re-Carpeted

After supper, most of us were lounging around in Buddy and Paulie's room. We were having a few drinks, talking a little golf, and talking a little trash; we were just having some fun. I think Buddy was down in the lobby getting our golf vouchers.

Johnny was walking around the room with one of my golf clubs. He was making a couple of swings with it and said, "You know, I used to swing left-handed when I first started. I think I was pretty good too."

"Why did you switch?" someone asked.

"When I moved to the States, I was told that only hockey players shoot left-handed and good golfers only shoot from the right," he came back with. Johnny dropped a ball down, in-line with the door opening, took a couple of practice swings, and wondered out loud, "I wonder if I still have it or not." He stepped back and stood behind the ball.

You could see him visualizing something. You could see his brain working overtime. What was he up to?

"What do you see?" I asked him.

"It would be a hell of a shot if it could be made. I don't know if I still have it in me or not," Johnny came back with.

Stewart and I were standing behind Johnny, and Stewart came out with, "Shannon, do you see what I see?"

"I don't know. What do you see?" I responded. "I can't see a fucking thing. It's dark out, stupid."

"Well, can you at least visualize it?" Stewart begged.

"Okay, okay. I'm thinking that we hit our golf ball from a tight lie on the carpet, through the door opening, up over the railing, keeping it just under the eave, and with enough distance to get to the pool. What's that? About a little over one hundred thirty yards, I think?" I pointed out the shot that I wanted us to make.

"No, it's well over one hundred forty, if not closer to one hundred fifty yards. I got ten-dollars says I can make it," Stewart bellowed as he dug a ten-dollar bill out of his pants and threw it on the bed. You must understand that Stewart was the best at this type of shot. It did not matter how dark it was out, how drunk he was, or how stupid the shot was. I'm sure he could have joined the Professional Miniature Golf Tour. Because putting and making that windmill shot takes talent. No matter what the shot was, he would always make it and walk away with all the money. Not this time, though. I thought I could do it.

"Well, I got ten-dollars." Throwing it on top of the other ten-dollar bill.

"To make it legit, I think if you make the shot, you have to retrieve and verify your ball out of the pool," Johnny declared.

Paulie, lying on the bed half-asleep, said, "I think that's fair. Can I shoot? I think I've got a ten-dollar bill somewhere." So he threw his ten-dollars onto the pile.

"Johnny, I think it was your idea. Are you not going to throw your ten bucks in?" I asked.

"Are you fucking nuts? Do you know how cold the water will be in the pool? I'm not that crazy. You are on your own, Kid," Johnny affirmed. "And besides, you hit it ten yards too long, and you will be pulling your ball out of someone's room across the way."

"Anybody else want to shoot?" I begged.

I think Pudden said, "Are you fucking nuts? The door is less than three feet wide, and you have a picture window on the left and the TV is to the right."

"And your point is? Not to worry, guys, this is Buddy's room," I cackled. "He won't mind."

"Or maybe you don't think you can get the ball up fast enough, or you can't hit it long enough to get to the pool? Or maybe you just don't like hitting it off that tight lie on the carpet?" Stewart chimed in.

Pudden and Kevin said that they couldn't watch anymore, and they were going back to their room before someone got hurt or before something got broke.

"Paulie, maybe we should we wait for Buddy. Do you think that he would like to play?" I wondered.

"No, he would just call it stupid and yell at us for being idiots. Let's just hurry up and do it before he gets back," Paulie hurriedly stated.

"I guess it's just going to be the three of us. All the rest of you are chic-chic-chicken," I boldly stated.

Stewart was going to go first. He grabbed his seven-iron, dropped his golf ball, a brand-new Titleist-3, and was about to hit when I piped up, "That's not enough club."

He backed away, glanced around the room, looked at me, licked his middle finger, and stuck it in the air like to check the wind. I think he was checking the wind.

"I got the right club. How about we make it twenty-dollars?" he asked.

"Paulie, are you still in?" I asked as I threw another ten-dollars in.

Paulie thought for a moment and came back with, "That's twenty-dollars Canadian, right?"

"Paulie, you are not in Kansas anymore." As I confused him with that statement.

"Kansas?" Paulie was trying to figure out where he was. "Were we ever, did we drive through Kansas?"

"Paulie, never mind. Do you not remember when we left Canada, we all agreed that all bets made in the United States are payable in US funds," I reminded him?

"Oh, that's right. I'm sorry; I guess I forgot," Paulie apologized. The thing was we never really discussed it, and yes, that's right, we were taking advantage of poor Paulie again, and it wouldn't be the last time. Paulie threw another ten-dollars in.

Stewart was about to take his shot again, and I piped up, "What if nobody makes the shot? Does the closest win?"

"Closest to what? Fuck, we are not playing horseshoes here. You have to make the shot to win, plain and simple," Stewart said.

"In that case, why don't we throw another ten-dollars in?" I asked as I dug another ten out of my pocket. "Paulie, you in?"

"All right, guys, this has to be the last time; I can't afford anymore," Paulie pleaded as both Paulie and Stewart threw another ten-dollars in.

Stewart started his pre-shot routine again. I jumped up and down waving my arms around as I interrupted one more time. "Wait! Wait! What if two of us make the shot? Do we share the pot? Do we have a tiebreaker? Or are we playing skins here, so one tie, all tie?"

"Fuck, will you let me shoot already? We are not playing skins here. We will have a shoot-out. Okay?" Stewart yelled.

"We should throw another ten-dollars in; might as well make it worth our while," I said. "That water looks cold."

Paulie pleaded again, "Seriously, I do not have any more money." He pulled his wallet out of his front pocket, opened it up, turned it upside down, and waved it around in the air. A few nickels and dimes fell out of the change pocket along with his key to his room.

"Is that a change pocket? Who has a change pocket in their wallet? Paulie, this is the first day. What do you mean you are out of money? How are you going to eat all week? Drink all week? Bet all week?" I asked, as I quickly picked up Paulie's key without him noticing.

"Well, I guess I didn't know it was going to cost this much. Who would have thought that we would bet so much, and I didn't expect breakfast to cost so much," Paulie said sadly?

"Paulie don't look at it as an expensive breakfast; look at it as an experience, maybe even a life-altering experience.

You fell in love. Also, aren't you glad that you didn't buy any chicken in Pennsylvania? If you did, you wouldn't even have money to be in this bet right now. And look, one lucky swing, and you could win all this money. So, Paulie, I'm going to raise this bet one more time; that's right, another ten. I will even lend it to you, because I have faith in you. I think, I know, you can do it," I advised him. I threw a twenty in for me and for him before he got a chance to decline the loan. So now we had one hundred twenty US dollars in the pot for a shot that shouldn't be makeable.

By now all the boys in the room were getting restless and started to chant, "Shoot! Shoot! Are we going to see this shot in my lifetime?"

Stewart swung; as usual, it was perfect. The ball came off the club just at the right angle, just making it over the railing, and just skimming under the eave.

The boys in the room looking out the picture window were all chanting, "Go! Go! Go!" The ball splashed into the pool for a hole in one.

"That shot was a thing of beauty. It sure was pretty." I looked at Stewart and acknowledged, "Great shot, Scooter."

I grabbed my eight-iron, threw my dirty old Top-Flite II down, and without any hesitation, made a swing. The ball went through the door, clipped the railing, ricocheted up toward the eave, hit the bottom of the fascia board, and careened back to my feet, landing inches from the spot that I had just shot it from. "Fuckkkkkkk."

There was a whole lot of heckling going on from the crowd.

It was Paulie's turn. He grabbed his five-iron and dropped his ball. It was yellow with black stripes. That's right; it was a fucking range ball.

"Paulie, that five-iron is way too much club. You will take out a window on the other side of the pool. And you can't use no fucking range ball!"

"Shut the fuck up. I'm using the five-iron, and I'm using my lucky yellow Spalding range ball," Paulie interrupted.

I told Paulie, "After you win the one hundred twenty dollars, you will not only be able to eat for the week, but you will be able to buy some good golf balls. You might even be able to buy some chicken on the way home or even stop for another motorboat breakfast."

"Chicken! Chicken! Chicken!" the boys were chanting in the background. "Paulie, if you win, are you going to buy chicken, or will you go for a boat ride? Bubububububu."

"What do you think? That's a no-brainer," Paulie answered. "I might even treat you all to a motorboat ride."

All of sudden, it got really quiet. Everyone was anticipating what was about to happen. Paulie was taking his time. He was weaving back and forth; he was pretty drunk. Paulie made a swing at the ball; at the same exact moment, Buddy came walking through the door. Buddy ducked just in time and hit the floor. He started to yell. "Paulie, what in fuck are you doing? I can't leave you alone for a minute?" He looked up at Paulie, and then his eyes moved slowly down to the golf ball, that Paulie had missed. There sat his lucky yellow range ball, with a torn piece of carpet lying over the top of the ball. Ladies and gentlemen, you call that a nylon beaver pelt. Stewart and I were just rolling around on the bed; we were just howling, as we couldn't stop laughing. The rest of the boys were just going wild. I'm not sure what was more amazing: Buddy coming into the room at the exact opportune time, him hitting the floor, or Paulie tearing the carpet from his tight lie.

Buddy was livid. He was so mad. Both eyes were watering and twitching. And those veins we talked about before had just connected into one. You could actually see the blood pumping through the throbbing bulge on his forehead. "How in fuck are you going to fix this? How are you going to pay for this? It's your first night. It's my fucking credit card." He just went on and on, and then he started to yell at me. "Why weren't you looking after him? How could you let him try this?"

"Buddy, I warned him, and I warned him. He just wouldn't listen to me, I told him that his five-iron was way too much club, and I told him not to use that range ball. Can you believe that? He used a range ball!" I tried to reassure Buddy with laughter.

Buddy exploded. "What the fuck are you talking about?"

"You heard me. Look at this shot; don't you think that a five-iron was way too much club? He could have taken out a window on the other side of the pool. And a range ball to boot. You know that it's not going to get up fast enough to get over that railing. I tried, Buddy. I even asked him to wait for you. He just wouldn't listen to me," I lied, scooping the one hundred twenty dollars off the bed to conceal the evidence.

Then it was like a big-o-lightbulb went off in Buddy's head. "You fuckers, you set him up again."

"No, no, Buddy. It was not like that at all. Stewart and I were just fooling around. I didn't want him to play. He begged us to play; ask anyone." I tried to convince him that I was innocent.

"I don't fucking care whose fault it is. What are we going to do about the rug? I'm not paying for it," Buddy informed me.

"Don't worry, Buddy. You are a carpenter. That rug is a Heuga carpet tile; you have laid thousands of these, over the years. We just have to find one in the motel that matches this ripped one. I'll look after it for you. Worst-case scenario, we just exchange a tile from under your bed," I suggested as I tried to ease his agony. "Don't lose any sleep over it."

"Fix this, and don't you dare touch another thing in this room," he came back with. "It is off-limits to you the rest of the week."

"Okay, okay. But can I come over at least and visit my good friend Paulie?"

"No, so just fuck off," Buddy bawled. "You just get that tile fixed."

"Okay, okay. Come on, Stewart. Grab that tile, and let's go tile hunting," I confidently said. "Hey Paulie, you want to help?"

"No, he's not going anywhere with you two," Buddy advised.

"Come on, Buddy. Let me go; I can help them," Paulie cried as he took a big inhale from his puffer. "You never let me have any fun."

"No, you are not going with them," Buddy warned him. "When will you learn? They are out to get you."

"No, we are not. We just want to see Paulie have some fun," I came back with. "Paulie, are you supposed to use that puffer that often? How many did you bring with you?"

"I hope I brought enough because I sure am having fun," Paulie said. "I'll be doing a lot of wheezing on the way home if I didn't."

So, we finally did find matching tiles. They were at the entrance to the restaurant. They were also in plain view of the front desk. So all I had to do was keep Sergeant Sally Sue busy while Stewart exchanged one of the tiles. Just as I went up to the front desk and started some small talk with Sally Sue, you guessed it, that song "Mustang Sally" started to play in my mind. I asked her for some directions to the various golf courses that we were playing that week. As I said before, her accent was so heavy, I could not understand her half the time. She took me around the corner to where there was this large wall map of the area. It had all of the golf courses, plus a few local attractions marked. I guess I kept her busy enough because as we walked back around the corner, the tile had been switched, and Stewart was gone. Stewart had done a fantastic job, as you could hardly see the tear in the carpet.

I catch up with Stewart, and all he asked was, "So what did you guys talk about?"

"I'm not sure. It was really hard to understand her. We talked about the weather for the week, directions to all the golf courses, and I think I have a date on Friday with her. She sure can be bossy and domineering at times," I responded with.

And Stewart came back with, "So, I have three days to get a date with her before Friday. No problem."

We got back to the room with the tile. Buddy and Paulie were gone, and the door was locked. "They're probably all over at Pudden's room. Don't worry. I stole Paulie's key," I let Stewart know.

"You did what?" Stewart laughed.

"Well, how else am I going to fix this dilemma?" We laid the tile, and it was perfect. Well, sort of perfect. The new tile was a little more faded from all the traffic to the restaurant than the tile from Buddy's room. I had Stewart help me move the bed an inch or so, so the impressions in the rug of the bed frame made it look like the bed had been moved. While we were moving the bed, I happened to notice that there were no carpet tiles under the two bed frames at all. This is usually done as a cost-saving practice. I thought to myself, *this is great. This will drive Buddy insane. He will think that I removed all these carpet tiles.*

We went over to Pudden's room; Buddy, Paulie, and Johnny were there as I expected. I tried to explain to Buddy, "Sorry. We just could not find a matching carpet tile, so we just exchanged one from under your bed."

"Like fuck you did. First off, how did you get in the room? It was locked," Buddy yelled. "Right, Paulie?"

"Yes, it was. I checked it; you saw me check it," Paulie replied.

"Remember, Buddy? We have adjoining rooms," I continued.

"Well, that door was locked also. Right, Paulie? Right, Paulie?" Buddy asked.

"Well, well, I think it was locked. Yeah, it was locked," Paulie stated.

Buddy gave Paulie a you-are-going-to-die look. "What's this 'I think it was locked'? Was it locked or unlocked?"

"I don't know now. I guess, I guess it must not have been locked?" Paulie said, apologizing to Buddy.

"Paulie, you have to remember to start locking the door, I tell you," Buddy reminded him. "You have to remember you are vacationing with those fucking O'Malleys."

"That's kind of harsh," I proclaimed. "Stewart, we're done here. Let's go find some nightlife. Johnny, are you coming?"

"Okay, but I can only come out for a little while," Johnny answered.

CHAPTER 9

Martha, There Must Be Another Canadian in the Pool

We were halfway down the stairs when Stewart inquired, "Where's my share of the money?"

"Johnny, did you not stipulate that to win, you had to retrieve the ball to prove that it landed in the pool? It was pretty dark out. I'm not sure I actually saw it land in the pool," I asserted.

"And how am I going to do that? The gate is probably locked, and that pool looks awfully cold," Stewart said as if he was trying to get out of jumping in. "You don't really expect me to go into the pool, do you?"

"Yes, I do. Go get it. It was a Titleist-3, was it not?" I tempted him with logic. "A bet is a bet."

It was dark, it was cold, and it had to be colder than forty degrees Fahrenheit; I really did not expect him to say, "Okay," but he did.

We were walking toward the pool, and Johnny was trying to talk him out of jumping in while I was trying to talk him into it. Johnny cautioned Stewart, "That water looks awfully cold. The water is going to be colder than you think. I'm not sure how you are going to get over the fence. The pool is barely lit. If you start to drown, I'm not saving you. And the Kid can't swim, so he is not going to jump in either. You will be on your own. I hope you know what you are doing."

Stewart pulled his golf shirt over his head, pulled his pants off, and handed them both to me; as I just let them both drop to the ground. He was standing there shivering in his tighty-whities. Funny thing, though: as we were trying to talk him out of it, we were helping him over the fence. Johnny was on all fours along the fence. Stewart was standing on Johnny's back as he tried to step into my cupped hands to lift him over the fence. Alley-oop, and he was over. This was not the first fence we had climbed to get to a pool or hot tub, and it wouldn't be the last. Next thing we heard was a splash, and he was in the pool. A couple curtains from rooms around the pool slid open to see what all the commotion was. I overheard someone saying, "Martha, there's another Canadian in the pool again." A few seconds later, Stewart came up with a ball.

"Is it the ball?" I questioned.

"No, it's some dirty old Top Flite. There must be another ball in here somewhere," he explained as he ducked in for another look. Still no luck, so he took a couple more dives but still came up empty-handed.

He had a confused look on his face as he climbed out of the pool and yelled at me, "O'Malley, I don't know how you fucking do it; I help you scam Paulie, and now you have scammed me. I was your partner. I'm your buddy."

He dragged a chair over to the fence to climb back over. He got about halfway over, and Johnny and I walked up right beside him on the inside of the fence and asked, "Why don't you use the gate?"

"I thought you told me it was locked," Stewart answered.

"I guess I didn't know. I guess I lied," Johnny replied.

Stewart was pissed, he was freezing, he thought he had just lost his share of the money, and he was tricked into climbing a fence to jump into a pool of freezing water to retrieve a ball that was not his. He gathered up his clothes and started to run to the room to get dressed and to get warm, all the while mumbling, "Fucking O'Malleys, I will get you guys if it's the last thing I do."

Johnny and I were sitting at a table at the pool having another beer as he rolled Stewart's Titliest-3 to me. "You know, he almost caught me exchanging his ball with that dirty old Top Flite. I sure thought that he would have noticed that off-white color of that fucking Top Flite of yours."

"Ah, he was drunk; we all were. It worked out perfect," I declared.

"So where is my share?" Johnny demanded.

I pulled out the wad of bills and handed him his share of forty bucks. "There you go; that should take care of you. It was great doing business with you, as always," I reckoned.

"Well, you didn't play that very well, Kid." Johnny was implying that I could have gotten more, a lot more.

"What do you mean? I emptied Paulie's wallet," I stated.

"Well, Kid, the way that I'm thinking—and the way it adds up in my head—is the following: You put forty bucks in for yourself; Stewart's got no money, so you put Stewart's forty dollars in; Paulie put thirty dollars in, and you loaned

Paulie ten dollars. I'm no mathematician, but if you get soft and still give Stewart his share of sixty dollars, plus my share of forty dollars, plus the forty dollars you put in for Stewart, plus the ten dollars you loaned Paulie, that comes to a grand total of one hundred fifty bucks you paid. Minus the one-hundred-twenty-dollar pot, so my backward math has you in the hole by thirty dollars. You do the math," Johnny explained.

"*What?* You were right about one thing: you are no mathematician," I asserted. "Also, can I use this math on Stewart, so I can try not to pay him? Have you not always told me that it is not always about making money, but you should at least try?"

"But, Kid, I have also said that if you don't make money, you're going to go broke," Johnny chided.

"Well, with your math, you must be one poor fucker. Hey, the night is still young, and I still haven't found any nightlife yet. Let's go see if Stewart is still talking to me," I blurted out as we walked back to the room.

"I think I'm done; I'm going to bed. I've been up for thirty hours, I've been drunk three times today, and I think our tee time is an early one in the morning," Johnny hinted. "If Stewart won't go, maybe you can drag Theodore out."

"Drunk three times? Johnny, you've got to start pacing yourself, like me. Just stay drunk," I replied, as we held each other up; while we staggered back toward the rooms.

"Yep. You're right, Kid," Johnny added.

CHAPTER 10

Theodore Meets Jack

We stopped back at my room, and the heat was cranked; it had to be one hundred degrees in there. Stewart was under all the blankets and shivering. He was still trying to get warm. "Stewart, ole pal, you still mad at me? You look cold. You want me to spoon with ya to get you warm?" I laughed as I reached down and touched his foot.

"Fuck off. Don't touch me. Don't even talk to me. Just leave me alone," he yelled as he kicked his foot away.

"Come on, let's go find some nightlife. You're going to miss something." I tried coaxing him. "You are going to miss some funnnnnn."

All he came back with was, "Fuck off."

"Well, okay then." I stuck my head through the adjoining door of Buddy and Paulie's room. I could see that they were in bed already, watching some TV. "Do you guys want to go get a drink?"

Paulie begged Buddy as he climbed out of bed. "Can I go, can I, can I?"

Buddy came back with, "No, no, you can't. Now go the fuck to sleep. Fuck off, O'Malley, and where are all my fucking tiles?" As I was shutting the door, all I overheard was, "Paulie, I thought you locked the door."

"I did, I did. I guess, I just don't know anymore," Paulie pleaded. "Buddy, I can't sleep; I usually play a few songs on my harmonica to help me calm down at night."

"Get over it already, and shut the fuck up," Buddy answered. "You keep this up, and you can sleep in O'Malley's room.

So we went over to Johnny's room, and there was Theodore, just getting ready for bed. I suggested, "Hey, Teddy, I'm thinking that I need to go have a nightcap. You in? I'll let you buy."

"Na, I should go to bed; it's been a long day. Oh, what the hell? Why not? I'm on vacation!" Theodore convinced himself into going. "It's not like I have to get up and milk the cows in the morning."

"I'm not sure where we are going, but there has to be a bar open somewhere," I told him.

The only place left open that time of night in Shady Hills was the Destination Dreamland Motel. It was just down the way across the road and was well within walking or stumbling distance home. It had quite a few rooms, a bar, and a great restaurant, which we ate at a few times that week.

When we booked our golf vacation, we had a choice of staying at either the Happy Holiday Hotel or the Destination Dreamland Motel. It was the same price. Don't tell Buddy, but prior to coming, I had called both the Happy Holiday Hotel and the Destination Dreamland Motel. And Sally Sue, although she was a little forceful on the phone, she was the only one who would agree to do the valet parking bit, along with some other pranks. It was like Dreamland had no sense of humor. Besides, the Happy Holiday Hotel also had towels with their logos on them that we would be able to steal. We all quit smoking, so we didn't need their fucking ashtrays anymore. Come to find out, the bar at Double-D's was the only place open after ten o'clock, and it was the closest thing to nightlife that you were going to get in this one-horse town.

Our bartender's name was Fanny. She was black, young, and very pretty. She also had a very thick Southern accent. She told us that she was there all week till two in the morning. I promised her that I would be there also.

"You'd better," she informed me, as I was listening in the background to George Thorogood's best drinking song ever: "One Bourbon, One Scotch, One Beer." The thing is, I believe it was on the jukebox because, as that song came to an end, it was replaced by Queen's "Fat Bottomed Girls." "It gets kinda quiet and lonely, late at night."

"Oh, I will. All you got to do is keep bringing me one bourbon, one scotch, and one beer, and I will be here.

"That's easy enough," Fanny answered, but you could tell that she had this puzzled look on her face about whether I was ordering these drinks or not.

Looking at Theodore, I gave him that little smirk and a wink, for Fanny, which did not register. I'm sure he thought I had something in my eye. Where was my best buddy, my go-to guy, when I needed him? All I can say is, Theodore was no Stewart.

I envisioned Fanny as my little French maid. She had that little black French maid's uniform on. It had white frilly trim, was low cut, and had a short matching skirt that exposed her white bloomers. She had a little matching bonnet on also. She was wearing fishnet stockings with six-inch stilettos. And of course, she spoke to me in a Southern Cajun French accent as she waved her feather duster around the room. "Quel est votre plaisir?" As I awoke from my daydream, she repeated herself one more time. "Sir, what is your pleasure?" You know, that Cajun French accent of hers is the international language of love. You got to just love the French.

"Why, you, of course, *mademoiselle*," I answered.

"No, no, I mean what would you like to drink?" Fanny blurted out as her face turned red from blushing.

We were sitting in the bar, and I was not sure what I wanted to drink. Theodore was telling me that he was having a problem finding a good rye to drink in the South. Besides beer, Theodore was a Canadian rye drinker, and only a Canadian rye drinker. Everything else would surely make him puke. After hearing that, I just had to introduce him to Jack, Jack Daniels, that is. I told him in the South, everyone drank Jack. Canadian rye drinkers, when they were in the South, they only drank Jack. It was the closest thing to rye that you would find. We ordered a couple of Jacks with beer chasers.

Theodore took a drink of Jack and made this unpleasant face look, like he was going to puke. He chased it back with a big gulp of beer to hide the taste of the Jack. "This is rye?"

"Yes, this is whiskey at the finest. Take a few more sips, and as you drink, learn to savor it. It will grow on ya." I raised my glass up to cheer him.

A couple hours later, Theodore piped up, "I thought we were only going out for a nightcap?"

"We did," I assured him.

"When did a nightcap become five Jacks and chasers?" he argued.

"It always is; it will help you sleep," I added as I finished off my beer.

"I shouldn't have too much trouble falling asleep tonight," Theodore reported as he tried to stand up but fell back into the chair. "I just have to get there."

"Are you going to be all right? Can you make it back to the room?"

"Why? You not coming?" Theodore pleaded as he got this troubled look on his face. "Those Jacks sure have caught up to me."

"Noooooo, I was going to stay and help Fanny clean up, if you know what I mean," I told him with a wink and a nod.

"I think I have to go," Theodore mumbled as he tried to stand up, again with no luck. "Can you help me back to the room? I'm pretty drunk."

"Hey, Fanny, can you call me a cab?" I yelled over to her, trying to get her attention. "My good friend here needs help to get home."

"Sorry, Shannon, but we have no taxicabs here. We are just a little town out in the middle of nowhere." Fanny set me straight as she walked over and cleaned the empties off the table.

"How is he going to get home?" I tried to come up with an arrangement so I could stay and help Fanny clean up; yeah, clean up. "Okay, I guess it's time for plan B."

"Plan B?" She wanted to know more. "What's plan B?"

"I'm not sure, so bring us another round so I can think one up."

"Another round? Shannon, I'm not sure if I can drink much more tonight," Theodore cried. You could see that all he wanted was to go home and go to bed.

"Oh, you will be fine. I will look after you," I promised as I put my hand out for him to shake. "I swear, one more drink, and we will go."

"I don't know. I think you promised me we would go three drinks ago," Theodore whined as it looked like his head was getting closer and closer to the tabletop with each passing minute. "If I pay the bill, can we go home? Bring me the bill. Please!" Theodore pulled out his wallet and threw two twenties down on the table. "That should cover it." Not being able to put his wallet back in his pocket, he got very frustrated with himself. "Lord Tunderin." Finally giving up, he just threw it onto the tabletop.

"I mean it this time. Here, Theodore, I'll hold onto your wallet for you. So you don't lose it," I reassured him. "You'll thank me in the morning."

"Thankssssss." Theodore showed his appreciation just as Fanny brought over another round of drinks.

Looking up at Fanny, I told her, "No matter how much money I offer you for another drink, you say no and kick us out, okay?" Winking without letting Theodore notice, I slipped her another twenty dollars to disregard my last statement.

"I'll cut you off and kick you out if you even think about ordering another drink." Fanny smiled as she winked back. "How's that?"

"That was perfect." I praised her, all for naught, as I looked over at Theodore, who had finally rested his head in the bowl of unshelled peanuts. Some would say that I wasted that twenty dollars; I would say that I had invested it for the future. "Fanny, you keep them coming till you got to go home, okay? Get yourself one; I'm pretty sure Theodore would love to buy you a drink too."

"You got it," Fanny agreed. Then jokingly, looking over at Theodore, she added, "Why, thank you, you kind, kind sir."

"I'm trying to come up with a plan B. Can you give us a ride home?" I asked as I emphasized *ride home*. "We are only staying over at the Happy Holiday Hotel."

"Sorry, not tonight. My boyfriend is picking me up in the three-wheeler. He will probably be here shortly," she answered with a smile. "Maybe next time, when you are not babysitting."

"Okkkkkkkkkay, you are on." I was surprised by the answer I just received; but to be honest, that was the answer I was looking for all along. "How am I going to get my good friend home? I don't think he can walk."

"But, Shannon, you don't have a car here?"

"Well, I guess, I'm just going to have to go get it," I informed her as I took another quick swig and stood up.

"Are you sure you are okay?"

"Yeah, no problem, it's only a couple of three-woods away."

"Huhhhh?" Fanny, puzzled by the statement, asked. "You are coming back for him, aren't you?"

"Yes, I'll be right back," I reported with a smile as I looked down at Theodore; I could see that he had peanut shell impressions all over his face. "Teddy, I'll be right back. Don't go anywhere." I'm not sure why I said that because I could see that he was incapable of going anywhere.

Just then Theodore sort of acknowledged me by turning his head in the bowl of nuts and pleading, "You are going to get me home? I don't care what it costs." The next thing I knew, he started to choke. I thought he might have accidentally inhaled a peanut or two. He stopped choking long enough to spit out the blockage. Then he quickly passed out in the bowl again.

"You all right?" I asked him.

When he didn't answer, I figured he was okay and out for the count.

"You'll be back, right?" Fanny pleaded as she got a worried look on her face. I'm not sure why she was so worried. Was it because I was not coming back, or was it that I was leaving poor Theodore in a bowl of her nuts?

"Oh, I would never leave my good friend Theodore," I said as I headed for the door. "I need him. We need him. He's our designated drunk for the week."

"Huhhhhh?"

I quickly got out the door to retrieve the van. I was there and back in a flash.

"Oh, good, you came back."

"Yeah, I told you I would be back," I confirmed as I walked in holding the Handicapped sign, which I had just backed over outside.

"Do you want me to give you a hand to get him in the van?" Fanny asked as she pointed over at Theodore. "So you can drive him home?"

"Nooooo, you know, I was thinking that I was okay to drive. Now that I am back, I know I was too drunk to drive. Don't let me do that again. That would be just stupid. I could never drive drunk with my good friend Theodore passed out in the back." I looked down at Theodore only to see that he had fallen out of the chair. There he lay motionless on the floor with peanuts scattered everywhere. "And besides, I let the air out of a tire. So I don't."

"You sure are looking after him."

"I feel sorta responsible for doing this to him," I added as I scrutinized Theodore just lying there. "I see he has made himself more comfortable."

"Yep, you had just left. I think he tried to stand up or something. And down he went," Fanny reported as she handed me another drink in trade for the crumpled-up Handicapped sign. "He wiggled around on the floor a little, just like a big old mud cat slithering in the mud looking for water. Luckily, he didn't break anything. Why don't you come up to the bar?"

Leaving Theodore under the table so I didn't disturb him, I bellied up to the bar to keep Fanny company. Or … or … After a couple of more drinks, she finally said, "Well, Shannon, it's time to go."

"How am I ever going to get Theodore home now?" Then it dawned on me. I was a card-carrying-member, of CAA, that is. "Fanny, can you call CAA for me?"

"CAA?"

"Yeah. Oh, I forgot where I was. Can you call AAA for a tow?"

"Why?"

"I have a flat tire. Remember, I let the air out of it?"

"Oh, that's right; you let the air out of it so you wouldn't be able to drive it. Good thinking." Confused, Fanny started to dial the AAA number.

"Yeah, I have a premier membership, and it includes a lot of extra perks."

"Extra perks?"

"Yeah, tell them to bring me a six-pack of Coors Light."

"Shannon, they are not going to bring you beer."

"Well, at least ask. That's why I pay for the premier membership—just for the extras," I told her as I tried to get Theodore to his feet. "See, back home, we used our CAA tow-truck drivers as our DD's. I would have even used the pizza delivery guy for a ride. But I don't want a pizza, and I don't think you even have a pizza joint here, right?"

"Right you are. There are no pizzas in this town," she agreed. "I wish there was; we sure could use a pizza joint here in Shady Hills."

"Come on, Teddy. We will go back to my room for one more drink, only one. Because, you know, you got to get to bed."

Theodore mumbled something in some foreign language that I could not understand, so I asked, "Hey, Teddy, when did you become bilingual?"

Within a few moments, in came this big, burly, black guy wearing coveralls. His name embroidered on the coveralls was Charlie. "Someone called for a tow?"

"Jesusssss, that was quick. Did you bring me any beer?" I greeted him as I tried to get Theodore to stand up. "Fanny, you better bring me a roadie."

"Beer? I was just parked down at the I-95 ramp," he answered. "Hey, girl. How you doing tonight? Where's that fucking asshole of a nigger you call a boyfriend at?"

"Oh, Charlie, why can't you just get along with your brother? Was he not outside when you drove up? He should be along soon," Fanny answered. I could tell that everyone knew each other or were related in this one-horse town.

"Well, I better hurry up and get out of here before he comes along. I might have to punch his lights out again," Charlie promised.

"Charlie, can we all not just get along?" Fanny cried.

"Hey, Charlie, can my friend here buy you a drink?" I said as I let go of Theodore so I could pull his wallet out of my pocket. Theodore, with no strength left in his legs, crumpled to the floor. "Teddy, will you quit fooling around? You keep this up, and I will just leave you here with all your peanuts."

"No, no, I'm working," Charlie responded, knowing full well that he really did want one.

"We've got Jackkkkk," I bragged as I motioned over to Fanny with my two fingers in the air.

"Well, in that case … No, no, I can't," Charlie maintained.

"Okay, suit yourself. But it's good stuff. Look what it has done to my good friend Teddy," I argued, pointing to the slug on the floor.

"It's his first time?"

"Yes, it was. He'll never be the same."

"What a lightweight."

"Yeah, I remember when I was introduced to Jack. It was my brother Johnny. My toenails all curled up underneath my toes," I answered as I tried to mimic my spindly fingers curling up underneath my hands. "And I spent an entire weekend lost in a cornfield. I never did find my way out. I think they had to finally send someone in on Sunday afternoon to find me."

"Yep. When you drink Jack, it reaches right up and grabs you in the short and curlies," Charlie answered as he started to lick his lips. You could tell that he really did want one … or two … or three … "I can never stop with just one."

"In that case, Fanny, bring him two," I ordered as I handed her money from Theodore's wallet. "Please hurry. Charlie looks like he is starting to drool."

He knocked back the two Jacks all in one gulp. He wiped his chin clean from any spillage that might have occurred. Then he slammed his glass down on the bar and had that surprised look on his face, like he had just tasted Jack for the very first time. But you could tell that he was a seasoned Jack drinker from way back. Because that surprised look of pleasure did not turn into a grimacing look of pain. "Thanks. I needed that." He gestured toward Fanny for a fill-up. "Fill her up this time."

"Charlie, you are working."

"One more, and we'll get back to work. I promise," Charlie begged as Fanny topped up his glass to the rim. And just like the last time, he guzzled it down in one drink. He slammed his glass down again and again had that astonished look like he had never tasted it before. "Come on; let's get that tire of yours fixed."

"I have a flat tire?" I questioned him, knowingly full well that I did.

"That's your van out there backed over that Handicapped sign, isn't it?" Charlie laughed as he started to walk toward the door.

"Yeah, it is," I answered as I followed behind dragging Theodore. "You know, I once had an uncle named Charlie. I used to call him Uncle Charlie. He died long ago. Can I call you Chuck?"

"Sure, I guess. But why?"

"I don't know. So I don't mix you guys up?" I tried to answer him. "And besides, you look like a Chuck."

"Okay, I guess. Let's get that tire of yours fixed."

"Buddy is just going to kill me when he finds out that I flattened his tire. Chucky, what am I going to do?"

"Don't worry. When I get done with it, you will never know you had a flat. He'll never know." Charlie shook his head as he tried to be helpful. "I'll get it fixed right up for you and get you on your way."

"Chuckles, don't you dare fix it. Can you give us a tow instead?" I snickered.

"Sure, I can tow you. Where do you need me to tow you to?" Charlie agreed, still shaking his head in disbelief that I was actually calling him Chuckles.

"We're just staying over at the Triple-H. You know, the Happy Holiday Hotel."

"That's not far at all," he answered. Then he stopped on his way to the door. "We probably have time for one more drink then."

That was like music to my ears. Without missing a beat, I ordered. "Fanny, Chuckles needs another Jack or two. You might as well bring me a couple also, seeing as he is twisting my arm."

"So let me get this straight. You don't want me to fix the tire?" Charlie asked just as Fanny brought us a couple more shots of Jack.

"That's right," I said as I was thinking that we had to get going. I didn't think Theodore could afford much more Jack for everyone. And besides, I wanted Theodore to have enough money left so he could tip Chuckles well.

I said my good nights to Fanny as she handed me a larger-than-large roadie. I told her I would definitely see her tomorrow night. I helped Theodore out the door, trying not to spill my drink and keeping him somewhat upright. "Come on, Teddy. One foot in front of the other. That's good; we are almost there. You keep up the good work, and I will let you play with the siren and lights." There was no response from him other than a few bubbles coming out the side of his mouth and some little gurgling sound—that nobody could hear but me.

As Charlie backed the tow truck up to hook on to the van, you could see the name on the tow truck, which said "BEAUFORD'S FILLING STATION." It also carried the AAA logo, so I knew I was in good hands and did not have to order a pizza. Although it was an older tow truck, I could see that it had had several modifications done to it over the years. The tow truck's lights seemed to be in sync with the loud disco music blaring from his cassette player. It sounded a lot like Donna Summers, but I was not sure because I was just getting the rhythm down, and his loud backup signal from the tow truck was interfering with the beat and tempo. As he climbed down out of the van, he was singing, "hot stuff, baby … gonna need …" Just as the song ended, Charlie asked, "Are you sure you don't want me to fix the tire? It won't take long."

"No, that would just ruin the surprise for Buddy. I know it, he'll just explode. I can't wait. I'm sure he'll want to blow it back up himself with Canadian air," I informed him as I took a big swig of my Jack.

"Who is this Buddy guy, anyways?" Chuck asked as he also took a gulp from his sippy cup. "He sounds a lot like my brother. He sounds a little anal-retentive."

"Well, Chuckles, he totally is. But he is one of my bestest, bestest friends. I would do anything for him," I agreed.

As I helped poor Theodore up into his seat in the tow truck, I was informing him of all the special responsibilities that he would have to look after, considering that our hands were full of drinks. "Now, Teddy, I think this knob controls all the pretty lights. And this one might be the air horn. And …"

"He sure is lucky to have a friend like you and not like my loser of a fucking brother," Chuck stated as he had just finished adjusting the hookup to the van. As he walked up toward the front of the tow truck, there was a loud air-horn blast, which must have startled him because Chucky screamed. "Now don't touch anything. No, no, no, don't put him in here. He'll puke, and then I won't be very happy. Put him back in the van; he can puke in there."

I finally got him repositioned into the driver's seat of the van. Theodore laid his head down onto the steering wheel, which made the horn blast. I had him safely buckled in so he wouldn't fall out and hurt himself. I always say, "You can never be too safe."

Chuckles bucked and jerked us out of the parking lot as he was looking for the right gear to use. He gave the air horn a couple of blasts to acknowledge Fanny waving goodbye. The music of Donna seemed to get louder and louder; it seemed to be trying to drown out the deafening sound of his big diesel engine. Within minutes, if not seconds, Chuckles had us home safe, and he expertly backed us up into our parking spot.

"Are you sure you don't want me to fix that tire?" Chuckles asked again.

"Nooooooo," I demanded as I pulled Theodore's wallet out again, looking for his CAA card. "I should have known. Farmers just don't need CAA."

"Okay, I just have to have you sign something," Chucky informed me as he went up to get his clipboard from the cab of the truck. "Have you got your card handy?"

"Here, Chuckles." I thanked him as I handed him the CAA card and a twenty for a tip. "Like I said before, if you are around here this time of night, we'll be visiting Fanny all week. I'm sure someone will buy you a couple of Jacks. And I'm sure I can let the air out of a tire, or maybe I will get creative and run out of gas."

"Sounds like a plan," Chucky agreed as he finalized the paperwork for me to sign. "Can I get your John Henry right here at the bottom?"

"There; that should take care of everything," I said as I scribbled on the dotted line and handed his clipboard back.

Examining the signature, Chuckles said, "I thought your name was Shannon, Shannon O'Malley?"

"It is."

"You can't sign it John Henry." Confused, Charlie tried to set me straight. "The name on the card has to match the autograph. My boss, he gets really mad when I bring this kind of shit home."

"Well, he's really going to get mad at you this time," I confessed as Charlie started to redo some of the paperwork. "'Cause I gave you Buddy's CAA card."

"Why? Why would you do that?" Charlie asked, annoyed.

"Because back home I have had too many flat tires, too many dead batteries, and I seem to misplace a lot of keys. Hell, I have even run out of gas a few times." I informed him of some of my shenanigans as I signed Buddy's name. "I guess I will have to start eating more pizzas."

"What?" Chuckles asked with a confused look on his face. I'm not sure if it was the statement of eating more pizza or because he started to read the signature of Buddy Parker. "This is good, right?"

"Of course. Remember—Buddy is my bestest friend. He'd want me to get home safe."

As Chuckles drove off, all you could hear was Disco Donna blaring from his stereo. A ways down the road, he was still trying to grind out a new gear that was not there. His old tow truck jerked and bucked all the way back to the thruway. He was never to be seen again. Maybe it worked out that he was just busy with other calls the rest of the week. Or maybe it was the eight Jacks that Theodore had bought him, which maybe put him in a ditch somewhere. That maybe got him fired. Or maybe it was his loser-brother who finally kicked the shit out of him.

I tried to unbuckle Theodore from his seat belt. The next thing I knew, Theodore fell out of the van, twisting and tangling his leg between the step and wheel well. "At least you didn't fall on your head."

The fall must have awoken Theodore a little, as he was able to precariously get to his feet, brushing himself off. "Holy fuck, that hurt. What happened?"

"Hey, Teddy, I sure could use a nightcap. You want to join me?" I joked, as I could see that he could not remember the last three or four hours of nightcaps.

"Oh, no. I'm way too drunk for that. But what the hell? Sure, why not? I'm on vacation." As Theodore changed his mind in midsentence.

"Okay, follow me," I said as I tried to head him up the stairs toward our rooms. "I know someone should have a drink for us somewhere."

He stood there at the bottom of the stairs weaving back and forth. "I can'ttttttt. My feet won't workkkkkk. Hic, hic." Theodore was in bad shape; he had no motor skills, his words were becoming slurred, and his hiccups had started again. I was thinking, I've got to get him to bed before he throws up. Where's Zackery when I need him? I knew Zackery would carry him up the stairs.

It was a struggle, but I did get him up the stairs; we were standing at his door, and he was fumbling around with his keys. He was weaving back and forth. He couldn't get the key to slide into the lock. Although he was extremely entertaining, it was getting really painful to watch. I finally got him into the room, and he flopped down on the edge of the bed. He was struggling with his shoes, and he tried to kick them off, but they would not come off. "They're not working. What is wrong with my feet? We don't have to do this every night, do we?" He incoherently asked for help.

"Yes, we do. We are on vacation, and so you'd better rest up," I declared as I reached down to pull his shoes off. "Teddy, where is your other shoe?"

"Huhhhhh?"

"Never mind. You are on your own for the rest … Or yell at your roommate for help. Johnny, Johnny, are you awake? Theo needs help."

"Theodore, did you meet Jack tonight? He usually introduces you to Jim (Beam) or Glen (Fiddich) first, and then takes you to Jack," Johnny mumbled from his sleep. "He must really like you."

I was heading out the door as I heard Theodore scurrying to the bathroom. I thought to myself, my work is done here; and then I made a promise to myself that I was not fucking babysitting tomorrow night.

When I got back to the room, Stewart was sound asleep. I tried to slip into bed quietly, and I tripped over the fucking cat and landed straight on my face. No, we did not have a cat. I wasn't sure what the fuck I had tripped over, but it sure did hurt. I guess I had drunk too much. No, never, I was just tired. That was it; I just needed some sleep.

I lay there in bed, thinking, "Wow. What a day! It could not have gone off any better. Well, maybe I could have had more music playing in my head. But this was only the first day. What music would be playing in my head tomorrow? What would tomorrow bring? Bring it on! I couldn't wait."

CHAPTER 11

Irish Wake

I woke up the next morning and tried to open my eyes. I was looking around and trying to focus. I couldn't remember a thing, and I was not sure where I was. I rolled over to make sure there was no one in bed with me. I looked under the blankets to find that I was naked. I didn't have any drawings or tattoos on my body. I had my eyebrows and my own head of hair as I felt around my face. I was not sure why I was checking all of this. Then it dawned on me. These were some of the pranks that I had pulled on my drinking partners who had passed out on me before. How dare they pass out on me? My head was pounding, my foot hurt, and my face hurt more. Why did my foot hurt and why did my face hurt? I was trying to unscramble all the events of the night before. Then I remembered: I tripped over that fucking cat.

I saw Stewart was out of his bed. Maybe he was in the washroom. As I looked at the closed door to the washroom, I called out, "Are you going to be long? You still mad at me?"

Still there was no answer. I was thinking that he must be really mad at me.

I had to have a dump bad. So I climbed out of bed and ran over to Buddy and Paulie's room to use their bathroom. There was Paulie getting dressed. I was thinking that Buddy must have picked out his wardrobe, as they almost matched. I slipped into their bathroom and asked, "Where's Buddy?"

"Buddy is pissed; he's looking for the tiles that you stole from beneath our beds. He made me help him move everything last night. He's a wild man; he's on a mission. I think he went to the van to look for them there," Paulie warned me.

"Oh," I confessed as I talked to him from inside their bathroom. "Paulie, I didn't steal them."

"Besides that, I have lost my keys; can you help me find them? Buddy is just going to kill me," Paulie pleaded.

"Where did you see them last, or when was the last time you used them?" I asked, but I knew exactly where they were; they were in my pocket.

"I don't know. I'm pretty sure I had them in my hand this morning," he came back with.

"Are you sure?"

"Yes, I'm … I don't know. Buddy will just kill me if I don't find them."

"Well, don't worry, Paulie. Until you find them, my door is always unlocked. So you can always come through there to get to your room," I explained.

Just then Buddy came barging into the room and retorted, "I'm going to kill him; they're not in the … Paulie, you fucking stink. Could you at least flush the toilet?"

"It wasn't me; we have ..." Paulie confided as he watched Buddy head toward the bathroom to flush.

As Buddy peered his head around the corner into the bathroom, he retorted, "I should have known. What the fuck are you doing in here? How come you are fucking naked? Where are my fucking tiles? Why don't you close the door? You fucking stink."

"What do you think I'm doing in here? Stewart was in our bathroom, and I had to go," I let him know.

Just then, Stewart stuck his head in the bathroom and said, "What are you talking about? I've been downstairs with Buddy ... and holy fuck, you do, you fucking stink."

"Paulie, why don't you come in also? One more person in here, and we can have a party," I remarked.

"Party? But you stink," Paulie complained as he walked into the bathroom. "What the fuck did you eat?"

"I was only kidding, Paulie. Has anybody made Caesars yet?" I inquired. "I sure could use one. Make it a good one."

"Here you go. I'll go make another one," Stewart said as he handed me his drink. "I found this shoe coming up the stairs. I think this is Theodore's. Is he missing a running shoe?"

"Is it a left or a right?" I asked.

"What difference does that make?" Paulie wanted to know.

"What difference does that make? Have you ever tried to put a left shoe on a ..."?

"Fuck off. We don't care," Buddy interrupted. He demanded, "O'Malley, you'd better hurry the fuck up; our tee time is at eight o'clock. The van is leaving at seven thirty, so we only have half an hour for breakfast."

"First off, Buddy, there is going to be a frost delay this morning. Did you see how cold it got last night? Ask Stewart how cold it got. I'm pretty sure we won't be teeing off till at least ten o'clock. Secondly, you know I don't eat breakfast. Thirdly, the course is only five minutes away. And fourthly and most importantly, who made you the fucking boss? Also, one last thing, and think real hard about this one: Who the fuck picked out Paulie's outfit for today?" I asked.

"What's wrong with it?" Buddy countered.

"Nothing, nothing at all," I responded as I slipped into my room to get ready for breakfast.

I got dressed and walked over to Johnny and Theodore's room with Stewart. There was Johnny standing in front of the bathroom door. He was just putting the finishing touches together for his wardrobe. He had Johnson & Johnson everywhere. Imagine a three-foot square of white baby powder sprinkled everywhere, except for two perfectly white silhouetted feet with toes from where he stood. Most men sprinkle their Johnson & Johnson from the canister, but not Johnny; he uses a twelve-inch powder puff that most would use to wash their car with. His bathroom at home is a hazardous and dangerous place. There's a quarter-inch layer of Johnson & Johnson everywhere, from the floor to the ceiling. You put that shit on tile or linoleum, and you have a skating rink. Talk about slippery; it's like the Ice Capades, only it's on powder. He should at least put up orange safety cones. And it can't be just any baby powder; it has to be Johnson & Johnson. He says it's finer, whiter, softer, and fluffier, and it smells like baby powder. Whereas most imitators have put smelly stuff into the formula. Who wants to smell like a vanilla bean or a lilac bush? It was the first; it was the original.

I asked him, "Did you get enough on, or do you need help? Looks like you might have missed a few spots by the way the carpet looks."

"Na, I'm dressed now, but maybe you could come over tomorrow morning and help me? It was hard for me to get my back end done. Pattie usually does the hard-to-reach areas for me," Johnny answered.

"Stewart, maybe you can help him. Seems like you both like your butts powdered," I offered.

"Hey, Johnny, I'll powder your butt if you tell me how you switched my golf ball last night," Stewart demanded.

"Okay, I'll tell you." Johnny chuckled, and then he lowered his voice and whispered, "It was all magic!"

"No, really, how'd you exchange the balls? I thought I kept my eyes on you O'Malleys all the time," Stewart said.

"All I can say, boy, is you've got to be reading, you've got to be reading all the time. Or just pay more attention next time," Johnny reasoned.

"Oh, never mind. Where's Theodore at?" Stewart inquired as he took a big gulp of his drink.

"Take a look." Just then Johnny pushed the bathroom door ajar to reveal Theodore lying in a fetal position in his old, faded-red, one-piece long johns, wedged between the wall and the toilet, his left arm hugging the john. "What a mess. I think he's been there since you left him, Shannon. He must still be alive; as every once in a while, I hear him hurl. I think I even heard him butchering the song "Hot Stuff." Did you guys go out to the Disco last night?"

"Uhhhhh, of course we did," I lied, but really, I couldn't remember what we did. "You could have at least given him his pillow to lay his head on or covered him up with a blanket or something."

"I did. I gave him his pillow and blanket when he first went in there," Johnny informed us. "Every time I went to check in on him, he was choking himself to death. He had his head in the bowl, and with the weight of his arm draped over the toilet seat, he was choking himself to death."

"That's what roomies are for."

"But it got a little hairy in the middle of the night, though. I had to piss real bad. It was dark. I came rushing in, forgetting that he was in here on the floor. I tripped and landed right on top of him. He didn't move, didn't even say a word. So, as I said, I had to piss bad. So, I was having my piss; I was trying really hard not to get anything on him. I finally turned the light on, and I got it everywhere. I'm not sure what took the biggest hit—the shower curtain or poor Theodore," Johnny added as he pointed to the pillow and blanket scrunched up over in the corner.

"Why didn't you turn the light on before you pissed? Or just piss in the tub?" I asked.

"Turn the light on? You know I can't piss when someone is watching me!" Johnny informed us. "You know, I didn't even think about the tub or sink or even outside. I guess I was relieved that I didn't have to shit."

"I think Theodore was probably relieved also," I reasoned.

"All right let's go get some breakfast," Stewart urged as Johnny took his Caesar from his hand. Stewart had lost another drink to the O'Malleys, and it surely wouldn't be the last.

As we walked down to the restaurant, I handed Stewart his share of the winnings from the night before. I apologized for trying to rip him off and told him how funny and perplexed his look was each time that he came up to the surface of the pool without his golf ball. I could tell that he still was somewhat mad. I figured he would get over it sooner or later.

"You won't believe it, but I found Double-D's last night," I bragged.

"Double-D's? You lucky bastard. Who was she?"

"No, not Double-D's, but Double-D's. And she wasn't a she at all; she was the Destination Dreamland Motel next door. But come to think about it, Fanny could have had Double-D's." I tried to explain. "I really didn't look that closely."

"Didn't look that closely? What do you mean? What have you done with Shannon?" Stewart reasoned.

I told him all about the Destination Dreamland Motel next door, and I told him about beautiful Fanny and her Cajun French accent. I explained to him how much I missed him and how I really, really needed him last night. I told him that Theodore was no right-hand man. These days you call them your wingman, but back then, they were your go-to guy or your right-hand man. They were your buddy, they assisted you, and they would help you score. Or they dragged you away from situations that you had no business being in in the first place. I told him that I introduced Theodore to Jack and that I was sure that Jack didn't agree with him. So tonight, I was thinking that we'd get Buddy to introduce him to his native drink, ta-ta-tequila.

We were all standing at the entrance to the restaurant for breakfast. The entrance had two French-doors, which were propped open with bottom door wedges. The one right-hand wedge was concealing Buddy's torn tile. The funny thing about standing there this whole time was Buddy was standing right on top of his torn tile. He hadn't even noticed. Stewart and I, we just looked at each other, and we started to chuckle.

One of the waitresses came over, pointed to an area in the restaurant, and said, "Have a seat at that large table in the corner, and I will be right over."

On the way over to the table, Buddy inquired, "Johnny, where's Theodore?"

"He was in the bathroom all night ralphing. Or should I say, singing some kind of disco music. I think he slept there. He's in pretty bad shape. I'm really not sure if he is going to make breakfast or anything else today." Johnny dared ask, "Shannon, what did you do to him last night?"

"I introduced him to Jack," I informed him. "I had to carry him home last night."

"So where is he now? And who in the fuck is Jack?" Paulie inquired.

Just then the waitress came over and introduced herself. "Hey, y'all, my name is Vicki, with an *i*. You all can call me Miss Vicki."

"Withaneye?" Paulie interrupted. "That's a weird last name, isn't it?"

"Paulie, just shut the fuck up," Buddy cried.

"What? I'm just wondering what her nationality is," Paulie inquired.

"Paulie." Buddy screamed at him to shut up again.

"You're on a golf package, right? Here are your menus, and your breakfast ticket will get you the first five items on the menu and the daily breakfast special, which is a cheesy cheese omelet. All breakfasts come with coffee, juice, toast, and grits." She went on to explain that she probably would be our breakfast waitress for the rest of the week. She was young and bubbly. I was thinking where in hell does, she get all her energy from so early in the morning?

As Scott and I looked at each other, I had Robert Palmer's "Simply Irresistible" playing in my head. By the end of the week, the song had changed to "Addicted to Love." I was thinking Miss … uhmmmm, did she just introduce herself as Miss? Was that her way of saying, "Hey, guys, I'm single, I'm available, and I'm horny. Which one of you lucky gents wants to take me home this week?" Both Stewart and I gave each other that little smirk and that little wink that Theodore could not conceive the night before. In my mind, I had her dressed in a teacher-type outfit. Her sexy white blouse skillfully unbuttoned halfway down. Which only revealed enough cleavage to say that there was more of that in the Valley of Love. Her eighth and ninth wonders of the world were beautiful. She had a short, sexy black skirt on. It had a slit going up the side, almost to her waist, which revealed her sexy, sequined pantyhose. Shoes? I had her in a big pair of clumsy Birkenstocks. Why not stilettos, you ask? It's my fantasy. Also, it's probably not safe to wear stiletto heels in school. She had big, round-frame glasses on that were pushed down to the tip of her nose, so she could look at you over the top of her frames. And I almost forgot, she had a yardstick pointer that she snapped across my ass. Stay in school, as I say; stay in school.

We all ordered breakfast, and I inquired, "How about getting some beers?"

She looked at her watch and said, "I can't serve beer till eight o'clock. That's only about twelve minutes away. Can you wait that long?"

Johnny piped up, "I can't. How about you just put a shot of vodka in my tomato juice?"

"I can do that for you," she conceded.

I came back with, "You might as well make seven of them; we might as well start the day off right."

"Okay, I will be right back," she replied.

By the time she made our drinks and delivered them with our breakfast, it was after eight, so it did not matter; we were legit. "Might as well bring us all a beer chaser when you get a chance."

"Ok, honey. Be right back."

"Hey, Paulie, why don't you ask Miss Vicki if you can order a motorboat with your breakfast?" Johnny dared him.

"You're joking, aren't you? No, we do not serve our breakfasts with a motorboat. This is not that topless place from up north," Vicki commented as she started to walk back toward the kitchen, all the while giving Johnny a glare.

"She's so fine. I'm sure we would all pick her to be our motorboater. Don't you think?" I recommended.

There were a lot of yeps, yeahs, and for sures. Except for Johnny, who finally piped in, "Nope, never. She's not in my weight class."

"Johnny, you've got to be a little less picky. At your age, you never know. You might miss a good one," I pointed out.

"Hey, Kid, don't you worry about me. You know, not everyone has to be built on speed." Having lost this argument with him once before, I decided that I would let him be in his little (big) fantasy world of his.

"Paulie, this is a much classier place. I'm pretty sure that they would offer them at lunch or might even offer them for supper," I suggested. "You know; like nipples and steak, like we enjoyed yesterday."

"Do you think?" Paulie came back with.

"Oh, I'm sure of it." I tried to urge Paulie on without laughing out loud.

"Miss Vicki, Miss Vicki." All excited Paulie yelled as he took an inhale from his puffer.

"Paulie, shut the fuck up; they don't have any fucking motorboats. You heard her. All they have is breakfast. Don't you dare ask her for anything more. And just shut the fuck up and eat your breakfast," Buddy warned Paulie.

Buddy glanced over toward me and said, "And you, you just leave the poor fucker alone."

Just then Miss Vicki came over to the table looking toward Paulie and asked, "Yes, honey, what can I get you?"

"Uh, uh." Looking for the words, Paulie looked over at Buddy for approval.

"Paulie, go ahead; tell her what you want. You know you want it. And don't worry about Buddy. He's not going to hurt you. Tell her. Tell her you need more pancake syrup," I teased him.

"Ah, ah, that's what I need. Can I please have some more maple syrup for my pancakes and ice cream?" Paulie pleaded.

So the rest of the week, like clockwork, Paulie would order pancakes and ice cream for breakfast, and Miss Vicki would always bring an extra serving of syrup for him. And Paulie, like clockwork, would always thank her; and as she walked away, he would lean forward, take a breath from his inhaler, and whisper, "The stupid bitch. I didn't even order this," as he would pour it on the rest of his pancakes. And just like clockwork, Buddy would lean forward and say, "Paulie, shut the fuck up and eat your breakfast."

By the end of each morning's breakfast that week, Paulie had either spilled or dripped pancake syrup on his shirt or place mat. This first morning, he dripped syrup all over his place mat, so between his elbow and everything else on the table, he got it everywhere. You really had to be careful what you touched or picked up because before long, you had this sticky shit everywhere.

The next think you knew, Buddy would get some sticky syrup on his hands, and then he screamed, "Fuck, Paulie. Will you watch what you are doing?"

Paulie, trying to be polite and helpful, tried to clean it up with his syrup-soaked place mat, which only made it worse and which made Buddy scream louder.

Keep up the good work, Paulie. Just keep it up.

We were trying to pick golf teams for the day, trying to decide who was going to play with whom, what games we were going to play, and most importantly, what the wagers would be. Our group's golfing ability ranged from better than average to downright awful. Theodore did not golf at all, though I would rank him better than Paulie, who was the worst of the bunch. But remember, he had a bad back and a bladder infection. So you can just imagine all the negotiating that went on at breakfast. It was like being ten years old, having a handful of hockey cards; you were trying to trade that old, folded, dog-eared card of Bobby Orr for a brand-new, mint-condition, Gretzky rookie card. I think Paulie's name came up on every trade, negotiation, or giveaway. In my mind, I was always going to have Paulie on my team. I was just trying to get Buddy to give me something for taking him, without him knowingly giving it to me.

I think I finally said, "I'm feeling really lucky today. I will take Johnny and Paulie, and we will take you all on. We will play a four-ball stroke-play match. Because we only have three players, our fourth player's score will be the average mean score between Johnny and me. You will give us two strokes a side, five dollars for individual birdies, double for eagles. Low man and high man added together will be worth twenty dollars each. We will have five-dollar greenies. Maybe longest drive is worth five dollars more. How about for every ball that we lose, that will cost you a dollar? That will go into a special pot for a tip for Zackery for ice. Did I miss anything, or do you want to add something?"

Buddy came back with, "Are you sure about these teams? You really don't have much of a team there. So let's make it three strokes a side. Also, what do you need the fourth player score for? You are just using the best score for the team, right? Tell you what; I don't want to take advantage of you on the first day. You keep that dummy fourth player, and we will have a total team aggregate for another five dollars. You keep Paulie, and we buy your team lunch at the turn."

"Does that include beer for everyone on the team?" I asked.

"No … Yes, that includes beer," Buddy declared, and then he thought about it and came back with, "No … well, we just better make it a two-beer limit."

"Okay, you're on. But what are we playing for?" I wondered.

"Oh, I don't know. Here's one: losers can only have coffee and grits for breakfast tomorrow," Buddy offered.

"Sounds like a deal," I approved as I shook Buddy's hand.

Paulie leaned over and said, "Remember, Shannon, I got no money, and grits will make me puke."

"Don't worry; you won't puke. That's why you are on my team," I confided to him as I handed him a fifty-dollar bill.

"Thanks. I will give it to you as soon as we get home, uh, as soon as I get it," Paulie confessed.

"No worries. I know where you live. Uh, I think I know where you live. Uh, somebody should know where you live," I confided to him.

We are just about to get up and leave, and in walked Theodore. He really did not look well. "You all right?" I questioned him.

"What happened last night? How did I get home? Who looked after me?" Theodore inquired as he looked around the room.

Paulie, trying to be helpful, piped up, "I think someone said it was some Jack fellow. They would not tell me who he was, though."

"You want some breakfast before we leave?" Buddy wondered out loud, even though he knew the answer already.

Theodore replied, "No, I'm going to skip breakfast. Are you guys all right to drive yourself to the course today?

Because I think I'm still drunk. I'm going back to bed … hic … hiccup …"

"No problem, Theodore. You might want to take a shower first. It will make you feel better, and it certainly will make you smell better," I suggested as I looked over at Johnny.

"Does anybody know why I'm so sore? And did we go to a disco last night? Because all I remember is Donna Summer and a lot of flashing lights." Theodore wanted to know what had happened to him last night. "Has anybody seen my running shoe?"

"Right or left?" I asked.

"Don't fucking start that again," Buddy cried.

"Oh, I think your shoe is in my room. Stewart found it in the stairwell this morning." I tried to enlighten him. "I couldn't keep you off the dance floor last night, literally. That's why you are so sore. Do you not remember having that dance off with some big black guy named Chuckles the Clown?"

"No, I don't believe you. Hic, hiccup." Theodore's jaw dropped in disbelief that turned into an I'm-going-to-puke look as he turned around and scurried off in a hurry. I think he had a date with the porcelain bowl.

Paulie leaned over and said, "Did you see him? He looked pretty rough, didn't he? I hope I never have to meet this Jack fellow."

"You might, Paulie, you might," I responded.

"I hope not. And I hope I never have to meet this Chuckles the Clown. Clowns scare me," Paulie cried. "Did you see Theodore's look when you mentioned that Chuckles the Clown?"

"We're already late; we better get going. It's already quarter after eight," Buddy interrupted.

Just then, Miss Vicki arrived with eight Coors Lights. She put two beers each down in front of Johnny, Paulie, and me and put the last two in the center of the table. She handed everyone their bill and advised us all to have a great day and that she would see us for breakfast tomorrow morning.

Buddy piped up, "Who's the fucking idiot that ordered these beers and why? We're going to be late. Do you see what time it is?"

"You did. And we are not going to be late," I interjected.

"I did not," Buddy argued with amazement.

"Remember, Buddy, when you said you would buy my team lunch with two beers if I took Paulie? Remember? I just figured you would want us to get them now just in case you forgot. And besides, you must have ordered them; they're on your bill," I responded.

Buddy glanced down at his bill. "Like fuck they are. Oh, I'm not paying for this, and what are the other two beers for?"

"Buddy, they are for the dummy you put on my team, remember? He's going to get thirsty too," I responded.

"I'm not paying for no two beers for no fucking dummy," Buddy yelled back.

"Buddy, why do you have to be like this? It's our first day. We all had a great breakfast except for Theodore. We had one hell of a lady wait on us. We negotiated in good faith on bets for the day. We shook hands. I just want to have fun. Five minutes in, you are yelling and trying to renege on the bet. Why you got to be like that?" I cautioned him. "Maybe you should ask your team before you start screaming? You know, you keep this up, and one of these days, you're going to give yourself a heart attack. It's going to be the big one. You are going to fall down, and I'm not going to blow in your mouth."

"O'Malley, why do you do this to me all the time? You know, one of these days, you are going to die, and you won't have any family or friends come to your wake or funeral. You will die lonely," Buddy promised.

"Buddy, this is where you are wrong. When I die, I'm going to have an Irish funeral," I said.

"Irish funeral? What's an Irish funeral?" Paulie asked in anticipation.

I came back with, "An Irish funeral is where you have an open bar at the wake. You drink till you pass out. And even though it is a little early, I've already started on my list. Right now, Buddy, I'm not sure if you are going to make it or not. I just might have to make you a special invitation or something."

"Open bar. I'll be there," Paulie promised as he took one of the biggest puffs ever from his inhaler. "Will there be any kind of music?"

"Of course there will be. It will be all the songs that have played in my mind over the years. I'm thinking I will have to come up with a theme song. I'm leaning toward Kim Mitchell's "Lager and Ale.""

Like clockwork, everyone at the table took their turn to say that they would be there. "I'll be there … I'm coming … Wouldn't miss it … What's the date going to be? … Will it be more than one day? … Can we bring a friend? … Are you feeling okay? … You sure don't look good … We sure are going to miss you …"

Even a couple of guys at the next table asked, "Where do you live, and do you need an invitation?"

I looked at Buddy and asked him, "You'll come, won't you, Buddy? You'll come, right?"

"Yeah, I'll come, but I know I'm not going to be very happy," Buddy assured me as he gave me a half-hearted hug.

"Okay, enough of the sad faces. Let's go golfing." That would assure everyone that I wasn't going to die anytime soon.

"Just remember, O'Malley, your beer for lunch is paid for," Buddy pleaded.

Buddy hurried us out of the restaurant. We got to the van, and the first thing Buddy saw was a big bucket of ice. "Looks like Zackery is looking after you, Buddy. You are just going to have to give him another twenty dollars for tomorrow," I said.

"Like fuck I will. Someone else can tip him tonight," Buddy yelled. Then he noticed someone on the other side of the van working on something. "Flat tire … how the fuck did that happen?"

"Oh, I forgot. Last night when Theodore drove home from the disco, he must have drove over a nail or something. We just made it home before it went flat," I informed him as I watched Zackery skillfully change the tire in under twenty seconds. "Jesus, Zackery, have you ever thought about being in a NASCAR pit crew? Christ, that was fast. You almost ruined the surprise."

"You would be surprised at what you can learn when you watch NASCAR every Sunday, like I do," Zac stated as he finished up, wiping his hands off with a grease rag. "I've learned a few tricks here and there. It's a good thing you had a spare. I have seen so many golfers come down here and never check their extra tire. You want me to take it down to the filling station and get it all fixed up for you?"

"Sure. Would you?" I agreed as I took Zackery to the side and whispered, "Zac, all it needs is air." I got to thinking that that drunk clown wouldn't have got it done that quickly or that efficiently.

"I know, I know. The valve cover is missing. I know it was on there yesterday," Zacho whispered back, giving me a skeptical look. "Somebody must have let the air out of it."

"God, you're good," I answered with a wink.

Buddy did not get as upset as I would have thought he would have. Maybe it was because he did not find it flat. NASCAR-Zach had found it and changed it and had ruined the surprise.

"You let Theodore drive drunk?" Buddy bawled. "What in fuck were you thinking?"

"Of course, I let him drive. There's no way in hell I could drive. I was way too drunk." I tried to bring him up to speed on what had transpired the night before. "And besides, I think that fucking Chuckles followed him home from the disco."

"Followed you home? Now the clown knows where we liveeeeeeee," Paulie cried, worried, as he took a swig from his puffer.

CHAPTER 12

If You Dress Like a Canary, You Must Be

Everyone climbed in as I threw the ice on the beer in the coolers.

Buddy wheeled out of the parking lot and inquired, "Does everyone have their golf vouchers?"

Almost everyone spoke up with a "Yeah."

Ten minutes down the road, we came across a big old sign that said "WYBOO GOLF COURSE … HOME OF THE BOO."

Paulie asked, "Why do they call it Wyboo Golf Course? What do you think *wyboo* means? And what do you think a boo is?"

"Maybe you should ask the clown." Johnny tried to scare Paulie.

"Nooooooo." Paulie emptied his puffer.

"Paulie, I think wyboos are those squirrelly like rodents. I believe they are a mix between a possum and a squirrel. They are blackish gray, with a black bandit mask over their eyes, with a white nose. And instead of living in trees, they live in holes in the ground. I think I read somewhere that locals believe they are possessed. If they called this course Wyboo, I would think there must be many of them here. So stay away from them. They will chase you, and they do bite." Pointing out the van window at one, I told Paulie, "There goes one. Just be careful if you see one. They like to play possum, and then when they get you close enough, they pounce and attack." I'm not sure where or why I came up with this imaginary tale, but it was almost like subconsciously I had heard something about wyboos before. No matter, just as long as it had scared Paulie.

"Boy, am I ever glad that I'm playing with you today. You sure can spot them before anybody else does." Paulie gasped for air from his puffer as he stood up in the van to get a better look out the back as one scurried past the van.

"I think that I have read that once they get you down into their burrow, they gang up, and they have a way to pull the dirt in on you. They won't stop until you are buried alive. It's one of the few squirrels that will eat meat. They have razor-sharp teeth that are compared to piranhas," I lied.

"Piranhas? I hope they don't have them here also," Paulie worried.

"O'Malley, will you shut the fuck up?" Buddy screamed. "Paulie, there are no piranhas here, and there are surely no meat-eating wyboos either."

"Are you sure? Because Shannon seems to know a lot about these masquerading varmints," Paulie cried.

"Okay, Paulie. If you are going to play stupid, then you'd better be careful out there," Buddy acknowledged.

"Because I have heard that they will gang up on small, stupid men."

"All I can say is, I'm sure glad that I'm playing with Shannon; he can spot them a mile away," Paulie fretted.

"I'll look after you, Paulie. Seeing no one else will," I vowed as I looked over at Buddy shaking his head.

Everyone else in the van knew I was making most of this up as I went. Not Paulie. He seemed scared but also enthusiastic to see one up close. He wanted to know more. I tried to keep it as real as possible or as believable as Paulie would take in.

Along the way, we passed a sign with an arrow pointing to the right that stated, "BAG DROP." A bag boy tried to get Buddy's attention to stop. But it was too late as Buddy turned into the parking area. We carried our clubs back up to the bag-drop area. The bag boy introduced himself as Ian and inquired of Buddy why he did not stop or use the bag drop.

I interrupted and told him, "He doesn't take direction very well."

Buddy retorted back, "Fuck off, O'Malley. I'm sorry. I really didn't see you, and to be honest, I was not sure what a bag drop was."

Ian went on to explain what a bag drop was and why we should use it. "It just makes the flow of incoming golfers move a little easier and faster. I answer a lot of questions to make the golfer's day a little easier and enjoyable. I direct golfers to the pro shop, restaurant and bar, beverage cart, and BBQ at the turn. I can tell you the weather report for the day or the rest of the week. I can tell you if your tee times are on time or even what's good on the menu. I can also tell you who won the game last night. And by the way, we also have a two-for-one sale on golf shirts in the pro shop, if anyone is interested."

I'm not sure if he was directing that toward Paulie or not. But I did overhear Buddy saying to Paulie, "You look fine."

This was the early 1990s. We were from Canada. We did not know what a bag drop was. We had never seen them, never at our golf courses. But after using the bag-drop area for a couple of days, I'm not sure why someone did not think of it sooner. It made sense; it made perfect sense. Tomorrow we wouldn't let Buddy make us look stupid, not again. We would do it right. We would make it look like we had done it all of our lives. "BAG DROP." Who would have thunk it?

We went inside at the pro shop to check in. There, standing at the counter, was an older gentleman. He was dressed in a white Wyboo-logoed golf shirt and black pleated dress pants, and he was wearing a pair of black and white golf shoes, which matched perfectly. Every pleat or crease was razor-sharp. His outfit was either brand-new, or his wife was up all night ironing.

We approached the front desk and set down our empty beer cans on the counter. It seemed all week, whenever we went to check in for golf or with a hostess for dinner, there was always someone knocking over an empty beer can. It made an unbelievable tinny sound, which sounded like nothing else. What it sounded like to me was, I'm empty and need a full one.

"O-Dare," he blurted out in his Southern drawl as he ushered us over to the front counter. "Welcome to the boo. My name is Calvin, and it sure looks like we are going to have some fun today." He must have been the pro for the course. He was dressed like a pro. He acted like the pro; hey, he even smelled like the pro. This was the time period when the pro usually managed and ran the pro shop. It was his merchandise to sell. That was how he got paid; that was how he made a living. Calvin was in his sixties, and he had been the pro at the Wyboo Golf Course for a number of years. He wasn't as uptight as other pros. It was not about making money to him; it was about having fun. He loved the game of golf, and he just wanted to make sure everyone who came through his door had a great time at his golf course. "You must be the O'Malley group. I've got you down for eight o'clock. You are a little late, but don't you worry about it, cause …"

"I told you, you would make us late," Buddy interrupted him as he gave me an angry look. I'm sure that he had put his angry eyes in. Buddy was always putting his angry eyes in.

"Buddy, it wasn't me. I think it was that flat tire that made us late," I answered.

"It's okay," Kevin continued. "We had one hell of a frost last night. You guys could have stayed in bed for a couple of more hours. Looks like some of you could have used it. We are going to try to get you out around ten thirty."

I glared over at Buddy as if to say I told you so without saying a word. Maybe I should have put my angry eyes in.

Calvin suggested, "Why don't we get you all signed in? The driving range is open, and you can hit as many golf balls as you want. There are some demo clubs over there, if you want to try them out. Also, the putting green should be open in about a half hour. It gets the early morning sun, so the frost will burn off quicker there. If you are looking for breakfast, Chrissy makes a mean western omelet. There's free coffee and doughnuts over there. Help yourself." A few of the guys headed towards the free coffee and doughnuts. "We also have some specials going on in the pro shop." He pointed to a rack of golf shirts in the corner, which had a sign on it that said, "2-FOR-1, ALL SALES FINAL."

Paulie looked at Buddy and pleaded, "What's wrong with my shirt? You said I looked fine."

"Paulie, you're fine; he wasn't talking about you," Buddy assured Paulie.

"Are you sure?" Paulie asked as he started to ruffle through the rack of shirts. "They all look pretty good."

Most, if not all, had the Wyboo Golf Course emblems on them. Paulie held up two putrid-colored golf shirts: a celery-green one, and of course his favorite, a bright-mustard yellow one. "What do you think? You must be right, Shannon, about the wyboos. They all have those pesky squirrels in their logos."

"Paulie, first off, I would never lead you astray. Secondly, you are looking in the ladies' section again. And thirdly, you already have a yellow shirt on. You look like a canary, and with those black fucking-tight shorts on, you look like you are about to race the Tour de France," I commented.

Calvin spoke up with a little chuckle and said, "Shorts over here are on sale also, all sizes and colors."

"Buddy, you said that I looked fine this morning," Paulie repeated.

"You do, Paulie, you do. Never mind what they think," Buddy blurted out as he tried to help Paulie with his choices.

Next thing I knew, Paulie was at the cash register with a yellow golf shirt, celery-green golf shirt, and pair of black shorts that he wanted to buy. "Are you sure they are the right size?" I asked.

"They're the perfect size. I'd better get a new hat while I'm at it. I kinda like that logo they have with the masked wyboos in it. It's neat," Paulie reported as he grabbed a black logoed hat from the rack at the front counter.

"Your total is fifty-one dollars and twenty-three cents," Calvin said after he hit the total button on the register.

The next thing I heard was, "Can I borrow some money, Buddy?"

"Sure, Paulie, what do you need?" Buddy asked.

"Fifty-one dollars and twenty-three cents. Didn't you hear him?" Paulie demanded as Buddy handed him a fifty.

"What happened to the fifty I gave you this morning?" I dared ask him.

"I'm going to save it," Paulie declared.

"Save it for what? Oh, never mind," I said.

"Buddy, do you have the one dollar and twenty-three cents? I don't want to change my fifty," Paulie asked.

"No, I don't, so fuck off," Buddy countered.

"Paulie, check your change pocket," I advised him.

Paulie pulled out his wallet and opened it up. He unzipped his change pocket and started counting the change out to one dollar and twenty-three cents.

"Twenty-five, fifty, seventy-five, eighty-five, ninety-five, dollar-five, fifteen—I got it; I got it. Twenty, twenty-one, two, and three. There you go, one dollar and twenty-three cents," Paulie asserted as he handed over his change.

"Paulie, that's Canadian change. They're not going to take that," Buddy blurted out as he tried to help Paulie as much as he could.

"Yes, yes, we will. Today only. Just for you, my little canar … sir," Calvin said as he started to laugh along with everyone else. He handed Paulie his bag of brand-new golf attire.

By this time, we were all standing at the front counter, and Kevin was starting to ring us all in for the golf green fees. "Who has all the golf vouchers?" Calvin asked.

We all handed over the vouchers except for Paulie.

Buddy stared at Paulie and chimed in, "Paulie, where's your voucher?"

"Don't you have it?" Paulie whined.

"No. Why would I have it?" Buddy countered as he put his angry eyes in once again.

"You told me last night you were going to be my roommate, you were going to look after me, and you were going to protect me from those fucking O'Malleys … Remember?" Paulie retorted.

"Paulie, were you not in the van this morning when I asked everyone if they had their vouchers or not?" Buddy wondered.

"Yes, I was there," Paulie agreed. "You know that I was there. How else would I have gotten here?"

"Then why didn't you say something?" Buddy argued. You could tell that Buddy was getting flustered.

"I didn't think you were talking to me," Paulie confessed.

"Paulie, do me a favor. I don't want you to ever think again," Buddy pleaded with Paulie.

"Okeydokey," Paulie sputtered. "I can do that."

"Calvin, not a big deal, is it? I guess I could go get it. The hotel is not that far," I offered.

"Yes, I need those vouchers to get paid from the hotel. But not to worry this time. I'll just get Sally Sue over at the Happy Holiday Hotel to fax me over a copy for my records," Calvin responded as he handed me the starter slip. I quickly passed it along to Paulie to hold on to.

Buddy snatched it from our hands and warned us, "I'll take that. Are you fucking nuts? He'll just lose it."

So, unknowingly, all week long, each time that Sally Sue had to fax the golf vouchers to each course, a ten-dollar surcharge was added to Buddy's credit card. We did not know. Or I should say Buddy did not know this until we went to check out—or I should say, not till he got home and got a bill.

A few of us went to the driving range, and a couple went to the putting green. They all wanted to work on various aspects of their game to improve, or maybe it was to perfect some of their bad habits. Our team, Johnny, Paulie, and I, went to the bar to perfect our bad habits. Drinking. I'm glad we did. This is where we met Chrissy.

As we walked over into the bar area, all of a sudden, that *Three's Company* soundtrack started to play in my head. Enough with that song; I had had enough of the old girls. How many Mrs. Ropers were going to be on this trip? I had that theme song playing in my head repeatedly, which made me think about Mrs. Roper, that unquenchable, sex-starved landlady.

We were sitting there waiting for our granny waitress to come out from the back. I was wondering, would she be able to do the job at her age? I just hoped she didn't forget to put her teeth back in before she came out to take our order. Suddenly, she came out from the kitchen. Eureka! She was not a Mrs. Roper; she was a young Chrissy. Finally, let that music play loudly. She was even a better-looking Chrissy than Suzanne Somers could have ever created. But was she as dumb? I was sure we would soon find out.

Chrissy was a beautiful, bubbly young girl of twenty-five. She said she was doing everything today and went on to explain that the course was a little slow today, so she was the main cook, dishwasher, bartender, waitress, and anything else that needed to be done. Hmm? If time allowed, she would also be out on the course riding the beverage cart when needed. I'd give her something to ride. I had Chrissy dressed in a little Catholic school uniform. She was so innocent looking. Her blonde hair was tied back in a ponytail. She was wearing small, dangly earrings. She had big, black-rimmed glasses on, which surely made her look more intelligent. Her little white blouse was buttoned almost all the way to the neckline. Her purple tartan kilt almost hung down to above her knees. The safety clasp on the skirt's pin was facing up, so I think that made her available. It was professionally pinned so nothing could unravel. She was wearing white knee-high socks, which almost came up to her knees. And it was all finished off with black, shiny shoes. I did not see any wedding ring, but all she talked about was her son, William. So I was thinking that she was a struggling single mother who was trying to make a living.

We were sitting there in the bar that overlooked the putting green. And over in the distance, we could see the driving range. I was not sure if everyone was killing time or if they were actually working on something specific. It was funny watching the guys hit balls at the driving range. One would go right, and one would go left. It was also like they were in a race to see who could hit their bucket of balls first. Maybe there was a prize for emptying your bucket first. Maybe it was just a bet. The faster they teed up a ball, the faster it was hit into the woods, missing the center of the driving range by miles. Speed golf. That game hadn't even been invented yet.

Johnny gave me that look and reported, "I think we have work to do on the putting green. The greens look fast, very fast. They might be the fastest greens that you have ever played."

I acknowledged him with an "okay," knowing fully what we were about to do. I stood up, grabbed my coat, and said, "I'm going to put my coat in the van. Anybody need anything?"

"Yeah, can you take my new clothes to the van?" Paulie asked as he handed me his bag of items. He made sure everything was in the bag. He took his brand-new black hat out of the bag and traded it with his lucky old fifties fishing hat. He had to adjust the size a couple of times to make sure it fit properly.

"Sure, I can. But aren't you going to change your clothes?" I inquired.

"No, I think I will save it for tomorrow," Paulie stated.

"Okay. I'll meet you guys at the putting green," I announced before taking a shortcut through the pro shop.

"Hey Calvin, Paulie got the wrong size. Mind if I get them a little larger? So he doesn't look like a French biker!" I asked.

"Go ahead." Calvin laughed. "His clothes looked a little tight this morning."

In reality, I got a size smaller. So tomorrow's outfit would look just like today's outfit but would have one of those Wyboo's logos on it. I made the exchange and hurried off to the van.

CHAPTER 13

Buddy's Masters Logo Ball

By the time I got to the putting green, all of my crew and the Canary had all congregated there. They were all taking their turn putting at the various holes around the green. They were not making many, if any. It had probably been about three months since anybody had had a golf club in their hand. Besides that, the green was a whole lot faster than any of us had ever seen before. It was smooth as glass.

I stated, "Can you imagine how fast they are going to be out on the course? By the time we get out there, they will have cut all the greens. Whereas this green has not been cut, so this green will be the slowest of them all."

"They are going to be lightning fast when we get out there," Johnny added as he walked over toward Buddy. "Hey, Buddy, you seem to be walking a little more upright. Or straighter or something."

"You got something up your ass again?" I joked. "Your walk seems to be a little more uptight. What gives?"

"Oh, I got my new insoles in my golf shoes. I just had to trim them a little to fit. I feel so much taller. And I don't know, it's giving me so much more confidence," Buddy confided. "You guys are going to have to play really hard if you are going to beat me today."

"Hey, Johnny, maybe we should stop on the way home and get you a pair. So you can look like you got something stuffed up your ass," I jested. "Buddy, can you get them in different thicknesses?"

"You sure can, from as little as a millimeter all the way up to two inches thick," Buddy bragged as he did a little walk and twirl to show off his new inserts. "I got the maximum you can get. You can hardly tell that I'm almost walking out of my shoes. It makes you think to walk. It makes you stand up straighter, I tell you. Look."

"I don't know, Buddy. I still think you have something concealed in your ass again," I teased. "But you might have something there. Can you give us another twirl down that runway of yours?"

"Will you just fuck off?" Buddy screamed as he picked up his ball and went to the other side of the practice green.

"We still have about an hour to kill before we tee off. We should each throw five dollars in and have a little putting contest," Johnny suggested.

Everyone agreed as they handed over five bucks.

"Hey, Paulie, you need change for that fifty yet? Or are you still saving it for that rainy day?" Johnny inquired.

Paulie responded with, "Hmm, maybe I won't play. I don't really want to change it yet."

"Will somebody lend the canary some money already? Oh, never mind." Johnny handed him fifty dollars. "Now,

Paulie, notice how they are in small bills, so you don't have to worry about changing the big ones."

It was the first day, Paulie was broke, and he was fifty dollars into Buddy, Johnny, and me. But he did have some brand-new golf attire that wouldn't fit. Now if Paulie played his cards right, I should be able to get everyone in the group to lend him money.

Johnny called the putting contest, "Around the horn." But I called it, "How am I going to get more strokes from Buddy without him noticing, and if I can get a beer or two, all the better." What a concept! What a great game! It would be the best game ever.

Basically, whoever went first leads you to all the different holes around the putting surface. You counted each stroke for each hole till you were in the hole. If by chance you happened to putt it off the green or sink it in the wrong hole, you were disqualified and out of the game.

Johnny was explaining the rules to everyone and stated, "Low score wins, and if there happens to be a tie, there will be a sudden-death playoff hole."

It was Johnny's game, so he led us off. Johnny was by far the best putter of the group. He read the greens like no other. Not only could he see the breaks; he could also adjust his speeds to take advantage of the grain of the grass. But after saying that, he blew by the first hole by ten feet, missed the next one coming back, and settled for a three on the first hole. Unbelievably, both Johnny and I could not get the speeds down for the rest of the contest. I think Paulie disqualified himself on the first hole by putting it off the putting surface. Stewart and Buddy tied for first, so they needed a playoff to decide the winner. Buddy eventually won but needed four extra holes to finally finish Stewart off.

Buddy was on top of the world; he had finally won something. He was waving his hands in the air; he pranced around like he owned it. He was doing his happy dance. He had thirty-five dollars in his hands, waving it around like it was a million. He was letting everyone know that he had won.

"I'm buying, I'm buying. What does everyone want to drink?" he boasted as he rushed off to the bar to spend his winnings. I watched him closely, as I was waiting for him to run out of his shoes and fall.

Buddy came back from the bar with eight beers, four under each arm, being careful so he wouldn't drop them. "That thirty-five dollars didn't last long. Eight beers came to thirty-six dollars with tip," Buddy complained.

"I told you, Buddy, when you win, you lose," I assured him.

"Hey, Buddy, let me help you. You don't want to drop these, from your first win and all," Johnny said as he carefully pulled four beers from under one of Buddy's arms. He quickly handed me two of them. Both Johnny and I tried to down our extra beer before Buddy noticed.

Buddy distributed the rest of the beer to the gang and realized that he had no beer left; he had given too many away. He turned around to face us and yelled, "Where in fuck are my beers?"

As he turned around, both me and Johnny handed him our empty bottles and stated, "These were yours? Are you sure? I'm sorry; I thought you had bought us all two."

"Yeah, Buddy, I'm really sorry. You want what's left of this beer?" I smirked as I tried to hand him my other half-empty beer bottle.

"No, I don't want your fucking beer. I want my beer. You fucking O'Malleys. Go get me a beer," Buddy yelled.

Johnny eagerly scurried off to the bar to get Buddy another beer. Or was it just to see Chrissy again? Or was it just to get another beer for himself? As Johnny returned, he found Buddy in a better frame of mind; he was still doing his happy dance. He was explaining his new putter grip to me. As he said, he couldn't miss. He was unbeatable. He had just read about it in the latest issue of *Golf Digest*. I think he called it a "crab claw" or something along that line. All I knew was that his new grip looked like a crab fucking another crab. I was showing some interest in this new style. I made him explain every detail. I wanted to know more. I thought I was going to puke! What I had to put up with. Just to get more strokes for Johnny.

"Buddy, but really, do you think it is the crab claw, or is it that you are two inches taller?" I inquired as I mimicked his new putting grip. "You might have something there. You know, being taller and more upright. That claw grip of yours and being more upright. And that pendulum action of yours; you make it look so precise. It'd make your center of gravity a little higher, and your line of sight would make it directly over your ball. You make it look so easy."

"Yeaaaah, you're right. Look; I can't miss," Buddy bragged as he sank another three-footer.

"Nooooo, I think you are still concealing something up your ass again." I laughed as I shook my head.

"Will you just fuck off already?" Buddy warned me. "I don't have anything up my ass."

Later, I said to Johnny, "You owe me big-time."

He came back with, "Kid, we are on the same team. It's a win-win situation."

Buddy was still on top of the world from winning the putting contest. He was taller, he had his new putting grip, a new style, he had game, and he thought he couldn't lose. He started to rethink the bet made earlier this morning and said, "You know, maybe we should give you guys a couple more strokes on the bet we made for the round. You guys sure didn't do well in the putting contest."

Paulie, he didn't even know it, but he was very pivotal in getting all of this renegotiating of the bet. We needed him to come in last, and he did. By him putting his ball off the green, he disqualified himself. It was perfect. It was probably the easiest five dollars that he had ever lost.

"What were you thinking, Buddy?" I questioned him.

"I don't know. Maybe we give you four strokes a side, and we up the team aggregate to ten dollars, and we keep everything else the same."

I looked over at Johnny. "What do you think?" Before I got the words out of my mouth, there was Johnny shaking Buddy's hand. I guess he got what he wanted.

Just then we heard over the loudspeaker: "O'Malley group to the first tee and take that canary with you." You could also overhear on the loudspeaker a lot of chuckling in the background; Kevin must have forgotten to turn the mic off.

"Buddy, why did you pick this outfit for me?" Paulie pleaded. "That's it; I'm going to change."

"Into what?" I asked. "All you have is that brand-new canary suit you just bought. So it's not going to help."

"Wellllll," Paulie said, trying to find an answer, "well, if one of you guys would lend me some more money, I could buy something that wasn't canary-like."

"They did have some nice cardinal-colored shirts," I replied as I reached for my wallet.

"I think I saw some blue and gray shirts. How do you feel about being a blue jay?" Johnny added as he also reached around for his wallet.

"Will you guys leave him alone? He is not buying anything more, especially if it makes him look like a bird." Buddy tried to comfort Paulie. "You look fine, and besides, there is not enough time. Now get in the fucking cart."

"Maybe you want to borrow my rain suit? It's orange," Johnny said. "But it's in the van."

"No, we don't want him to look like a new arrival at a maximum-security prison," Buddy cried back. "Will you guys leave him alone? He looks just fine."

"Hey, Paulie, what would you rather look like: a canary or a fresh piece of meat with a tight ass?"

"Neither. I just want to look normal. Like one of the guys," Paulie whined.

"Too late."

We finally got over to the first tee, and I wondered, "Hey, Buddy, have we got all the bets lined up yet? I don't recall setting up any junk yet. We haven't even talked about brownies, sandies, woodies, arnies, or even pussies."

"O'Malley, it's the first day; let's just make it simple. We're not playing any more garbage, and besides, there's no more room on the scorecard," Buddy stated.

"All right then, Buddy, you might as well take your group and go," I retorted. "Get going."

"Not so fast. I think I'm going to drop back and play with you guys, just to keep you honest, and of course, to protect Paulie," Buddy joked as he moved his golf clubs into Paulie's cart.

"Speaking about honesty, did we do an Honest John?" I asked.

"Yeah, I guess we should do at least an Honest John. How's five dollars a man sound?" Buddy replied.

"So what's everyone's Honest John score?"

Everyone shouted out what they thought they were going to shoot. Stewart started with eighty-two. Kevin came up with an eighty-four. Buddy boasted a ninety-eight. Pudden stated a one hundred three. Johnny announced an eighty-nine. Paulie agreed to a one hundred fourteen. And I finished it out with a seventy-nine.

I quickly wrote down everyone's scores. I knew full well that everyone bragged on the low side. I believe I did also. It seemed they forgot that they had not had a golf club in their hands for months. I did a quick little calculation and told Buddy, "It looks like your team is down twenty dollars already."

"What do you mean?" Buddy asked.

"Well, I just totaled them up, and if everyone shoots what they say they are going to shoot, your team score came to three hundred sixty-seven, and ours came to three hundred sixty-six. With my math, you just lost your first bet by one stroke," I reported.

Buddy pondered it for a moment and came back with, "Okay, change my Honest John to ninety-six. There; you lose by one."

"Are you sure? It is bad luck to change your Honest John score," I reminded him.

"Yes, I'm sure. Now fuck off," Buddy boldly predicted.

"You know, Buddy, if you play with us, who's going to keep your team honest? Who are you going to trust with that entire scorekeeping? And besides, we're just going to fuck your game up," I promised.

"Pudden, he'll keep score. And he's trustworthy. He will only cheat and fudge the numbers enough to win. Right, Pudden?" Buddy said as he nodded and winked at Pudden.

"Right, Pudden?" Buddy echoed again.

"Oh, yeah, right," Pudden acknowledged.

Buddy handed over the starter slip to the starter. He introduced himself as Alex. He was an older gentleman, retired and divorced. As he said, he only worked six days a week so he could golf the other day for free. That did not sound like retirement to me. He went through all the do's and don'ts on the course, some yardages, and some helpful hints. Basically, he told us to just go have some fun. He also told us that it was going to warm up and be a beautiful day out there, but that there was a chance of a little storm that should blow through in a couple of hours and it should not last long. He said that he would blow a horn if the thunder and lightning got too close.

I piped up, "Paulie, did you ask him where the washrooms are? You know you will need them."

"I was just about to do that," Paulie replied.

Alex told us that there were washrooms on hole five and hole fifteen. He went on to explain hole one. "It's a long par four, slight dogleg right, with water all along the right. Water comes into play on the right all the way to the green.

It's slightly uphill, against the wind, so take an extra club or two. And for heaven's sake, stay left because everything slopes to the right, right into the water. If you are ready, your first group can hit."

All three—Pudden, Kevin, and Stewart—mishit their drives right. We could only see one splash, but with the look on Alex's face and his thumbs-down gesture, I would bet that all three went in the water.

As they drove away, I yelled up to them, "Number 11 will be our long-drive hole, okay?" I looked at Buddy and said, "That doesn't look too good for your team."

"Oh, fuck off. It's just one hole," Buddy retorted.

It was finally our turn to hit. Buddy was first, and you guessed it, straight into the water. I egged him on. "Hey, Buddy, four out of four on your team drowned. Also, did you know, four out of four dentists would say you lose? Also, that's four dollars for Zackery for ice."

"Maybe you will need longer clubs now that you are taller." Johnny laughed as he imitated Buddy swinging on his tippy toes. "You should have hit a few more range balls into the woods."

"Oh, fuck off," Buddy mumbled under his breath.

Paulie got up to the tee and teed up a yellow range ball, at which Alex chuckled. "Laddie, that range ball better not be from this course. So you better aim more lefter. You wouldn't want me to have to make you go swimming for it."

Paulie, not knowing if Alex was serious or not, responded with, "Oh no, sir. All these yellow range balls in my bag are from my home course."

"And what home course exactly are you from again?" Buddy wondered out loud, knowing full well that Paulie could not afford a membership at any golf course, even if he was given it.

Johnny added with puzzlement, "Shannon, do you have a golf course up there with the initials WGC?"

"WGC? They are not marked … Oh, they are. Um?" Paulie responded as he picked the yellow golf ball off the tee to examine it, only to find the initials WGC stamped on it. "Shannon …"

I quickly came back with a lie. "Yeah, that's the Watertown Golf Course; Paulie and I played it sometime last November. Remember, Paulie? They were selling all their range balls because they were getting a new shipment in the spring. Or, something like that."

"We did? Oh, yeah, now I remember. Yeah, that's where I got them from. I bought a dozen, I think," Paulie lied when he finally clued in. "I think I still have about ten in my bag."

"Well, laddie, if you want more, you just let me know. 'Cause I have thousands of those Watertown Golf Course range balls for sale." Alex laughed, as he knew Paulie had stolen the yellow golf balls from him earlier.

"No, no thanks. But if you have any more of those Wyboo Golf Course range balls, I might take a couple more for souvenirs," Paulie offered.

Alex just stood there with puzzlement on his face. I'm sure he was thinking, "Where did this Canadian come from?"

Paulie set his ball back on the tee and took a couple of practice swings. He tried his damnedest to keep it left, but he followed Buddy right into the water.

Alex repeated himself. "Keep it left, fellows, keep it left."

Johnny and I both hit it so far left, we might have been in a different zip code. But we were dry. We were the only ones that were dry.

As we drove up to our balls, I was thinking. We were on vacation, first day, first drive, and Buddy was wet and frazzled. What else could you want? Ah, maybe I could use another beer.

We got up to the edge of the pond to have a quick look for Buddy's ball and, of course, Paulie's Watertown Golf Course range ball. Now I could see why Alex wanted us to hit so far left, as everything sloped to the pond. Even though we had thought Johnny's and my balls were hit too far left, they in fact had actually made their way to the center of the fairway. Not too bad of drives after all. Not bad at all.

We were all fishing with our clubs around the edge of the pond looking for Buddy's and Paulie's balls. They were looking in each clump of grass, hoping to find them. We were finding the odd ball or two. But we had no luck finding Buddy's or Paulie's.

"Hey, look at this," Buddy shrieked as he pulled a ball from the water. "It's a Master's logo ball. Wow." As he held it up to show everyone his new prized possession, he proclaimed, "This is my new lucky ball."

At the first, Johnny made an unbelievable par. I got a disappointing bogey five, and both Buddy and Paulie scored a triple. Off to a great start. Other than Buddy's triple on the first hole, he settled right down and parred the next seven holes. He was maybe having the round of his life. I did a quick calculation and a little speculation on what the group up ahead was doing, and I thought we were down in the match a little. Johnny suggested to me that maybe we should pick our game up a little. We did not want to lose the first day. I told him not to worry as Buddy was playing way above his head and that he would eventually come back to earth sooner or later. Or we would bring him back, I promised.

On hole nine, all four of us were out in the middle of the fairway. Johnny was about two hundred yards in. I think I got about 196, Paulie got about 191, and Buddy had an unbelievably long tee shot and probably had less than 180 yards in. The hole had a large sloping green from back to front, a large pond guarding all along the front edge, and there was a huge, deep bunker in the back. The flag was about center left.

Johnny had to jump all over this shot if he planned on getting over the pond in front. He dubbed it, and it rolled perfectly up to the edge of the pond in front. I think we all yelled at him, "Great layup."

"Just the way I planned it," Johnny offered.

I grabbed my three-wood, went next, and just barely made it over the water. The ball bounced a couple of times past the pin, then started to trickle back toward the pin and water. "Sit. Sit," I yelled at the ball. The ball ran by the pin and headed toward the pond. It slowed down just enough to get caught up in the fringe. "Wow, that was a close one. How I stayed out of the water, I don't know," I commented.

"Yeah, there is more slope there than you think. Did you see it pick up speed?" Johnny said.

"Holy fuck, I can't believe it's playing that long. I hit that on the screws," I boasted. "I'll take it. I'm safe."

"Partner, you better take an extra club," Johnny told Paulie.

"Yeah, it looks long," Paulie said.

And wouldn't you know it? Paulie deposited another one of his stolen range balls into the middle of the pond. "Shit, I didn't think I hit it that bad," Paulie exclaimed.

"It's okay, Paulie. At least you're losing the balls here at the course where you stole them from," Johnny revealed. "Was that a Wyboo ball, or was it a Watertown ball?"

Buddy got over his ball, and he was wondering, "Should I choke down on a three-iron, or maybe I should swing a full five-iron?"

"Are you nuts? Did you not see our shots? I was thinking you should hit a baby three-wood or a full five-wood," I retorted. "You know you hit your woods better than your irons."

"Yeah, you're right. But I don't think I need a three-wood. I'm going to choke down on a five-wood," Buddy boasted.

Buddy took a couple of practice swings, then took dead aim and swung. The ball never left the flag. It sure was pretty in the air. "Is it enough club? Is it?" I teased.

The ball flew completely over the green. "Wow. That has to be the best five-wood that you have ever hit, Buddy," Paulie stated.

"Yeah, I hit that pretty good," Buddy stated.

"Pretty good? That's the best five-wood that I have ever seen you hit," I reassured him.

"Do you think that I'm okay? What do you think is back there behind the green?" Buddy worried about where he had ended up.

"Yeah, I think you're okay. It looks to be a bunker back there," Johnny confided as he examined the picture of the ninth hole on the back of the scorecard.

I'm sure that as Buddy drove up to the green, he was saying to himself, "Boy, did I ever make a great shot. That has to be one of the best shots ever." But I'm sure doubt had crept into his mind also. "What the fuck am I going to do now?"

We got to Johnny's ball; he wedged it over the pond. It landed about twenty feet past the pin, then rolled back past the pin to about a foot away.

"Great shot, Johnny. Pick it up," Buddy yelled as he pointed to Johnny's ball. "Is there ever a lot of slope there, eh?"

"Yep, I thought I hit it way too hard, but I guess it was just about perfect," Johnny offered.

Paulie got up and deposited another ball into the pond and screamed, "Fuck."

"You must be out of all those stolen range balls by now?" Buddy asked.

"Na, I got a few more," Paulie boldly stated as he dropped another one.

This time he skipped it three times across the water, and it came to rest about two feet from the pin.

Buddy yelled, "You lucky bastard. You can have that one too."

"Nice shot," Johnny added.

And I came back with, "Great shot, partner. I'm not sure if I would have done it like that."

Buddy and Paulie took the cart around to the back of the green to take a look for Buddy's ball. The green sloped so much from back to front that you really could not see the guys back there. Sure enough, the bunker had caught his ball. This bunker was huge. It was a great collection area for balls hit too long. Anything hit too long ended up in the woods behind. It was not only huge; it was deep, and everything sloped from there to the pond in front. Buddy grabbed his sand wedge and wandered down into the bunker to hit his ball. He aligned himself and was about to address his ball. Even with his extensions, he was still so short he couldn't even see out of the bunker, let alone see the flag.

"What the fuck? I can't see the flag. Where is it?" Buddy screamed as he jumped up and down a couple of times to see if he could see the position of the flag.

"No worries, Buddy." As if to be helpful, Johnny went over to the flag, lifted it out of the hole, and waved it around. "Can you see it now?"

"Yes. Are you sure? Is that where the hole is? I know what you are like," Buddy retorted.

"Come on, Buddy. I'm not always like that. I'm just trying to be helpful here," Johnny responded.

Looking back at that shot of Buddy's, the degree of difficulty and such, out of a hundred times, he would dub it and leave it in the bunker ninety-two times. The other eight tries, I would think he would deposit it in the pond in front. There would be no way in hell that he would be able to put enough spin on the ball to keep it on the green. There was no chance. No chance at all.

In the beginning, Buddy was not a good bunker player. I have to think he is a thousand percent better now. And I want to think it is because of Johnny and me. We would always put him there; we wanted to see him throw a club. Sometimes you would have to duck, and other times you would just have to jump out of the way. Anytime we had a chance, when he was not looking, we would toss or kick his ball into a sand trap. I remember on a couple of occasions where I tossed his ball into a bunker on the other side of the fairway or on the other side of the green. He would always have this drunken, puzzled look on his face. Then he would swear. Then he would accept it. Then he would throw his club—because he had made a poor shot—and then he would swear again.

One time we were playing a course that advertised that they had 113 of the most challenging bunkers. We put Buddy in seventy-one bunkers that day. Actually he had only landed in about nineteen of them. We had placed him in the rest. As usual, one of us O'Malleys would keep him busy, while the other would do the dirty work. We would not just throw it in the middle of the bunker; we loved to put it in the bestest of the worstest spots. You know, up against a lip, downhill lies. Sometimes it was a matter of placing his ball beside a bunker so he would have an awkward stance, like one foot in and one foot out. We were very busy that day. He just didn't have a chance. He threw his club forty-two times that day. I believe he also broke his sand wedge. It was just another club he had to replace without Marilyn finding out. How do I know these numbers? I keep scorecards, especially important ones. For days like that, I keep a sand bunker column, a club throwing or dub column, and even a column to count the beer he could drink in a round.

I remember at the end of one round, we were all sitting in the clubhouse having a beer. We were all bragging and crying about our rounds, and Buddy grabbed the scorecard to question something in his round. "I didn't take a seven on eighteen; I'm sure I took a six. See, I was in the fairway bunker on the drive. My next shot landed in the right-hand bunker at the green. I wedged it across the green to the other bunker. From there, I was able to get it out onto the green, where I two-putted for a six. See, I get a six! And by the way, what are all these numbers and columns beside my name?"

As he handed me back the scorecard, I claimed, "My scorekeeping is usually pretty accurate; let's see what I've got you down for. Yup, I still have you at seven, and my gosintas is usually pretty good too."

"How's that? Show me," Buddy questioned.

"Let's see. I got you at one plus one beer, one dub, three sandies, and one helicopter, equals seven. And I have you down also for seven fucks, which verifies that the score is right," I surmised.

"What the fuck are you talking about?" Buddy screamed.

Coming back from the bar with a round of beers, Johnny grabbed the scorecard and interrupted with, "Buddy, I was not even in your foursome. But I think I can tell you shot for shot or at least pretty close. You drove the ball into the fairway bunker on the right; you said fuck, went to the cart, and opened a beer. You shot from there to the bunker at the green; you said fuck. You wedged one over the green to the other bunker and said fuck. Your next shot probably landed on the green, and you probably two-putted from there. You probably said fuck-fuck as you put your putter away. Now I see on the scorecard, you had a dub, and you threw your club once, and I'm still missing two fucks somewhere. So this is just an educated guess, but I'm going to back you up to that first bunker shot. I would think you had a dub in that first bunker. You said fuck, and then you threw your seven-iron into the woods. After you calmed down a bit, you hit your next shot to the green side bunker. You went to retrieve your club from the trees, and you could not reach it. You threw things up into the branches to knock your club loose. You were so mad you threw an unopened beer up at it and it worked, but when the beer hit the ground, it exploded. When you saw all that beer pouring out of the can, you said fuck one more time. How's that, Buddy? Am I close?"

Dumbfounded and confused, Buddy said, "But you weren't there. How did you get all of that out of his scorecard? And you were right; I did take a seven. I forgot all about that dub in the bunker and that beer; what a fucking waste. And how the fuck did you know it was a seven-iron?"

"Who do you think taught him?" Johnny responded. But he also did not want to divulge any more information, like he was in the foursome right behind him, watching it all unfold.

So in the long run, I think Buddy owes us money on all the lessons or practice that we gave him in getting out of a bunker all these years.

So back to the shot on hole nine that Buddy was about to make. He backed out of the bunker and came around to the side to see that Johnny was indeed actually holding the pin directly over the hole placement. Because the sand was so steep and fluffy, he could not come forward to check the pin placement and said, "Okay, okay. At least there's one honest O'Malley today. No, no, I mean this minute."

Buddy positioned himself in the bunker once more and took a couple of practice waggles and swings. An explosion of sand flew up, and the ball went straight up and came straight down, hit the top lip of the bunker, and trickled forward. What an amazing shot, as it rolled toward the pin.

Both me and Johnny were screaming at the ball. "It's got a chance. It's got a chance. Look. It might go in." It lipped out and stopped on the edge of the hole. I quickly picked it up and put it in my pocket.

By the time Buddy got back around to the edge of the green to see his great shot, both Johnny and I were over at the front edge of the pond, to make it look like we were fishing for Buddy's ball. We are using our putters to see if we could dig Buddy's ball out of the water. We were having a back-and-forth conversation with each other. "It looked like it was going in for the longest time."

"Did you see how much speed it picked up as it went by the hole?"

"Grain will do that."

"Yeah, you're right, but you know everything goes to the water."

"I almost had it there. Fuck, it's gone now," I said as I thought I hit his ball with my putter in the murky water.

"Hell of a shot, Buddy. I thought it was in," Johnny reported.

"Yeah, I thought it was in also," I added.

"Fuck, fuck, fuck," Buddy screamed; he was about to throw his sand wedge again.

"You can't be mad. It looked good all the way. It looked great, and don't throw your club either. We're too close to the water. Remember the last time you threw your sand wedge in the water, you had to borrow money to replace it, so Marilyn would not see it on your VISA bill. By the way, I don't think you have paid me back yet," I scolded Buddy as he was walking around gesturing, about to throw his club.

"Yeah, you're right. But I'm still not happy," Buddy assured me.

We finished the hole, and Buddy was still not happy; he was still at the water's edge fishing around with his club, trying to stir up his golf ball from the murky bottom. He was like a little dejected kid who has just lost his best friend. "I guess it's gone now. That was a lucky ball. I found it on one, and I was playing my best round ever. It was a golf ball from Augusta; it had that bright yellow Masters logo on it. I knew I shouldn't have played with it," Buddy cried, as he was still upset with himself for losing such a great souvenir.

We walked off the green. I got my four, Johnny got his four, Paulie got his seven, and by the time Buddy was all said and done, he also had a triple, instead of his actual par.

As we walked toward the carts, I boastfully and proudly stated to Johnny, "I just talked Buddy out of throwing his club in the water."

"Yeah, I can't believe it. I think you're getting soft," Johnny responded. "Sometimes I just don't know about you."

Buddy bought lunch and, of course, beer at the turn just as he had promised. He forgot that he had bought beers at breakfast. But there was no tricking him into buying for that dummy he had put on our team.

After a short lunch, we got back out to the tenth tee. I was thinking that I had to plant a seed in Buddy's, mind, so I told him, "Other than your bookend triples, you have a great round going. I got you at a forty-two for the front nine. You will never win your Honest John that way."

"You had to tell me my score, didn't you? Now I'm going to be scorekeeping in my mind," Buddy said.

As the back nine went along, Buddy just got worse hole by hole. I'm not sure if his golf game was catching up with him, or if he was just getting drunk. I know Paulie was getting drunker by the minute.

A couple of holes later, we are on the tee. It was Buddy's turn, and he drove his ball straight into the adjoining lake. He was stomping around, smashing his driver into the ground. He was pissed. "Fuck, fuck, fuck," Buddy screamed.

I couldn't believe his driver had not broken. "Here, take a mulligan. You deserve it. See if you can hit this one," I suggested as I pulled a ball out of my pocket and tossed it to him.

Not thinking, he caught it, placed it on the tee, and said, "Thanks. I deserve this mulligan."

He aligned himself, took a couple of practice swings, and stopped. He was standing there quite still. You knew he was thinking about something, but what? "What the fuck?" He said as he reached down and picked his ball up from the tee.

He examined the ball real close as he rolled it around in the palm of his hand. He had a puzzled look on his face. "Where did you get this from? How did you get this?" He drilled me on how I got his Master's ball.

"What are ya talking about? I found this a couple of holes ago. Ask Johnny. Remember, Johnny? I showed you," I responded.

"Yeah, I'm pretty sure it was on number nine." Johnny laughed out loud.

"You fucking asshole. I oughta just kill you now. How close was it?" Buddy screamed.

"Well, Buddy, what do you think? I could tell you that it went in. Or I could tell you that I stopped it; I saved it just before it went into the water. You decide," I proposed as I tried to paint a picture that he could understand.

"You fucker. You cocksucker. Paulie, did you see it? Where were you?" Buddy pleaded.

"No, I was back there with you, behind the green. Remember?" Paulie replied.

"Well, I'm changing my score to a birdie-3," Buddy chimed in.

"Buddy …?" I argued as I tried to bring him back to earth.

"Yeah, you're right. There was no way to keep it on the green. I'll keep it as a triple. That's what it was. Wasn't it?" Buddy justified his question.

"Okay. But at least you got your lucky ball back," I answered.

"I'm not playing with it now; I don't want to lose it again." Buddy went to put it away in his golf bag for safekeeping.

"But you were playing so well with it. You were shooting par with it and triples without it. It sounds pretty lucky to me." I tried to coax him a little to play with it.

"Yeah, you're right." He changed his mind and placed his new lucky Master's ball on the tee. You guessed it; he drove his Master's ball right into the middle of the lake. "Fuck, fuck, fuck," Buddy swore as his driver helicoptered toward the water.

His whirling driver landed in the cattails short of the water. "Hey, Buddy, you were almost three for three into the pond."

"Oh, fuck off," Buddy yelled as he hurried toward the cart to retrieve his thrown driver before it got lost for good in the murky water. As Buddy got closer, you could see the club falling, zigzagging down the stalks of the cattails.

"Hurry, Buddy, hurry."

Paulie scampered after him puffing from his puffer. He yelled, "Buddy, wait for me. What's wrong? What did I do?"

"Paulie, he'll be all right. Right now, he just needs some alone time." Johnny pulled up alongside Paulie and said, "Get in."

Buddy finished the hole with a snowman even with the mulligan. I was thinking my work was almost done on this round but not quite yet.

CHAPTER 14

The Canary Meets a Posse of Wyboos

All day long, Paulie was looking over his shoulder, watching where he stepped, even where he stood. I can't tell you how many times Paulie came running out of the woods, screaming, "Those pesky wyboos. They are everywhere."

"Try hitting it in the fairway. There are no wyboos there," I told him.

I'm not sure what hole it was, probably hole twelve. From the tee, Paulie had shanked one to the right, right into the woods. The cart path ran along the left all the way to the green, and it was the only cart path on this hole. We pulled up as far as we could, keeping his ball in line from where it entered the woods. I told Paulie to grab a club, and we would go and see if we could find his ball.

"I don't know what I need. I don't know the yardages," Paulie argued.

"Well, bring a couple then."

Paulie started to go through every club and their yardages as he picked through his bag of clubs. By this time, he had six clubs in his hands. So I asked him, "What if you can only chip it out sideways, or what if you are up against a tree?" Next thing I knew, he had eight clubs and a putter in his hands.

"Paulie, why don't you just bring your whole bag? That way, you will have all the clubs you want. And you won't lose any," I told him. "Like last time …"

"Yeah, I guess you're right," he confirmed with me as he put all the clubs back into his bag. He then unstrapped his bag from the cart, threw it over his shoulder, and carried it all the way to the other side of the fairway. "Have you seen any wyboos lately?"

"No, now that you mention it, I haven't seen any since the front nine. I think that's when you have to worry. I think that's when you have to be on your toes. When you don't see them; that's when they start to gather, to swarm together. You know, to posse up. They almost become invisible. That's when they are planning their attack." I told him.

We got over to the edge of the woods, and I went in search of Paulie's ball. I was thinking that Paulie should have been right behind me, but he was not. I looked behind me to see that Paulie was frozen along the tree line, looking up, standing there statue-like. "What's wrong, Paulie?"

"Can you feel them looking at us? Look. There are two of them, up there in the tree," Paulie whispered, scared to death, pointing up into the tree. "I feel they are watching me very, very closely. I think they are ready to pounce. What do I do?" Paulie tried to take a puff from his inhaler quietly but clumsily dropped the inhaler to his feet.

"I see what you mean. Just stand still; don't move," I warned him as he reached down to try to pick his inhaler up off the ground. "Maybe it's the canary color? You know, like bulls and the color red."

"Do you think? I knew I should have changed. I can't go in there," Paulie said as he started to step back one step at a time. "Shannon, can you see the second one? He seems to have disappeared."

"I see it, Paulie. I see it. It's in the tree above you. Be careful. Uh-oh. He's got a third buddy up there," I warned Paulie. "Oh shit. There's more."

Just then Paulie turned and started to hightail it back to the cart. He sure was funny looking. You had this canary; he had his old, outdated, brown leather golf bag over his shoulder, running across the fairway. He looked like a yellow bird with short spindly legs running, with his golf bag swaying back and forth. It was like watching a yellow Tyrannosaurus rex running on his short hind legs and what looked like his tail swaying back and forth. It was quite the sight. He left a trail of golf clubs, balls, and tees, which had fallen from his golf bag. "Run, Paulie, run. They are right behind you." I tried to encourage him to run faster. Then his golf bag went flying. He had everything strewn across the golf course.

Paulie almost made it back to the cart, but he tripped and planted his face in the turf. Johnny and Buddy came running and met me at Paulie's fall. Paulie lifted his head from the ground and was panting for air. He lost his brand-new wyboo hat in his fall and knocked the wind out of himself. He had sod stuck to his glasses and chin. There were grass stains down the front of his yellow shirt. He was still gasping for air and demanded to know, "Am I okay? Did I make it? Where is my puffer?" Paulie cried as he removed his glasses between gasps and gulps to clean the dirt and grass from them. His eyes were watering, and he was still struggling to breathe. His look had changed from dismay to relief when he found out that he had made it.

"Make it from what? And what the fuck were you running from?" Buddy screamed as he tried to knock some of the dirt from Paulie.

"Did you not see them chasing me?" Paulie gasped as he tried to dig out his spare puffer from his pocket to get some kind of relief for his breathing. "I think there was a group of them."

"A group of what?" Buddy demanded to know. "Did you ever look stupid running across the fairway and then falling, you idiot."

"Why, wyboos, of course. Did you not see them? I think there was at least a dozen." Paulie was still gasping for air.

"Now, Paulie, I don't think there were a dozen of them. I think I counted eight. And I believe that any more than three wyboos together at a time is called a posse."

"A posse? That's just weird," Paulie remarked as he was still trying to regulate his breathing.

"Yes, posse. Actually, I think that's where the word posse, as we know it, came from. They would gather together to hunt down, and then they would overtake." I offered up another lie.

"Wow," Paulie babbled.

"The main thing is you are all right. You made it out alive. Not too many can say that. Especially someone wearing yellow." I lied again.

"O'Malley, will you fuck off and leave the poor bastard alone?" Buddy barked as he tried to brush the grass and dirt off Paulie as he got to his feet.

"What did you trip over anyways?" Johnny inquired as he looked around for his hat. "You almost made it."

"Did you not see the big one? It got tangled in his feet and tripped him up. They do that; that's how they bring down their large prey." I lied again.

Buddy looked around, and he finally stated. "O'Malley, will you just fuck off? Paulie, there are no wyboos, and a group of them are not called a posse. The word *posse* did not come from wyboos, and they do not like yellow. He is lying to you. He is making this all up. Look, you tripped over that gopher hole. And look, there is your hat." Buddy pointed to his hat lying beside a larger-than-normal hole in the ground.

"Buddy, you don't know. You didn't see it. You weren't there," Paulie cried out, still trying to catch his breath.

Johnny joined in. "Paulie, are you ever lucky! That's one of those wyboo holes. They go for miles underground, and all interconnect with each other. They almost had you down it. Boy, are you ever lucky!"

"You could be, maybe, the only one to survive a wyboo posse attack. And I'm positive that you are the only one to be halfway down the shaft and live to tell about it." I coaxed him on a little more as I picked up his wyboo hat and brushed it off.

"Will you leave him alone? How can you pick on him like this? He is your partner. He is going to have nightmares tonight. And I am not going to hold his hand," Buddy warned.

"That's okay, Paulie; you can sleep in our room. Buddy, why you got to be like that? You are always so down on poor Paulie," I told him.

"Are you fucking nuts? He's not sleeping with you fucking O'Malleys," Buddy screamed. "Paulie, just go hit your ball and let's get out of here.

"I never found it. Are you crazy? And besides, I can't go back in there," Paulie pleaded.

"Paulie, I found it just before you got attacked. Um, there's not much of a shot. Do you want me to hit it for you?" I asked.

"Would you? You sure are brave," Paulie told me.

"Hey. Buddy. Can I hit it for him?" I begged as I headed toward my cart to get a club.

"Noooo. Oh, go ahead; just so we can get out of this fucking nightmare!" Buddy growled.

"I know what you mean. The farther away we can get, the better," Paulie agreed.

I grabbed my three-wood and went in to find Paulie's ball once again. The ball was nestled in a clump of pine straw, about two hundred yards through a maze of fur. I got about a six-foot opening and would have to slice it some forty yards. It couldn't be hit higher than twenty feet off the ground but would have to carry two front bunkers in front of the green, and the pin was tucked right behind those two guarding bunkers. There was no bailout shot unless you wanted to chip it backward. "What's Johnny Miller say? He's in jail. He's got no shot." I thought to myself, I got this; this is my normal three-wood shot, and besides, it's Paulie's ball. But the real trick to the shot was how thick was that nest of pine needles, and how was the ball going to react coming out of that stuff?

I heard Paulie in the cart yell over, "Hurry, Shannon. Oh, please hurry. I know you can do it. Get it on the green." I took a couple of practice swings, and the pine straw felt a little thicker and fluffier than normal. I took a full swing and took the shot. I picked the ball cleanly from its bed of needles. The shot was like watching it in slow motion. It started to rise a little quicker than I wanted. It ticked off the bottom branch that I figured I needed to be under. The ball kept going and hits just above the front bunker lip. The front lip took all the velocity off the ball as it bounced forward twice. That was all I could see from the view I had.

Next thing I knew, Paulie was out of the cart jumping up and down and screaming. "It went in, it went in! Holy fuck! I got an eagle. Boy, am I ever lucky on this hole? I got an eagle and survived an attack of wyboos."

Paulie bragged about it, hole after hole. Buddy was at his wits' end by now, and he just wanted Paulie to stop. Paulie was telling him every little detail, every little lie. Every few minutes, all you would hear was Buddy yelling at Paulie, "Will you shut the fuck up already?"

"You weren't there," Paulie responded. "You can ask anybody about those pesky wyboos. They are dangerous, I tell you. Just ask Shannon."

Then Buddy would grunt at me. "O'Malley, see what you have fucking started?"

CHAPTER 15

Johnny-on-the-Spot

We were getting close to the shit-house hole fifteen, and Buddy and Paulie zoomed by. We decided that we had to race after them; even though we knew exactly why they were hurrying to the shitter, Johnny yelled, "What's going on?"

Buddy yelled back, "He's got to go … He's got to go."

"I should have known." I responded as we chased after them.

Their cart had not even come to a stop, but Paulie had jumped out and hurried into the Johnny-on-the-spot!

Ten minutes later, Buddy yelled into Paulie, "Will you hurry the fuck up? What's taking so long?"

"Well, I can't just go like that, with you guys outside listening and all," Paulie stated as we even heard him taking a puff from his inhaler.

"Okay, then, I won't listen, and don't you guys listen either," Buddy warned us.

"Does that help, Paulie?" Johnny asked.

"It helps a little. Hey, they have *Golf Digest* in here, and, Buddy, there is an article in there about your new grip claw for your putter. They call it the crab-claw grip. Wow, I can't believe that they stole your idea!" Paulie reported. "But they don't say anything about lifts or insoles."

Johnny came back with, "Am I ever glad that they don't have any of those *National Geographic's* in there?"

"But if you don't hurry up, I'm going to tip this fucking shitter over," Buddy promised.

"You wouldn't do that, would you?" Paulie pleaded.

"Yes, he would, and if he doesn't, us O'Malleys will do it," I maintained.

"Okay, then," Paulie anxiously said. "I'll try to hurry."

"Watch this. This will get him out," I stated as I grabbed my ball, tee, and driver and went over to the shit shack. I teed my ball up, about five feet away from the shitter, and took a couple of practice swings.

When Buddy asked, "What are you doing? Are you crazy? You are going to break something."

"Nah, you have to hit it just right. The sound is unbelievable. It's just like a shotgun going off in your ears. It's loud. It will be funny as hell," I retorted as I tried not to laugh too hard. "Watch. Paulie will just shit himself."

"What are you guys up to out there?" Paulie asked.

"Let me do it. You can't have all the fun, you know," Buddy insisted.

"Okay, but get your own ball," I told him as I bent down and picked my ball up from the tee.

Buddy pulled his ball from his pocket, placed it on the tee, and took a couple of practice swings. "Take this, you motherfucker. This is for all the fucking headaches you have caused me today."

"Hey, what's going …?" Paulie was interrupted by the loud noise of the golf ball coming off the face of the driver.

"Bammmmm." Buddy had missed the green shitter; the ball flew deep into the woods, never to be seen again.

"Holy fuck, Buddy, how did you miss it? You were only four feet away. If it's any consolation, that was one of your best drives today," Johnny alleged. Then he grabbed the ball out of my hand, placed it on the tee, and pushed Buddy aside. "If you can't do this, I will."

"No, no, I got this," Buddy promised.

"What's going on out there?" We heard this faint question from Paulie again from within the toilet.

Buddy moved a little closer and took dead aim. He swung with all his might. Just then, Johnny positioned himself behind me for cover in case it ricocheted backward. "Bbbbbbooooooomm." Not only was it loud, but it echoed through the forest. It was like an explosion. He not only hit the shitter; it went right through it. Talk about funny. Johnny and I just looked at Buddy with disbelief on our faces. He actually did it. But he shouldn't have. He should have just walked away.

From inside came a faint, "What the fuck was that?" as Paulie's eye peered out through the three-inch puncture in the side of the potty. "What the fuck happened? I didn't do that, did I?" Then we heard from within, Paulie taking another puff from his inhaler.

I yelled over to Buddy, "Hey, Buddy, how are you going to explain this to Marilyn?"

"How did I do this? Why? O'Malley, why would you let me do this?" Buddy cried out as he got a worried look on his face.

"'Cause I can," I came back with. "Don't worry, Buddy. I'm sure you can pay for it with a credit card. So then, all you have to do is hide that extra charge."

"I didn't know it would go through it. Did you know? You were going to hit it. Johnny was going to hit it. Why did you let me do that?" Buddy wanted to know.

"I don't know. I don't think I would have swung so hard." Johnny tried to ease Buddy's thinking. "It's only made of plastic."

"All I know is you must have hit that right on the screws. And besides, you wanted to do this. There was no stopping you. You wanted to get back at Paulie—poor, poor Paulie. Remember?" I explained. "The last time I did this all it did was bounce off with a big bang."

Just then, Paulie came stumbling out of the toilet. He was struggling to do up his piss-stained shorts. My golf ball in his hand, he asked, "Who belongs to this? You know, that almost hit me."

"Never mind about all that. We have to get out of here. Paulie, get in the fucking cart," Buddy cried.

"We can't leave it like that. They will know you did it, Buddy; and Paulie will get blamed somehow," I explained as I took my golf ball back from Paulie.

"How are they going to know that I did it?" Buddy objected.

"I don't know. Paulie might talk. He might let it slip," I warned him as I pointed at Old Bucket Mouth.

"Let what slip? Buddy, what's going on? What did I do? All I know is I'm minding my own business, having a shit, reading about your new putter grip, and I almost get hit with a golf ball. And you're screaming at me to shut up and get in the fucking cart," Paulie claimed.

"What am I going to do now?" Buddy wondered.

"Hey, Buddy, give me a hand. I will try to help you fix this," I suggested to him as I pointed toward a branch lying on the edge of the tree line. It looked about the right size. Its thickest limb was about three inches in diameter where it had broken off the tree above. We tipped the outhouse on its side, and then all the green, slimy, stinking stuff seeped out of the bottom. Buddy was tiptoeing around this stuff so as not to get any on his golf shoes.

"Fuck, Paulie, you stink," Johnny chimed in. "What did you eat yesterday?"

Paulie piped up, "What are you doing? It wasn't me. I haven't gone yet. Can we tip it back up so I can go?"

"I don't think you want to go back in there," Johnny told him.

With Buddy's help, we grabbed the branch, and we lodged it in the hole in the side of the shitter. We had this Porta Potty lying on its side, seeping green slime out of all of its seams. And it had this limb growing out of it. My thinking out loud was, "The wind picked up, almost like a microburst. It broke a limb off from the tree above. As it fell, it planted itself into the side of the shitter, knocking it over onto its side." I was standing there admiring my work, and I said, "What do you think, Buddy? Is it plausible?"

"Yeah, I think it will work," Buddy spoke up.

"What the fuck? Maybe you guys want to plant some flowers around the base also?" Johnny suggested. "Let's get the fuck out of here."

"All I can say, Paulie, is it's a good thing you got out of there before this all happened. It might have killed you. You sure are lucky today."

"You can say that again," Paulie added. "I don't think we need any flowers at the base; it would be a little overkill, wouldn't it?"

As I got in the cart, Johnny said, "Well, that could not have worked out any better."

"Yes, you are right. My work is done here," I boasted as I started to drive to the next tee.

"How come we are always helping him get out of all the jams that he gets himself into?" Johnny added.

"Because we are his bestest friends," I answered.

We got to the next hole, and we all played that hole pretty bad. Buddy was quiet, he was worried, and he was scared. But above all, he was pissed. He was pissed at us O'Malleys for tricking him. He was also pissed at himself for letting his guard down. I'm sure in his mind, he was saying to himself, "How could I be that fucking-stupid?"

The next hole was number seventeen, a short par three. It was playing around 135 yards today. All four of us hit the green. It had only taken seventeen holes for the four of us to actually look like golfers. Well, three of us looked like golfers; the other one looked like a fucking canary. Paulie was the farthest away from the pin, at over a hundred feet. Both Johnny and I were around twelve feet away, and amazingly, Buddy bounced one in close to under eight feet.

I yelled over at Buddy, "Looks like you have a real good chance for your team's first greenie."

"What do you mean?" Buddy asked.

"Well, there have been no markers on the greens on any of the par threes or par fives, so far. So I'm thinking that they were unable to validate any of them with a par? Also, while I have you in this frame of mind, there was no marker out on number eleven for the longest drive either. So, Paulie wins that with that puny drive of his. He was the only one in our group that was in the fairway," I reported.

"There is no way in hell I'm paying Paulie for that fucking drive on number eleven. He was less than a hundred yards off the tee. I'm sure there was someone who had a longer drive or a greenie up ahead. They better have," Buddy responded.

"Buddy, you know the rules. You have to mark the greenies, and you have to validate them, and long drives have to be in the fairway. You know that," I explained to him once more.

"Yes, I know. I know all that," Buddy moaned. "Is this fucking day ever going to end?"

"No, Buddy, we're not done with you yet," I declared.

"Not by a long shot," Johnny added.

"Blah, blah, blah, @#&/@%$, blah." Buddy was rubbing his eyes and walking around in circles, twitching and bitching. He was not very happy. "You know there's no way in fucking hell that I'm playing with you guys tomorrow."

"Why, Buddy? What have I done wrong?" Paulie asked.

"It's not only you. It's all of you. It's every one of you," Buddy responded. "You're all a bunch of O'Malleys."

"Oh, I don't know. I have only been the luckiest guy ever to play today." Paulie then started to tell him why he was so lucky. "I'm on vacation. I'm playing golf. I had pancakes and maple syrup this morning. With ice cream, no less. I even had beer for breakfast. I have had free beer all day. I was able to play golf without my golf voucher. I got a brand-new favorite outfit. I've only lost eight balls today. Well, I really didn't lose any, because they were all range balls from …"

"Will you just shut the fuck up? We don't fucking care. We don't care where you stole those range balls from … and just so you know, it was nine balls that you lost," Buddy interrupted.

"Don't worry, Paulie. You stole nine balls from the Watertown Golf Course, and you lost them all here. Who would have thunk it?" Johnny added.

Paulie kept going on without losing his rhythm from the interruption, kept on telling us how lucky he was today. "I won the longest drive. I got attacked by vicious Wyboos and survived. I learned about posses. I made an eagle from almost two hundred yards. I almost got hit with a golf ball while I was on the shitter. I barely got out of that shitter before that microburst went through, planting a tree limb into the side of it and knocking it over. I could have been hurt. Or worse. I could have got that green slime on me. And most of all, I'm playing golf with my best buds. And the day is not even half-done yet."

"I know what you mean, Paulie. Hasn't it been a great day? I don't know why Buddy has to be like that," I reckoned.

Paulie went to putt first. He was lining his ball up, and then he rolled it up to about a foot away. We were all amazed that he was able to get it that close for being so far away and for being so drunk. He tapped in for his first par of the day.

Both me and Johnny made great putts for birdies, and I confided to Buddy, "Boy, am I ever glad you put that dummy on our team. Not only did Johnny and I birdie this hole, but our dummy did too. That will cost you fifteen dollars a man for birdies on this hole alone."

"What in fuck are you talking about now?" Buddy screamed as he removed his glasses so he could rub his eyes.

"We had two birdies on this hole, so I figured the dummy had to have one also," I maintained.

"How's that possible?" Buddy asked sternly.

"The dummy's score is the average of my and Johnny's score," I reminded him. "Remember? You are the one who put the dummy on our team, and I'm pretty sure you are the one who said that his score was the average of my and Johnny's."

"Fuck you. I'm not paying for no fucking dummy," Buddy yelled as he backed away from his putt.

"We'll see, we'll see," I concluded.

So, Buddy had this important putt. It was less than eight feet away; it was downhill, down grain, broke almost two feet, and lightning fast. All he had to do was make this, and he would salvage his round, maybe even save his team's round, and I made sure I let him know it. He was all lined up and took a couple of practice swings. He took a couple of strokes with his new claw grip and then took a couple with his conventional grip. Next thing you knew, he took dead aim and stroked his ball with the conventional style. He under-borrowed, hit it way too hard, and the ball just kept rolling and rolling. It never had a chance. It rolled by twelve feet.

"Holy fuck, Buddy, you hit that way too hard, and how come you used your old grip?" Johnny scolded him.

"Yeah, what happened to this new fancy grip of yours?" I asked.

"I don't know; it just didn't feel right. And besides, there is no rule saying that you can't go back and forth between grips," Buddy stated.

"There should be. You're farther away than when you started," I insisted as I tried to make fun of him by mocking his new putting stroke.

Now he was lining up his putt again, and he was acting like he was unsure what grip to use. His practice strokes consisted of a couple of the crab grip, and then he took a couple with his old grip. Now he was really unsure. He backed away a couple more times.

"Buddy, hit the fucking ball," I screamed.

His round probably was unsalvageable, but maybe, just maybe, he could stop the bleeding. Maybe it would help the team. His putt this time was going uphill, against the grain, and wouldn't you know it? It came up almost three feet short.

"Fuck, fuck, fuck," Buddy screamed.

"Buddy, pick it up. You have shot yourself in the foot enough," Johnny told him. "Pick it up before you hurt yourself."

"Yes, Buddy, you have suffered enough," I added. "We have all suffered enough watching you."

Buddy responded with, "I've got this. I'm going to make this if it takes me the rest of the day."

Paulie came back with, "Please, please, pick it up, Buddy. I don't want to be here after dark with that posse lurking and all."

"Paulie, fuck off. Don't you get started again. I've got this," Buddy proclaimed.

Buddy was fucked now. He was not in the right frame of mind; he had two putter grips that didn't work. He had two fucking O'Malleys, that had been in his head all fucking day. He had Paulie, whom he was going to protect, thinking a little masked rodent was going to eat him alive. And the worst was he was losing a match that he should have won. He just couldn't make a putt, and he was not going to make this one either.

He finally made his stroke, missed, and took a five. "Fuck," he screamed as he picked up the ball, threw it in the air, and took three attempts to hit it baseball-like into the woods with his putter. With each miss, he swore. "Fuck, fuck, fuck."

Johnny sarcastically said, "If you are going to hit that ball into the woods, you might be better off throwing it."

Now Buddy was mad. He tried one more time without luck. So he picked up the ball and threw it away toward the woods but only got about halfway. "Fuck, fuck," he swore again as he helicoptered his putter into the woods. "Fuck."

"There is no fucking way that I'm playing with you two fucking-O'Malleys tomorrow," Buddy stammered.

"Come on, Buddy, we weren't that bad, and besides, I think we warned you," Johnny responded.

Paulie ran over to the tree line to grab Buddy's putter and yelled, "I've got this for you, Buddy."

"Leave it fucking there, Paulie. I don't want it. It's useless," Buddy warned.

"Then can I have it?" Paulie asked as he skipped toward the cart with his new putter in hand.

"No, you can't fucking have it, you idiot. Just put it in my bag," Buddy screamed.

Now the most important hole of the round was about to take place. The nineteenth hole. We would get to see Chrissy, have a drink, and of course figure out how much Buddy owed. Buddy just wanted to go; he couldn't take much more. He did not want to be around when they found that shitter. He had to get Paulie out of there also. Not because of his heroic wyboo attack, but because he had a tendency to let things slip. That would be the last thing that you would want was Paulie here when they found that outhouse overturned.

We got back to the van, loaded the clubs up, and Buddy was yelling, "Let's go, let's go. We've got to get out of here now."

"What's your hurry?" Just as I said that, the music started to play again. "We all want to go inside and see Chrissy. You know, to have a beer and settle all the bets."

Buddy was pleading with everyone to get in the van and go. And Johnny and I were trying to oppose the idea. We wanted to go inside; we were trying to get everyone to stay. We were slowing things down. What we were doing was making Buddy sweat. He was pacing; he had his glasses off. His eyes were red and puffy from all the rubbing he'd been doing. He was walking in circles and piped up, "Please, please, guys, can we just go? I will buy the first round wherever, just not here."

"Okay, only on one condition, Buddy. Does that include our dummy?" I asked.

"No, no, you just fuck off with that dummy," Buddy reasoned. "Don't start that again."

"Okay, Buddy, we are going in to see Chrissy. You can stay here in the van if you like. But I would think you would want to be around when we settle up all those bets that you've lost," Johnny stated.

"Come on, Paulie, let's go inside for a drink," I interrupted with as we started toward the bar. "You can brag about surviving that vicious wyboo attack and how Buddy put that big hole in the shitter. Remember? You were there."

"Okay, okay, I will buy that fucking dummy a fucking drink. Now let's get the fuck out of here," Buddy pleaded.

Johnny sarcastically spoke up. "Does that include a chaser?"

"No, Johnny, I would think that it doesn't. Or does it? And besides, we do not want to press our luck," I jested.

"No, there is no fucking chaser. So let's get in the fucking van and go. Please, please get in the van," Buddy pleaded.

"All right, but only because you said please, Buddy." I rejoiced as we climbed into the van.

Johnny looked at me and said, "I'm starting to think that you are getting soft or something. No chaser? What are you thinking?"

"But I got him to say please," I responded.

"Being polite does not help my thirst. You know," Johnny argued, "sometimes I think you just don't use your brain."

CHAPTER 16

Is It a Vulgar styrenga or a Syrinaga vagina?

We all climbed into the van and opened a beer. Everyone was either bragging or bitching. Most were crying about their round. We must have sat there for at least ten minutes or so before anyone noticed that nobody had climbed into the driver's seat.

Then everyone interrupted with, "Who's driving? … Where's our DD? … He's back at the motel getting over that Jack attack. Who is this Jack anyways? … I can't drive … I'm drunk … Where are we? … Who's got my beer? … Did you see my game today? That was not my ability that shot that one hundred thirteen … I can't, I'm drunk, I played with the O'Malleys today … I'm an American … I can't hold the steering wheel because I have a beer in each hand … Buddy, you told me you would never, ever let me drive, no ifs, ands, or buts … Buddy, you drove us here … O'Malley, you know me. I'm always to, and someone else is always fro, remember? … What's the legal limit in South

Carolina? … It's got to be twelve or fourteen beers, I would think? …" Then you heard a couple more beer cans open … "I'm way over that; this has got to be number seventeen … Um, what was the question? … Guys, how are we going to decide? … Thumb-wrestle? … Rock-paper-scissors? … Flip a coin? … I like games," Paulie finally concluded with.

I got out and walked around to the driver's side and got in, and all I heard was … "You can't drive; you are drunk … We are all going to dieeeeeee … How many beers did you have today? …"

"I'm not worried about the beers I had … It's the Jack I had last night that I'm worried about … I'm still drunk," I responded.

"You're drunk? … You can't see? … How many fingers are you holding … No, no … I mean, how many fingers am I holding up?" Buddy quizzed me by holding up one hand that was missing his middle digit.

To make a long story short, about Buddy's missing finger. He always says, "I was young and stupid and got it caught in some heavy farm implement, and it ripped it off." He was right about two things: young and stupid. He gave the finger to someone he should not have, someone he owed money to. So they cut it off. He must have paid up because they only cut half of one finger off.

"I see nine and a half fingers," I confessed.

"You're good to go. You can drive," Buddy retorted.

"But, Buddy, you were holding only one hand up. I think I counted four and a half," Paulie broke in with.

"Maybe you should drive. Or maybe you should shut the fuck up," Buddy suggested.

"Close enough. He's good to go," Paulie agreed as he used his puffer one more time.

Other than a little speed bump leaving the Wyboo, I think I did a pretty good job commandeering the van home. I did not kill anybody, and no animals were hurt, but there might have been a little vegetation killed. Examining the van when we arrived, I noticed a partial tree limb caught up in the roof rack, wedged to the green Happy Holiday Hotel awning. There were also some colorful petunias lodged in the front grille of the van. I was thinking, I don't remember hitting anything on the way home, but I knew I might have cut that corner a little close leaving the entrance of the golf course. Other than that, it was clear sailing all the way home … I thought. Later in the week driving by the Wyboo Golf Course entrance, we noticed that someone had driven through the flower bed. There were two perfectly aligned tire tracks down the center, with the little crab apple tree missing most of the branches to one side.

I remember Paulie piping up, "Look at that mess; I hope they got the fucking hooligans that did that. Why would they do that? What a fucking mess."

"You never know, Paulie; maybe they had to leave in a hurry. Like maybe a posse was chasing them," I answered.

"Oh, I almost plumb forgot about them," Paulie cried out.

"O'Malley, fuck off and don't you get him started again," Buddy warned me.

I pulled into the entrance of the Happy Holiday Hotel, right up under the green awning, for what else? Valet parking.

As I pulled up under the awning, Buddy blurted out, "What are you doing? Never mind; don't answer that."

As everyone opened their doors of the van to get out, empty beer cans rolled out everywhere onto the pavement. But Buddy couldn't open his door to get out, as I had pulled up way too close to the pillars holding up the awning. Each time he would bang his door in to the post, and each time he would swear," Fuck, fuck, fuck. O'Malley, where did you learn to drive?"

We no sooner climbed out of the van, and like clockwork, out rushed Zackery to park the van. "Looks like you guys had fun today."

"We sure did; but I can't tell you about it because someone might get arrested. Right, Buddy? Other than that, I don't remember good," Johnny informed him. "Hey, Buddy, tell him how much fun you had today."

"Oh, fuck off, will you?" Buddy cried. "I'm never golfing with them again, ever. I hope they all die."

Then Paulie piped up in a drunken slur, "It was so much fun—until we got tangled up with those blasted wyboos."

"Wyboos?" Zackery asked, puzzled.

"Don't worry about them. They don't know what they are talking about. They are all fucking nuts," Buddy interrupted.

I was trying to dislodge this tree branch from the roof rack, and I said, "Zackery, can you help me with this? I'm not sure where it came from, and these petunias, I'm thinking maybe Buddy is trying to play a joke here. He's such a jokester."

"Sure. What were you doing? Were you backroadin'?" Zackery asked as he climbed up on to the van roof to dislodge the branch wedged underneath the roof rack.

Everyone was drunk. They were trying to hold each other up. But they were like dominos. As they bent over to pick up their beer cans, they would fall into each other. The next thing you knew, they were rolling around on the ground laughing their guts out. When they would try to help each other up off the ground, someone else would accidentally drop a beer can, and the process would start all over again.

Paulie finally got to his feet and scurried over to the edge of the driveway, where the flower bed was separated by the curb. He was bent over, with his hands resting on his knees so as not to fall over, weaving back and forth.

"Paulie, what are you looking for? Loose change or something?" Johnny asked as he followed him over to the flower bed. I wasn't sure if he went over to maybe help him, get sick himself, or maybe he just wanted to see the pretty flowers? Or just maybe he was going to have a leak. You could tell that Paulie, weaving back and forth, was going to throw up any minute now.

"What are you guys up to?" Buddy yelled over to them. "I didn't know you guys were into flowers."

Just then Paulie leaned forward and hurled—total projectiles. He lost his hat in the bushes in the process. Johnny didn't move an inch. I was thinking he was going to do the same at any time. But then, suddenly, it was like he got his second wind or something and offered up the following. "You know, they should have never planted these red dahlias so close to this *Syringa vulgaris*. They need the sun, and they need a lot. There's no way they would get enough sun from the shadows of this bush. They are also water hogs, so planting these so close together just doesn't make any sense at all. And the colors ... reds and purples. Are they color-blind? The hues and color pigment make an ungodly contrast. And the smells—don't get me started, as they just do not do themselves justice."

"Huh? What did you say? And what the fuck is a *Vagina styrenga* or whatever you said?" I asked.

"It's pronounced *Syrinaga vulgaris*, and that's Latin for lilac bush. I thought everyone knew that. Mom sure didn't spend too much on your edgamacation. You know what I mean, though; you can't plant on the north side of a building. There's no sun, and what sun they do get in the afternoon, this big old lilac bush is blocking it from the red dahlias much of the day. I'm sure putting those *Rosa-sinensis* scattered around among the *Hostas* must have been an afterthought. They could have saved this flower bed if they would have just planted some gladiolus flowers. Look at the colors. It looks like the Red Hats are having their annual garden party or something. And the smells, I'm sure they don't smell much worse than Paulie's party that he had going on in his mouth a moment ago."

"Johnny, I didn't know you were a horticulturist?" Pudden wondered.

"He's not," I butted in just as the song "If I Die Young" started to play in my noggin. As the music began, I was thinking that maybe the hotel gardener was going to come rushing out; I wondered if she was going to give us trouble.

"Why do you say that? He sure sounded knowledgeable to me," Buddy argued as he sauntered over to the flower bed.

I walked over to the flower bed to examine the flowers that Johnny had just been talking about and said, "Look, Buddy. It's January, and they're plastic."

Buddy reached down and pulled a handful of the pretty red dahlias and some *Hibiscus* to look at and remarked, "Sure had me fooled."

Just than Sally Sue stormed out of the front door and yelled toward Buddy, "Sweet Jesus, Mr. Parker, what do you think you are doing, sir? Step away from that flower bed."

Taken aback by Sally Sue's presence, Buddy tried to explain what had just happened. "It was not me. Johnny thought that they were real. He's into gardening. He's very knowledgeable. Ask him, ask him anything. I don't know how he did it, but Shannon did it." Buddy looked around to point a finger at me. But I had slipped around to the front of the van to help Zackery dig out those petunias from the grille.

Sally Sue, standing there with her arms folded and crossed, would not have anything to do with what Buddy had just said. She rebutted with, "Mr. Parker, all I see is you're holding a handful of my flowers, from my flower bed, from in front of my hotel. I've got three golfers rolling around on the ground looking for their beers trying to get to their feet. I have a big bird trying to regurgitate a worm that is caught up in its throat, and you are trying to blame poor Shannon for all of this. Hmm, and I don't see MR. O'Malley anywhere. So what do you have to say for yourself?"

Buddy went back over to the flower bed, replanted the fake flowers from where he had just pulled them, and said, "There, it wasn't me."

"Sweet Jesus, Mr. Parker, all I can say is I'm going to keep my eye on you," Sally Sue warned him as she gestured her two fingers up to her eyes and then pointed at him. "You just better be careful now. You hear?"

"Fuck, O'Malley, is it ever going to end? Can this day get any worse?" Buddy pleaded with us to stop.

Paulie, with perfect timing, hurled one last time— "Rrrrrrralphhhhhh"—all over Buddy's golf shoes.

"Paulie, you fucking idiot, watch what you are doing," Buddy screamed as he did a Texas two-step to try to avoid the projectile of vomit toward him. "You are going to clean these up," Buddy added as he took his shoes off and whipped them toward Paulie.

Paulie, between gags, tried to apologize. "I'm … I'm … so … sorry … Yes … I … will."

Buddy started to stomp toward his room, and I questioned him, "Where are you going? We haven't settled up any of our bets, and you promised to buy the first round. Zackery hasn't got any tip money for ice either. You know the lost-ball bet? And don't forget about Paulie. Remember, he is your roommate, and you said you would look after him. You are going to have to hold his head tonight when he pukes." I laughed.

"I don't fucking care. I gotta get out of here before I hurt someone. You fucking O'Malleys, now you have Paulie on your side," Buddy accused us.

So Buddy, rethinking what he was about to do, said, "Come on, roomie. Let's get you to bed." He grabbed Paulie's hat and repositioned it on his head so it wouldn't come off again. He then threw him over his shoulder. Even though Buddy was a small man in stature, he was a very, very strong man. He was quite the sight. Here he was stumbling toward his room in stocking feet. He had a yellow canary draped over his back, and occasionally, you would see Paulie heave or gag, and a little vomit would run down Buddy's back.

And all you would hear was Buddy saying, "Will you just fucking stop that already?"

With Buddy and Paulie gone, I looked at the rest of my drunken crew and said, "Well, I don't think Paulie will miss his harmonica tonight. Who needs a drink? Let's just go in the hotel's bar. We will see if Miss Vicki is still teaching. Or I should say working. Remember, Buddy is buying. I will get her to charge the drinks to Buddy's room."

"I thought you would never ask," Johnny boasted as he staggered for the door.

As we moved inside, I leaned over toward Johnny and asked, "So, how long have you had that one saved up for?"

"What do you mean?" Johnny wondered.

"About the flowers. You're not that smart," I told him.

"But I am. Pattie and I have been going to the horticulturist society meetings in Penn Yan every week. I've learned so much," Johnny came back with.

"Do they serve beer?" I quizzed him.

"No, but …" he responded.

"Johnny …?" I interrupted him.

"Okay, I've been saving it for a while now. You know, for that special, one-of-a-kind moment," Johnny stated. "You didn't play it very well. I was thinking that Buddy could have or should have been kicked out of the hotel. That would have been ideal."

"Come on, Johnny. It's only been the first day. We have almost a whole week to go, and besides, we need his credit card at this hotel," I retorted.

"Yeah, I guess you're right. Maybe I should have waited a couple of more days before playing this one out," Johnny suggested.

We went to the bar and ordered a round of drinks, making sure we got one for Buddy, Paulie, and Theodore, and of course that dummy Buddy so delightfully put on our team.

I told Miss Vicki, "Charge it to Buddy Parker's room and give yourself a big fat tip." I explained to her that after the day that he had had, he would want her to have at least 20 percent, if not more.

I was so happy that Miss Vicki was still working. And she was still wearing that teacher's outfit from this morning. The only difference was her blouse was strategically unbuttoned by at least one more button. One more, and it would be coming off. I could help her.

I was checking the scorecards with Pudden, and one glaring mistake became apparent. The reason that we never saw any long drive or greenies markers on the course was because they had forgotten to place them. I asked Pudden, "Am I going to tell Buddy, or do you want to do it?" He said he would rather not be around when I told him.

Our team was a clean sweep on every bet; but the most important thing was, they had to eat grits for breakfast and Paulie could enjoy his pancakes, ice cream, and maple syrup. It was a good day, it was a great day, it was a fantastic haul, and as usual, when you win, you lose.

"Looks like we are buying supper, maybe all week," I reported as I glanced over at Johnny.

"And quite a few drinks also," Johnny added.

"It's four o'clock now. So, any of you lightweights that need to take a nap can. Why don't we meet back here ... let's say around eight o'clock or eight thirty for supper?" I suggested.

Everyone agreed as they started to stagger toward their rooms for a nap.

CHAPTER 17

There Is More Than One Way to Skin a Catfish

I told Stewart that on the way home from golf, we happened to pass a tavern that I thought we should check out. It was only about a mile from town. I told him that on the sign, up front, it said something about serving topless and free pool during happy hour.

"What are we waiting for?" Stewart concluded.

We headed out the front door, and there lay Buddy's golf shoes laden with puke in the flower bed. I suggested to Stewart, "Maybe you should take them up to the room for Buddy. You know he has those new inserts of his."

"Fuck him, I'm not babysitting him now," Stewart babbled.

"But I had to babysit him all day," I retorted.

"Fuck you. Oh, they will be there when we get home," Stewart countered.

Our walk didn't turn out to be very long. I had figured it was two beers to get there, two beers home, and two in case we got lost coming home, sidetracked, or ran into a slow bartender. That was just about perfect, as I had brought six apiece.

As we got closer to the bar, one of those rent-a-sign on wheels came into view:

FREE POOL

HAPPY HOUR

4:00 to 6:00

WE SERVE OUR OYSTERS TOPLESS

We walked into a small, dingy, very smoky bar. The bar would have held under fifty patrons. There were maybe six barstools around the bar; four seats were taken by some locals. As we walked in, you could see them glance over at us. They gave us the stare, the once-over. It was like, "This is our bar; what the fuck are you doing in our bar?"

Behind the bar, there was a great big nicotine-laced mirror. In Canada, in front of that mirror, you would have found a fully stocked bar with various forty-ounce bottles of booze. Not in South Carolina. Their liquor laws were different, and they only let them sell those little airplane bottles of liquor. So, basically, there were only about a half dozen of these bottles of each kind. I was thinking that they were going to have to restock after Stewart and I left. I think there were only Miller Lite beer on tap and a couple of other brands in the bottles. Around the mirror there were one-dollar bills from around the world pinned to the wall. Stapled to the ceiling, I could see a few different-colored bras of various shapes and sizes. There were white ones, pink ones, and black frilly ones; there was even a pink polka-dotted one. I was thinking, it must have been one hell of a party. Did we miss something special the night before?

Looking around the room, I could see that most of the beer posters were set around NASCAR advertisements. There was even an orange crumpled-up hood from a NASCAR racing car bolted to the wall. I think I spotted about twenty various state license plates from around the United States. Did they want one from Ontario? I was wondering how I would get the plate off the van without anybody noticing it missing. Or would I be able to get home without getting caught, or more importantly, what was it worth? What could I get in return for it?

Everything looked dirty, old, and dingy. A few bar signs were scattered haphazardly around the room. There were a few tables and chairs scattered around the room. Along the wall, there were a couple of dartboards and two outdated pinball machines that looked like they still worked. But most importantly, in the center of the room, there sat a five-foot-by-nine-foot bar pool table, which looked like it had seen better years. Over the pool table, a couple of antique brass lights hung from the ceiling lit up the room. Although I feel I'm very lucky at golf, I am also one of the luckiest on green felt. The great thing about this pool table was it was free. We had arrived just in time to take advantage of their happy hour. A sign over the bar stated:

HAPPY HOUR
4 to 6
50 CENT DRAFTS
75 CENT SHOTS
FREE POOL

AND WE SERVE OUR OYSTERS
"TOPLESS"

"I think I have gone to heaven," I told Stewart.

Our black bartender introduced herself as Latisha and recognized us as being Canadian, probably down to play golf. Did we stand out that much? She was cute, big breasted, and very flirtatious. Stewart looked over at me, gave me that nod, and winked twice. So that really told me he approved and had fallen in love again. I was fantasizing about her as well—what else? A slutty bartender. She had a very tight, white T-shirt on. On the back of the T-shirt, it said, "WE SERVE OUR OYSTERS … TOPLESS WITH A SMILE." The T-shirt had seen better days; it was stained and worn thin. The thin fabric was almost see-through, and I saw, and everyone else could see, that she had no bra on. Wow! Latisha had on a little black skirt that was way too short for her height and figure. She was not hiding anything. The black boots she had on had three-inch heels and were the type that said, "Come over here and fuck me," I'm not sure if I was in love with her or the free pool. Suddenly, the jukebox lit up and came to life as it started to play "Girls Girls Girls" by Mötley Crüe.

We ordered a shot and a beer chaser and were amazed that the total was only a couple bucks for both of us. The thing is, those little bottles were an ounce and a half, not like a regular one-ounce shot. We argued about who was going to pay for the first round. I suggested that we settle it on the pool table. Whether it is playing golf or playing pool, I think Stewart has more talent in both, but I am a little luckier. As Stewart says, luck can only take you so far. I always say I would rather get lucky than get good.

Stewart yelled, "Okay, winner buys, right?"

I came back with, "Of course. When you win, you lose."

Not only did the locals at the bar have amazement on their faces, but they were totally confused by that statement.

"Who's breaking?" I asked.

"Whoever downs their drinks first will break," Stewart replied.

"Okay," I said as I turned around and handed him my empty shot glass and beer mug.

"How did you do that? That fast? You must have been really thirsty," Stewart declared.

"Yes, it was a long walk," I reasoned.

"Then go ahead and break," he offered as he finished racking the balls.

I broke, got lucky, and sank a couple of stripes on the break and ran the rest of the table. I yelled over to Latisha, "Get everyone a drink. I'm buying."

At the bar, there was a large brass bell that customers would ring when they wanted to buy a round of drinks for everyone at the bar. Latisha reached up and gave her a good ring. The locals looked up from their conservations long enough to smile as they anticipated what was to come. As they got their drinks, they all gave a nod or a gesture of a thank you. But they still all wore puzzlement on their faces. It cost me less than four dollars for the round; money well spent. By the time I got back to the table, Stewart had the balls all racked up and ready to go again. I got really lucky this time, as the eight ball fell in the corner pocket on the break. I went over, rang the bell once more, and waved my arm in a circular fashion to get Latisha's attention. "You better keep them coming."

A few more locals had just come in the door and ordered a drink. They tried to pay for them, and someone at the bar told them, "Put your money away. We have some crazy Canucks in the house, and they are playing pool. And the best is, they are buying." They went on to explain the game and the rules of the wager for playing pool.

Latisha asked, "That was quick. Are you always this lucky, or are you just this good?"

"Yes, and yes," I answered her with a flirting wink as I handed her five dollars for that round. I got back to the table, and Stewart was ready for me to break again. He had a perturbed look on his face. I was not sure if it was because he had not had a shot or because I was flirting with his new girlfriend? I won the next three games. But these games, I really had to work for them this time. Stewart took me down to the eight ball each time. Each win, I would go up to the bar to ring the bell for another round. The cost of each round grew a little as more and more regulars came through the door. With the ringing of the bell each time, I noticed that I was getting more and more of the regulars' attention.

Latisha looked over at one of her regulars sitting at the bar and said, "Hey, Mudcat, don't you think it's time you showed these Canadians a thing or two?"

Just then, a local stood up and gave Latisha a little nod, then looked at me and inquired, "All righty if I play ya?"

"Sure, let's play," I said as I reached over to shake his hand. The look that Latisha and Mudcat gave each other, I just knew he was the local bar pro. I was wondering how long it would take for him to step up. I was waiting for this.

Mudcat was his name. I don't think it was his real name, more likely a nickname. But that's where it got confusing.

Was he called that because he was a local fisherman, who fished for those monster Catfish in Lake Marion? Or was it his resemblance to looking like a bullhead? If you took off his fishing cap, he had a shiny, smooth, receding hairline. He had two slits for eyes, which seemed to almost look from the sides of his face. His forehead sloped down to his flat, wide nose with huge nostrils. Underneath his nose was a handlebar mustache that curled to a point at the ends. Under his mustache was the start of his mouth, which had no upper lips that you could see. His bottom jaw enveloped his upper lips. I think this look was the cause of him having few or no teeth. He had no chin and very little neck, so his sloping, chiseled face looked like it just sat on his shoulders. When he stood up, you could see that he was a short man. He was shorter than Buddy. He would have made Buddy look tall. You could see he had a pair of green rubber bib coveralls on. He wasn't wearing a shirt, and I'm not sure if he had anything else under this rubber suit. There was only one shoulder strap fastened, with the other one just dangling down to his waist. They looked like they were two sizes too big. He had a pair of matching green rubber-boots on. They even looked too big on him. I thought for sure when I shook his hand, he was going to walk out of them. But maybe he had that nickname because he just stank like a rotting fish.

"All right with you if we play the same rules? Winner buys?" I asked.

"Sure, why not? You Canadians sure are weird," Mudcat exclaimed.

There we were; I was going to have to play the game of my life against Mudcat, their local pro. He had the home field advantage. This was his bar. This was his table. He knew every shot and how it would react from every cushion. He knew every drift on the table and every dead cushion. I knew this, and I hadn't even seen him take a shot, let alone pick up a cue. I knew I was in trouble as soon as he smiled at Latisha. From behind the bar, she grabbed his pool case and handed it to him even before he asked for it. They had done this before. I was wondering how much money he had taken off unsuspecting tourists.

I was about to brake, and I noticed that the regulars had taken up better positions around the pool table to view the game. The crowd had grown to maybe eight or nine by now. They were all chanting, "Mudcat, Mudcat."

I knew they had done this before. I was stickhandling the cue ball with the tip of the cue, waiting to break. I looked around for my one and only fan, and he was nowhere to be seen. I finally spotted him over at the corner of the bar. He was in a deep conversation with Latisha.

I yelled over at him, "I sure could use some support over here."

"You will be all right. Just don't let him get on the table," Stewart yelled back. "You'll be all right."

I looked over at Mudcat as he opened his black leather case to reveal a two-piece cue, various types of chalk, and a little container of Johnson & Johnson baby powder. He screwed his cue together, looked down the length, and rolled it back and forth on the table to see any imperfections. The thing is, he knew there were no imperfections in the cue as it was straighter than straight. He was only doing this out of instinct or habit. He rubbed a little baby powder on to his hands and then transferred a little to the length of the cue.

"That smells like Johnson & Johnson," I said. "I sure could use some."

"Sucks to be you. You should have brought your own," he said as he pointed to various signs on the wall.

**NEVER LEAVE HOME WITHOUT IT.
DO YOU FEEL LIKE YOU ARE GOING
TO GET LUCKY TONIGHT?
MAKE SURE YOU BRING IT.
YOU KNOW YOU HAVE POWDERED
YOUR BUTT WELL
WHEN YOU FART AND ALL YOU SMELL IS
JOHNSON & JOHNSON.
IS THAT A BOTTLE OF JOHNSON &
JOHNSON IN YOUR POCKET
OR
ARE YOU JUST HAPPY TO SEE ME?**

I was not sure which sign he was pointing at, but I read the first four, and I guessed each one of them could have been the one. I knew Stewart always powdered his butt well, so I yelled at him, "I sure could use some baby powder over here."

"Well, I don't have any, and you're sure not sticking your hands down my pants, not like the last time," Stewart came back with.

"Now don't be like that. You know you like it." I laughed.

That first game, you're always a little nervous. I'd started to perspire a little. But I'd been here before. I had been on the other side of the table also. I'd been the local pro. I had the home table advantage before. I had the hometown crowd on my side. One thing you have to remember about playing the bar pro. Even though you want to beat him badly, you don't want to beat him too bad. You have to remember, you are on his table, and you are in his bar. These are all his friends. This is his territory. It can get downright nasty. So you have to be careful.

Just before I broke, I looked over at Mudcat, and we gave each other that good-luck nod.

I heard a cry out in the crowd. "Go get 'am, Fishy."

I broke, got real lucky, and ran the table.

Mudcat cried, "Dang nab it."

I rang the bell one more time for a round of drinks. This time the round cost me a few more bucks as the crowd had grown again.

"Keep up the good work, O'Malley. But can you win a little faster next time, as me and Latisha, we're getting thirsty over here," Stewart pleaded with me as I noticed that a new bartender had taken over for Latisha and that she had planted herself in a seat right beside Stewart at the end of the bar.

The crowd in the bar was growing. It was like someone had put a flashing sign on the outside that stated: "Mudcat has lost a game of pool." Interested spectators were growing around the table. There was a buzz around the table. You heard things like, "Who is this lucky Canuck?" … "Mudcat has never lost a game on this table." … "I can't believe the winner is buying the drinks." Then they started to chant: "Go get 'am, Fishy, Fishy, Fishy."

By the time I got back to the table, Mudcat had the balls all racked up and ready to go. I sank a stripe on the break, but in doing so, had hooked myself on the next shot.

"Looks like your luck has just come to an end, Luckyyyyyy," Mudcat crowed.

I missed, and with ball in hand, Mudcat cleared the table. Proudly he went over to the bell to ring it and boldly stated, "There. Lucky is not so lucky anymore. Get everyone a drink on me."

Mudcat went over to his case and started to unscrew his cue, and I inquired, "Maybe we should have just one more game. You know, a best of three. Just to make sure that Lucky is done."

"Rack 'em up," he yelled. "It's your funeral."

He broke, made a couple of balls, then missed an easy shot and cried, "Dang nab it." Maybe he was not as stupid as I thought. My stripes were positioned perfectly around the table. I was thinking with the large crowd and with the wager the way it was, the last thing that I wanted to do was run the table. I made it look good, though. I made it to the eight ball and sewered and lost.

Mudcat went over to the bell and rang it. Not once, but twice. He screamed, "Lucky is not lucky anymore! Lucky is done! Get everyone two drinks! I'm buying!"

I shook his hand and said, "Great game."

A couple of his friends went up to him and said, "Wow, I have never seen you lose a game on this table before. Are you feeling okay? Can I play ya?"

"Sure. Rack 'em up," Mudcat confidently stated. "Let's show these out-of-towners how the game is really played."

I went over and tried to position myself between Latisha and Stewart, and he uttered, "Don't you have someplace to go?"

"Yes, I think we should leave," I warned.

"Leave? Why?" Stewart questioned. "I'm just getting started."

"We should just leave," I answered him. "Come on; we should go."

Next thing I knew, Mudcat reached over my head to ring the bell once more and growled, "Get everyone another drink. Fishy is on fire."

Latisha got up from Stewart's lap and went around the bar to help Harold get the next round of drinks. She advised Mudcat, "It's about time you went home. Ethel's going to wonder where you have been, and besides that, I don't think you can afford to win much more."

"What do you mean? I have only won three games," Mudcat argued.

Latisha rang up his bar tab for the last four rounds, and the cash register tallied a whopping $123.76.

"Dang nab it. What … how's that possible? I don't have that kind of money," Mudcat cried out. "Ethel is going to kill me."

Harold, the other bartender, who just happened to be the owner, reminded him, "Look around, Mudcat. There must be over thirty people in here now, and happy hour ended when I came on duty about three games ago. I can't carry your bar tabs much more."

Mudcat and Harold started to argue back and forth, so I warned Stewart one more time and gave him the old head gesture toward the door. "Stewart, our work is done here. Let's get out of here before it gets ugly."

I was sure Stewart did not want to leave, but I was thinking it was time before it got messy. We said our goodbyes and stated we would be back. I told Latisha I would be back for some of her famous oysters served topless.

"You better. You better come back and see me," Latisha begged us.

I passed by Mudcat one last time as we headed out the door. He was still in a heated argument with Harold. I interrupted them both to shake Mudcat's hand one last time. I thanked him for the game and lesson and pointed to the wall with all the signs and declared, "You know, maybe you need one more sign up there?"

"What's that?" he wondered with puzzlement on his face.

"You know, there's more than one way to skin a catfish," I bragged as we quickly slipped out the door.

We laughed and chuckled all the way home. I bragged about my game, the ruse, and how little it cost us to get drunk. All Stewart wanted to do was talk about—what else? Latisha's breasts. I didn't mind talking about them either.

CHAPTER 18

A Taller Buddy Will Have to Play Short Today

The next morning, I was having my morning ritual, my customary dump in Buddy's room. I was in no hurry to get down there this morning as I really don't eat breakfast as a rule unless there are some extracurricular activities like motorboating or I am very, very hungover. But to be honest, this morning, I really just wanted to leave Buddy a little something special in his porcelain. A calling card, if you will. All I needed now was a cigarette and a coffee. Oh, that's right; I had quit smoking. We had all quit smoking; that was why we were all down there.

I was sure that everyone had already headed down for breakfast. I could visualize them all there, waiting for me to join them. Paulie was wearing his new yellow outfit, which still made him look like a canary, but it seemed to be wearing a little tighter. He was enjoying his flapjacks and extra syrup. Oh, and I almost forgot his ice cream. Buddy and his losing team were huddled at the other end of the table, complaining about the way that they played golf yesterday. Buddy, of course, had not even noticed that he had dried-on puke stains down the back of his golf coat from carrying Paulie home last night.

They were all bitching at each other for having to eat grits for breakfast. I was sure that Johnny had suggested to them that they order some sausage gravy to put on them. "It will help the grits taste better, or at least, if anything, it will help let them slide down your throat easier."

And I was sure Paulie had added his two cents. "Just put some maple-syrup and ice cream on them; that usually fixes everything."

By now, they all had taken their first slurp of grits. Some had spit them out, while others had forced themselves to swallow the granule morsels. All four who had to order them I'm sure were making the most god-awful face. And knowing Johnny, he had probably ordered a couple extra sides of grits, just to show the guys that they didn't taste that bad. He had crumpled up a couple handfuls of his beloved pork rinds and saturated it all with some sausage gravy. He said, "You have to have the right ratio of extra ingredients to make it all work." Johnny, for most of his life, has had a mustache. So there has always been some kind of a remnant of grits, gravy, or pork rinds encrusted in there for a later snack. In the past, I have watched him pick up the bowl and lick it clean.

For the drink of the day, I was pretty sure that Johnny had already ordered eight screwdrivers for the crew.

I had just finished leaving Buddy that little extra-special something. I had locked everything up and put a "Do Not Disturb" sign on his door handle. That should let that special gift fester and ferment in his toilet bowl until he got home later today. I believed it should smell quite ripe in about six hours. I was going to leave him a note, but I was sure he would know that this special gift was from me.

As I walked in to join the group, Miss Vicki greeted me at the front door, and she was just as beautiful as ever. She had her best teacher's outfit on; as this morning's outfit was a little tighter than yesterday's, it accentuated her figure to the fullest. Boy, would I like to serve her breakfast in bed.

"Morning, Shannon. What did you do to them yesterday? Look at them; they are all pretty quiet," she said as she reached for the coffeepot. "They all look half-dead this morning."

"Oh, they all are lightweights. They all are in training." I laughed. "I believe some won't make the end of the week."

As she was walking away laughing, I added, "Oh, can you bring us eight beers? You know, for my winning team."

"I'll get that right up for you, Shannon," she answered as she hurried off, looking at her watch.

As I walked over to them, I could see that everyone was hungover. They all looked a little rougher than normal. Some couldn't see, or let's just say they couldn't keep their bloodshot eyes open. A few were wearing sunglasses to cut down on the glare of the overhead lights. It all seemed pretty quiet around the table. So it must hurt to talk. They all looked like they were going to die at any minute. "Did you guys get into some bad grits?"

"Nooooooo." Someone asked, "What the fuck is grits, anyways? And why does it taste so bad?"

"Grits? All it is, is well, basically, it is corn all ground up. And it gets its taste from …," Johnny alleged, "well, big fat Indian women stomp all over the corn in their bare feet. You know, something like how fat Italian women stomp all over grapes to make wine."

"That explains it. That's why it tastes like toe jam, Indian toe jam, that is," Stewart added.

"I think I'm going to puke." someone said. "Whose fucking idea was it that we were going to drink yesterday?"

"It was that fucking O'Malley," Buddy piped up.

"And who made that stupid bet about eating grits?" someone asked.

"Oh, I'm sure that it was that fucking O'Malley also," Buddy answered.

"Whoa, whoa, whoa. Back up the bus for a minute. I'm sure it was not all my fault. And besides, I don't think you guys could have donated any more money to dinner or, for that matter, the ice fund for Zackary." I looked over at Theodore. I hadn't seen Theodore in two days and said, "Nice of you to join us this morning. I would hate to see you stay in bed for all of your vacation. You feeling better?"

"A little. How can someone be hungover for two days? Did you put something in my drinks the other night?" Theodore cried. "And how come I stank so badly?"

"Theodore, it was just a little Jack. You have officially met Jack. Stink? Jack doesn't usually stink. Oh, yeah," I tried to explain as it dawned on me why he stank, so I tried to change the subject. "Tonight, we will introduce you to Jim (Beam), or would you prefer to meet Glen (Fiddich)? … Or here is an idea. Buddy, how about you introduce him to that beautiful, beautiful lady, Margaret."

"No, I do not want you to introduce anybody to me ever again. I think I will just drink beer the rest of the trip. You know, the lighter, the better." Theodore tried to reassure us all as he started to pour his beer into his half glass of water.

"Suit yourself, but Jim, Glen, and Margaret are really good people. They are all special, and they all want to meet you. They're not like that fucking-Jack," I argued with him. "Someone should lock that fucker up."

"Who is this Jack?" Paulie asked from the end of the table. He was getting his sugar fix as he was devouring his flapjacks and ice cream. Paulie seemed to be the perkiest of the bunch, and if I remembered correctly, he surely had to be the drunkest. All I remembered was this big yellow canary being carried over Buddy's shoulder, regurgitating all of his lunch with every step that Buddy took. He was one pretty drunk Big Bird.

"I tell you what. You stay a little soberer today, and I will introduce you to him," I promised as I took a seat beside Buddy.

It was all just as I had envisioned it. As Paulie looked up again with a big smile on his face, between smacking and licking his lips, he said, "Smack, smack, wow, smack. Was that ever fun yesterday. Can we do it all again? Smack, smack."

Perturbed, Buddy cried, "No. Will you just fuck off? And can you lick your lips a little quieter? Can you see that we are all not feeling well?"

"Smack, smack, smack." Paulie looked like he had just had an orgasm, and he licked his lips again. "You know, just that little extra syrup makes all the difference."

"Paulie! "Buddy screamed.

Paulie had picked his plate up off the table with his two hands and started to lick the plate clean, only to drip syrup down the front of his brand-new canary shirt. "Oh, shit, I was going to wear this tomorrow again. Oh well." Paulie set his plate down, picked out the spot from his shirt, and licked it clean. "I don't want to waste any. Uhmmmm. Uhmmmm. Uhmmmm. This should fix it. Just like brand-new. Just like yesterday's shirt, but with a …"

I interrupted him. "I can see that you must have done this quite a few times this morning, as there seems to be more than a few syrup spots down the front of your shirt."

"Oh, it cleans up real good. When it dries, you won't be able to tell where I spilled any syrup," Paulie explained as he looked down at the unsightly stains. "I hope."

"Paulie, maybe you should start wearing a bib to catch all that extra syrup you spill. It would make it easier for you to lick off," I told him.

"No … I'd just look stupid." Paulie claimed as he looked down the front of his shirt. "I'd look like a Babbbbbyyyyyyyyy."

"Suit yourself, but syrup stains don't come out very good," I informed him. "All you got to do is look at yesterday's shirt."

"Huhhhh?" Paulie, trying to change the subject, bragged, "So who wants to be on my team today? Who wants to be a winner? More importantly, who wants to eat grits tomorrow?"

Buddy interrupted, "What? Oh, you are a captain now?"

"No, I was just trying to get negotiations going so we can pick some teams and get going. I just can't wait. It was so much fun yesterday," Paulie informed him. "Other than those pesky wyboos, it was the best day of my life. No, it was the second-best day. Motorboating the day before at breakfast has to go down as the best day of my life."

So negotiations started and ended quickly as Buddy finally demanded, "Fuck that; we will have the same teams. You can't win two days in a row with Paulie."

"Do we get beer to take, Paulie?" I asked.

"Fuck you. There's no extra beer today," Buddy argued. "And I'm going to play with my own team today, so you don't fuck my game up."

"So, what about poor Paulie? Who's going to protect him today if you play in the other foursome?" Johnny asked.

"You got Paulie. He's all yours. He's fair game. Have at him. I don't fucking care," Buddy disclaimed. "You do what you want with him. He's all yours."

"What about our dummy?" I asked.

"I told you. You got Paulie," Buddy cried.

"No, no, I mean our dummy. You know, the one you bought beer for all day yesterday." I laughed.

"I told you there is no dummy, and there is no extra beer," Buddy cried again.

With perfect timing, Miss Vicki showed up with eight beers and placed them in front of Paulie, Johnny, and me. "Sorry, Miss Vicki. You can take two back, as Buddy says he is not buying for no dummy today."

Us being polite, we acknowledged, "Thanks, Buddy."

"Thanks for … They better not be on my bill," Buddy screamed.

"They must be," I lied as she laid our bills in front of each one of us.

"Holy fuck. I'm not paying for this. You better not have," Buddy emphasized. "Take them back. I'm not paying for this."

"But, Buddy, they are open. You have to pay for them," Paulie argued.

"I'm not paying for them," Buddy demanded. "Miss Vicki."

"We have to keep them," I said.

"Someone's got to pay for them. I just finished my first one," Johnny informed us as he set his empty beer bottle on the table.

"Vicki, Vicki," Buddy screamed again. "You can take them off my bill. I'm not paying."

Miss Vicki interrupted, "But …"

"But nothing," Buddy argued. "Take this bill and shove … fix it."

"Buddy, will you stop screaming at her? You are going to make her cry," I warned him as I tried to stick up for Miss Vicki.

"But, Mr. Parker, the beers … I already have …" Miss Vicki tried to answer him as her voice started to crackle under the pressure.

Buddy, blowing his stack, interrupted her one more time. "I don't care. I don't care what he has promised you. I'm not fucking paying for them. His, theirs, or that fucking dummy's. I'm not paying for them. Understand?"

"But, sir, Shannon bought them. They are on Shannon's bill. Not on yours. Look," Miss Vicki argued as she grabbed Buddy's bill from his clenched fist.

"Oh, I'm so sorry. Will you ever forgive me for being such an ass? They make me so crazy at times. I'm not sure what got into me," Buddy apologized as he tried to grab Miss Vicki's hand to console her.

"It's okay. It was an honest mistake," Miss Vicki said.

"Oh, here is twenty dollars for the beer." Buddy expressed remorse for acting so stupid and reached around for his wallet.

"As I said, Buddy, thanks for the beer," Johnny said.

"Yeah, thanks," I echoed.

"Why? Why do you do this? Stop me next time," Buddy apologetically cried.

"Buddy, you did it to yourself. All I did was walk in to have a lovely breakfast with my best friends. I wanted to buy everyone a beer, and you started yelling," I tried to reason with his stupidity.

"Never mind. Let's get the fuck going," Buddy cried.

"But, Buddy, I haven't had my breakfast yet," I told him.

"Don't get me going again," Buddy warned as he stood up to leave, tossing the keys toward Theodore. "Let's go. Theodore, you're driving."

"How do you expect me to play on an empty stomach?" I said as I reached down for some of Johnny's crumbs on his plate. But I think I could have made a full meal from all the bits and pieces of pork rinds in his mustache. "You could have saved me something besides your burned crusts."

"What are you doing? Look at you. You don't even eat breakfast. Get in the van," Buddy screamed at me as he headed toward the door, and everyone started to follow. "We are leaving now."

"Buddy," I tried asking for more time.

But just then Paulie interrupted and said, "I can't. I've got to go get my new lucky hat from the room."

Just as he said that, I reached around and pulled his hat from my back pocket and handed it to him. The last thing that I wanted was for them to go back to the room and find that special surprise that I had left for them. "Here you go, partner. You must have left it in my room last night."

"I did?" Paulie babbled as he took the hat from me and positioned it tightly on his head.

"Yeah, you must have forgotten it sometime yesterday," I reasoned. "It was on the television."

"I guess I just don't remember," Paulie stated with a puzzled look on his face. "Who put me to bed?"

"I did. I put both you and Buddy to bed last night." I laughed. "As a joke, I was tempted to put your Spider-Man pajamas on Buddy. You were pretty drunk last night. You were both pretty drunk."

"Boy, I would have paid money to have seen that," Johnny added. "You guys, you were really drunk."

"Oh, well, it doesn't matter now I guess." Paulie cackled as he adjusted the curvature in the bill to make it fit just right.

As we almost get to the van, I motioned over toward Buddy. "Look, I don't think you can get any more ice in that cooler of yours."

"How much money are you giving Zackery today?" Johnny sarcastically asked, as he could see Buddy's cooler filled to the brim with ice, sitting right next to the van.

"Will you guys all fuck off? I told you, I'm not tipping him today. Someone else can look after him," Buddy cried as he lifted the cooler up and threw it into the back seat. "But it sure is nice having cold beer all the time."

"I know. Thanks, Buddy," I agreed with him.

"Fuck off. Has everyone got their golf vouchers? Paulie?" Buddy screeched as he looked around at the group.

"Why are you asking me? You know I don't. You got them. Remember you put them all together last night. You said I could not touch them ever again," Paulie cried as he took a puff from his puffer.

"I know, I know. I was just teasing you," Buddy joked.

"Well, don't tease me like that. You know that I get very sensitive when you start yelling at me." Paulie whimpered at the thought.

And the thing was, Buddy didn't have all the vouchers. I had Buddy's in my back pocket. I stole it last night. I knew Buddy would just explode at the course when he found out that he didn't have them all.

Theodore finally got us to the course and dropped us off. He was on his way to do some snooping. He was going to drive around and find a farmer or two to talk about—what else? The weather.

This day was no different than the rest; there was another frost delay. Buddy exploded one more time as Johnny said, "Hey, Buddy, I think the rest of the week we should just come two hours later for these frost delays. I know most of us could use that extra couple of hours of sleep."

"Yeah, but with our luck, there wouldn't be any frost delay that morning, and we would miss our tee time," Buddy said as we all walked up to the front counter.

"You must be the O'Malley group, right?" the head pro asked as he looked around at us all in varying states of hungoverness. "Let's get you guys all checked in. Who has all the golf vouchers?"

I could see that his name tag stated "CARL," so I came back with, "Oh no, Carl. This is the Parker group. But it just so happens that the O'Malleys are playing with the Parker group today. Can you not see that Mr. Parker is the one in charge?"

"Oh, I'm sorry. Who's Mr. Parker?" Carl asked as he looked around the room for someone to step up.

"Never mind him. Carl, here is what you are looking for," Buddy stated as he stepped out from behind Pudden.

As Buddy handed over the golf vouchers, Carl started to do a quick head count. Then he recounted the vouchers and seemed to be coming up one short. He inquired, "You are all golfing, aren't you, guys? I seem to only have six vouchers, and we have you down as seven golfers."

Like clockwork we all turned our heads toward the tight-fitting canary, and Buddy screamed. "Paulie …"

"Don't blame me. You knew I didn't have it. You have it. Remember? You put them all together last night," Paulie tried to explain as he emptied out his pockets to show that he didn't have it.

"I know I did. So where is it?" Buddy cried as he started to take everything out of his pockets, looking for that last voucher.

"It's not me. It's not me this time," Paulie cried in jubilation as he did a little happy dance.

Buddy started to take everything out of his wallet and said, "I don't understand. This is not like me. O'Malley?"

"Don't look at me. I couldn't have taken it. Remember? You got your place locked up tighter than the Virgin Mary." I tried to explain that it couldn't have been me.

"If I don't have it, Paulie doesn't have it, and you don't have it …" Buddy started to say as he looked around the room and eventually made his way back to me and yelled, "O'Malley, I don't know how you do it. But I better not find out that it was you."

"Hey, Carlton, is there any way to find out whose voucher is missing?" I asked. "So I can prove to him once and for all that it's not my voucher that he is missing?"

"Oh, yes," Carl said as he started to lay down all the vouchers in order. "See, right here at the top left-hand corner? See? This is your room number and the last three letters are the initials of your name."

"There you go. This will prove it." As Buddy continued to arrange the vouchers by room number, he was coming to the end of the pile and said, "234SAW and 234SPO."

"Yeah, that's my and Stewart's room," I confirmed. "See?"

"235PUG," Buddy said as he put the last voucher down on the counter. "What? That doesn't make any sense. It should say 235BMP."

"Hey, Paulie, what's the *U* stand for?" Johnny interrupted. "Useless?"

"No, it's Urian." Paulie proudly said.

Stewart chuckled out loud. "You got to be kidding. And you never wanted to change it to Useless? Ha-ha-ha."

"Noooo. I got it from my father, who got it from his papi; it was their middle names," Paulie proudly argued. "It's been handed down for many years."

"So Paulie, who are you going to hand it down to?" Johnny asked, knowing full well that Paulie was not married and didn't have any kids. And sure as hell wouldn't have any in the future. "Are you getting a pet or something?"

"Well, you never know. But I'm still looking for that very special lady, you know," Paulie acknowledged.

"Urine. Now it's all starting to make sense," Buddy added. "Did they have problems with urinary tract infections also?"

"Not Urine. Urian … U-R-I-A-N, Urian," Paulie protested as he spelled it out to explain. "They are spelled differently."

"Urine or Urian, it doesn't matter to me. You can spell it however you want. It still sounds and smells like piss to me," Buddy informed the group.

"Buddy, Buddy, old pal. You know it's not always me. And don't worry about it. It's all good. I'm sure Sergeant Sally Sue could fax a copy over," I said, trying to address the missing voucher problem.

"Yeah, no problem. I'm sure she won't mind. I'm sure she has had to do it on more than one occasion before," Carl agreed as he tried to defuse the problem.

"Yeah, she had to do it just yesterday, right, Paulie?" I tried to explain.

"Uhhhh, don't you bring me into this," Paulie answered as he looked up from the ladies' two-for-one rack, taking a puff from his inhaler. "Didn't we decide yesterday that it was Buddy's fault? He was the one who forgot the chit yesterday."

"All I can say is I better not find out that it was you," Buddy tried to warn me one more time as Carl handed him the starter slip.

"Come on, Buddy, let's go get a drink. I'm feeling generous so, seeing you have your wallet out, I'll even let you buy," I said as I put my arm around him and started to guide him toward the bar.

"Nooooo, I'm thinking that it has to be your round," Buddy replied.

"Okay, okay, sounds fair. We will let Johnny buy," I suggested. "Johnny, it's your round."

"Yep, I sure could use a drink," Johnny agreed as he headed right behind us for the bar. "Buddy, unless you want to go out on the practice green and win some money like yesterday."

"No, we all are staying put. I'm keeping my eye on everyone, so nobody makes any more stupid bets, right, guys?" Buddy stated as he sunk down into one of the big tub chairs in the bar.

"That's right. Right, Buddy," Pudden added as he agreed with him.

"What are you talking about? Are you saying that every one of your bets that you made yesterday was stupid?" I joked as I slunk down into my chair.

"Can we get a couple pitchers of beer over here?" Johnny ordered as he fell down awkwardly into his chair. "Wow, are these ever low! But they sure are comfy."

"It's amazing how comfortable chairs can be when your feet lie flat on the floor, and they don't dangle in the air," Buddy bragged as he squirmed around a little to get more comfortable.

"I know what you mean. Nothing worse than having a shit on a toilet that is too high," Johnny added as he tried to explain his preferences when having a big dump.

"Worse is when you get a urinal that is mounted way too high. And you have to get on your tippy-toes to have a piss," Buddy complained.

We were all sitting around having a drink before our round, or as some would say, a drink or two to kill some time for that fucking frost delay. The teams were all set, and no one wanted to practice. It seemed everyone was quite confident on how they lost yesterday.

The next thing you knew, Carl came into the bar area and said, "If you guys want to get out now, I can get you out on the back nine."

"Thanks, Carlie. That was quick," I said as I tried to dig myself out of the deep chair to stand up. "Johnny, just bring the beer pitcher with you. We'll put it in our cart."

"Like fuck we will." Johnny cried at the thought of having to share as he tipped it up to his mouth and guzzled it all down to the bottom. Without spilling a drop, he took the back of his sleeve to wipe his mustache dry. "There. You can get us a six-pack to go."

"Carl, we just have to get our golf shoes on, and we will be on our way," Buddy agreed as we walked out from the bar area. "Where are my shoes? Okay, O'Malley, where are my shoes?"

"I don't have them," I answered as I tried not to smile. "Why are you asking me? I'm not your mother."

"Because between you and your brother, you are the ones that are playing all the practical jokes," Buddy stated. "Oh shit, my new insoles, they were in them."

"I haven't seen them since you had them on your feet last," I tried to lie without smiling. "And you played so well yesterday. Remember, you almost had a great day."

Thinking back, Buddy tried to find the answers that he was looking for. "Paulie, what did I do with my shoes yesterday?"

"Don't look at me. You told me that I was useless. And besides, you told me that I was drunk. Remember?" Paulie tried to explain but could not come up with any answers that Buddy wanted to hear.

"O'Malley, when was the last time that I had them on?" Buddy asked. "I believe I had them on right up to when I went to bed, right?"

"Did you wear them to bed?" I tried to help.

"Nooooo, you fucking idiot. I didn't wear them to bed," Buddy screamed.

"Don't swear at me. I'm just trying to help you narrow down where you lost your shoes," I pleaded with him. "I think I took them off you when I tried to put Paulie's superhero PJs on ya."

"Fuck off, will you?" Buddy cried as he had a concerned look on his face that he might not ever be tall again. "Don't start with all that again."

"Come to think of it, I'm sure that you swore at me when I hosed you down last night."

"Hosed me down? What the fuck are you talking about now?" Buddy argued. "You never hosed me down last night."

"Don't you remember puking yesterday all down the front of yourself? And you got it all over your shoes. Your shirt had stains all down the front just like Paulie's," I informed him.

"Nooooooo. But I sure can't get the smell of puke out of my mind." Buddy smacked his lips as if he was trying to maybe taste the puke, which was never there. "I'm sure I can still smell it."

"And I don't know how you did it, but there is puke all down the back of your golf coat. Look." I tried to embarrass him as I pointed to the back of his coat. "So I had to hose you down. I guess I didn't do a very good job. You want me to hose you down again?"

"You're wrong," Buddy argued as he tried to pull the bottom of his coat around to take a look at the dried puke stain.

"Yes, you did. Me and Paulie almost had to carry you home last night. But we couldn't. You had that shit everywhere, and besides, you were all wet from the hosing," I tried to explain.

"Fuck off, O'Malley. You never hosed me down," Buddy cried.

"Oh, okay, that must have been another night that I'm thinking of," I reasoned as we rushed out the door.

"Now it's all coming back to me. Paulieeeeee, where are my shoes?" Buddy bawled.

"Uh, in your golf bag?" Even Paulie was trying to find answers now as he took a large puff from his puffer.

"They better be. They just better be," Buddy claimed as he walked out of the bar toward the bag-drop area. We all noticed, as he walked away with dried-on puke splattered down the back of his black coat. I was thinking that Buddy was going to kill Paulie; I could already see it. Buddy was pulling everything out from his golf bag, trying to find his golf shoes and of course his inlays. "They are not here. Paulie, why do I think you had something to do with all this?"

"I don't know why you think I had anything to do with this. You know I don't remember anything, and the only thing I do remember is Shannon carrying me home and putting me to bed." Paulie answered. "For some reason, I think he put you to bed also. Right, Shannon?"

"Right, Paulie," I agreed with him. "It was something like that. At times I think that I am the only one who cares about everyone else."

"He didn't put you to fucking bed, Paulie," Buddy disagreed. "And he sure as hell didn't put me to bed either."

"Sooooooo, where are your golf shoes?" Paulie tried to stick up for me as he took another mouthful from his puffer. "Why do you have to argue all the time? He continually tries to help you and me, and everyone else for that matter."

"Now you are on his side?" Buddy started to argue again. "Fuckkkkkk. Never mind. That's not the point. Where are my golf shoes?"

"We were getting it narrowed down to where they are. Did we decide if you slept with them on or not?" I egged him on.

"Will you fuck off? I didn't sleep with them on," Buddy answered again.

"Okay, now we are getting closer. How about Paulie? Did he sleep with them on?" I asked again.

"No, I don't think I … Well, I don't remem …" Paulie answered.

Buddy interrupted Paulie before he could finish. "Never mind, you fucking assholes. I hope they are back at the hotel for your sake."

"Okay, good. We have that settled then," Paulie said in relief as he found out that he was not responsible for Buddy's shoes, as of yet. "Let's go play some golf."

To make a long story short, we kicked their ass again, even worse than yesterday. Buddy probably played the worst game of his life that day. He couldn't figure out that he was playing a little shorter than yesterday, when he had his lifts in his golf shoes.

When we got back to the hotel, Buddy was on a mission. He wanted to find his golf shoes and his new insoles that made him half an inch taller but made him feel like he was the tallest short guy out there. And not to mention that it helped him play better golf. He tore everything out of the van with no luck. Then he started to check everybody else's golf bags in case someone was playing a terrible joke. As he was going through everyone's bag, he found something unusual that did not belong there. "Johnny, what's this pink shit in the peanut butter jar?"

"Get out of my bag. I don't have your fucking inserts," Johnny jumped in as he went over to pick up some of his prized possessions that Buddy had strewn around. "I get heartburn really bad. So I use this Pepto Bismol sit as a chaser with my first beer in the morning. You should try it."

"You whattttttt?" Buddy chuckled.

"Hey, you didn't happen to find a baby food jar with some calamine lotion in it, did you?" Johnny asked as he took a big swig of the pink shit, wiping his mouth off with the back of his sleeve. "Sometimes I get those two mixed up. One tastes really bad, and the other tastes really, really bad. But they both work really well on snakebites."

"That's what I must have drunk a couple days ago, I had heartburn so bad," I informed them. "That explains why my throat dried up, I was spitting dust for hours, and I had to drink so much beer just so I could swallow."

The next thing Buddy did was he made everyone take their golf shoes off so he could examine them all. Just to make sure no one was playing taller than he had all day. "Buddy, do you not think that maybe it would have been, uhhhhh, sweeter-smelling if you would have checked everyone's shoes first thing this morning?"

"I don't fucking care. I want my insoles back," Buddy argued as he threw Pudden's shoes at him. "Holy fuck, these stink. What the hell did you step in today?"

"Oh, I don't know. There was a pile of this stuff; I ran into it. I think it was hole twelve or so. Remember? I asked you what you thought it was. And you told me to fuck off for the fourteenth time. Remember? I don't think I stepped in it, though. Well, maybe I did just a little. I don't know. I'm not sure what it was, but fuck, did it stink! Johnny, taste this. What do you think it is?" Pudden cried as he handed Johnny his shoe to lick."

"Oh, that, that's wyboo shit. It won't hurt you, but you better get it off because it will stain your shoes if you are not careful," Johnny warned him as he took the shoe and wiped it off on the back of Buddy's shorts.

"Will you fuck off? Why you got to be like that?" Buddy yelled as he quickly tried to move out of Johnny's range.

Not finding his shoes, Buddy headed up to his room. There, sitting at the base of his door, were his golf shoes, sitting on a cooler of ice with a note attached that said

Mr. Parker,
I think these are yours.
I found them in the flower bed covered
in this yellow chunky stuff.
I was able to get most of the dried-on chunks off.
They sort of cleaned up real good, but the tongue
on the left one might be stained for good.
And you can never have enough ice …
The Iceman

"That Zackery, what a guy! You will have to tip him really good today," I added. "He not only found your shoes. He got you more ice to boot. What a guy!"

"But where are the insoles? Someone has stolen them. Who would have done that?" Buddy screamed as he almost tore his shoe apart looking for his inserts.

"Buddy, I would think that whoever stole them would have to be shorter than you" I tried to console him. "But I know for a fact that you have to be the shortest troll in this hotel. So that rules out anybody in this place from stealing them, right?"

"O'Malley, will you just fuck off?" Buddy cried as his eyes started to water for the sixth time today. "This is serious shit, you know."

"Buddy, I know. I can feel your shortness." I laughed as I tried to cheer him up. "Maybe you can check the lost and found?"

"Fuck off, will you? I got to go find Zackery to find out where he found them," Buddy growled.

One thing about our group, we always had a tendency to misplace things after golfing. We could lose almost anything, from golf shoes to jackets, to even one of us; sometimes on purpose, sometimes not. The thing is, if we didn't change our golf shoes and put them away immediately, they could or would eventually walk away.

I remember one time we were playing in a tournament over at the Thousand Island Golf Club, which is situated on Wellesley Island. The weather was perfect for a beautiful boat ride home after golf. Of course we are all drinking quite heavily to celebrate our win. I had forgotten to change my shoes at the course; what a mistake that was. To get more comfortable for the boat ride home, I decided to kick those shoes off and go barefoot. All I know is when we finally did arrive home at the dock, no shoes could be found. Buddy finally did pipe up and said something to the effect, "I warned you, shoes can't walk on water. Payback is a bitch. Next time you might be wearing them."

I'm not sure what he was trying to pay me back for, but I'm sure it was nothing.

CHAPTER 19

You've Got to Get Out the Back, Jack

Friday finally came. Sally Sue had reminded me all week about our randieview (rendezvous), our get-together, our date. Over the week, I found out that she lived only a couple of miles down the road. "Shady Hills Estates" was what it was called. It sounded like a cemetery or a very expensive gated community. As Granny from the *Beverly Hillbillies*, would have said, "Surely they all must have cement-ponds in the back for their ducks and geese to live."

Earlier in the week, Sally Sue had confided in me that she did have a live-in boyfriend. His name was Samuel, but most everyone who knew him called him Sammy for short. He was a sergeant in the military, a lifer. Sammy was hardly ever home. He was always on maneuvers. He was gone for days at a time. These training exercises that he was involved in took him away for five to seven days at least three times a month. As she said, she was not very happy as it cut into her playtime. She felt that he was neglecting her all the time.

Anyways, he was going to be away till at least Monday. She had told me that she would pick me up out front of the Destination Dreamland Motel at eight o'clock, and if I knew what was good for me, that I would not be late.

As I walked up to the Dreamland, I saw that I was about five minutes late, but no matter, because our song had already started to play: "Mustang Sally." There she was, my Mustang Sally Sue sitting in her car waiting for me. I was hoping that she had not been waiting long, as I rushed up to her parked car. She was driving a beautiful red Mustang. Although it was not brand-new by any means, it was a classic. But what made it even more sexy, it was a convertible. Thank God, the top was up, considering that the temperature was dropping, but I sure was hoping that it would get hotter as the night went on.

She waved me over to get in. I was thinking she was not even going to buy me a drink first. How easy did she think I was anyways? She must know me better than I know myself. Just as I opened the car door, "Mustang Sally" abruptly changed to a Rolling Stones' classic, "Start Me Up."

As I got in the car, she gave me a great big hug and kisses and said, "You're late. We better get out of here."

"What do you have in mind?" I asked her as I noticed a pair of shiny handcuffs dangling from the rearview mirror.

"You will see. You will see," she warned me. "Hurry, get in."

Pulling out of the parking lot, she squealed the tires, which laid a nice streak of rubber down the center of the road. We had only gone about a mile when she started to put the top down. And all I was thinking about was that was not the top that I wanted down. It was kind of chilly out to be going a hundred miles per hour in a convertible.

"Is that all she's got?" I knew as soon as I asked it, it was a mistake, and I was going to be in big trouble.

"I'm sure this little pony has a lot more," Sally Sue bragged as I looked over and saw the needle hovering around the 120-mile-per-hour mark. As the needle kept moving up, I had to readjust my white-knuckle grip on the dashboard. This racehorse was a real thoroughbred as it maneuvered around all the corners to her house. Maybe she missed her calling? The way she handled that car, maybe she should have become a NASCAR driver. Was she just trying to scare me, or did she just want to show me that I was going to be in great hands?

We pulled left into an entrance with a big old sign that said, "SHADY HILLS ESTATES." The headlights from the car lit up the once grand sign. It needed paint, a whole lot of paint. Some of the raised letters were either missing or broken. Some were just unrecognizable; a few were even dangling upside down. The power to the sign had been cut off long ago. The new sign was one of those portable rental signs that have the wheels attached to the bottom frame. The thing is the wheels had been stolen long ago. You could tell that by the way the weeds and vegetation had grown up around it. There was no electricity to the portable sign to light it up, so they had just gone back to the old floodlight shining up at it. Well, it was not even a gated community; it was not even a large community of houses. It was a fucking trailer park, and not even a good one. There weren't even any double-wides there, and most of the trailers looked like they were twenty to thirty years old. The trailers were all packed in there like sardines. I was sure if you farted in one trailer, you could not only hear it, but I'm sure you could have smelled the stench in the other trailers. They were that close.

She apologized as she was explaining her home. "It's not much, but it's all mine. I grew up here, and my best friend, Tomeka, lived next door. We were known as the Shady Hills Girls. We were the camp's kids. Inseparable we were. We did everything together. And you know what? She still lives next door. I hope you don't mind. She might be joining us later."

"Mind? I don't mind at all. The more, the merrier."

"I would love to introduce you to her. My biological father lives three trailers down. My momma, God rest her soul, left the trailer to me and me alone. Thank God all my brothers and sisters have all moved out of state. I really wouldn't have wanted to have shared this place with the other seven."

She hurried me in the front door, as if for no one else to see. All in one motion, the door shut, and the light switch flicked on. She started to unbutton her full-length coat to reveal her outfit. As she ripped her coat open, I could see it all started with a white silk scarf tied around her neck. Her white fishnet body suit contrasted with her dark skin, revealing everything. This suit went from her neck down to her toes. Over that I could see she was wearing a black, matching, sexy, tight, crotch-less corset, which held and displayed her beautiful, busty cleavage. With all of her essential extremities tied up tight, I wasn't sure how she would have gotten into this outfit, but I was sure glad that she did. She stood there in black, killer, six-inch-stiletto heels, impatiently tapping her toe. As her coat came off, she grabbed for her black silky robe to throw on. Her robe shrouded most of her body. As she reached into one of the pockets, out came her riding crop. Her black fingerless gloves rode all the way up to her elbows. She was a dominatrix. I was right all along. My fantasy was bang-on. She was going to be my mistress for the night. This was going to be the best night everrrrrrrr, I thought.

"What are you waiting for?" she yelled at me impatiently with her arms crossed. Sally Sue stood there with a mischievous smile and had a naughty twinkle in her eyes. I knew at that moment that even though I was afraid, I was going to be in good hands for the night. And then, she snapped that fucking whip at me. Just at that moment, I knew I was done for. The leather riding crop missed me by millimeters. It even sounded like pain as it snapped back. Wow, that was close; I knew I had better do everything she told me to do, as I didn't do pain very well.

I rushed toward her. She stopped me in midstream and commanded me, "No; stop. Hurry; get undressed *now*!"

She snapped that riding crop at my ass this time and connected. "Owwwwww. That stung."

"Now you will listen, right?" She barked at me to get my attention. She went on to say, "I'm in charge; I'm in total control of you the rest of the night. You are just a naughty boy who needs to be taught a lesson, right?"

"Right!" I cried as I started frantically to undress as I did not want to get whipped again.

"Now you will address me as Mistress Sally Sue and Mistress Sally Sue only. You can only talk when I tell you to. You cannot look at me. Ever. Or touch me unless I tell you to. Right, you lowlife? Now give me a twirl. I've got to see what the fuck I'm working with here," she vowed and then stated, "I guess this will have to do. Now get down on all fours, slave."

"Right. I'm so sorry. I'm just a lowlife. I've been a bad boy. I really should be taught a lesson." I tried to explain, as I thought we were playing a role-playing game or something. Not being used to playing on this side of the whip, I obliged and got down on my hands and knees.

"And," she yelled at me once more as she snapped that riding crop at my ass.

"Ouch. I'm so sorry, Mistress Sally Sue." I pleaded for some understanding and sympathy as I writhed in agony. I was thinking I had to get either quicker or smarter because this was not fun, and it was starting to fucking hurt.

"Sweet Jesus, boy, you've got to be learnin', learnin' all the time, boy," she screamed at me as she thrashed me a couple more times for good measure just to show me that she was in total control. Then she tied her white scarf around my neck and led me like a fucking dog slowly into the back bedroom.

"Fuck. I will try," I said as she interrupted me with another smack to my ass.

"Try? What the fuck is this try shit?" she screamed as she gave me an unsympathetic stern look.

"I will do better, Mistress Sally Sue." I bellowed that it had hurt. But in a sort of kinky way, I was starting to enjoy it. I was being bossed around; I was being restricted on what I could and couldn't do; I was being controlled, totally controlled, even if I didn't know why. And I would be punished and punished a lot if I didn't do it right. Usually I was the one who was in charge. I was the one who was in total control of the situation. This was something different for me, so maybe that's why I was starting to enjoy it. I was starting to like fear; it was because you never knew where it was going to go next.

"Were you looking at my crotch?" Sally Sue demanded as she snapped the whip in the air. She herself seemed to be getting off at flogging me.

"No, no, I wouldn't," I cried as I looked down at her feet.

"What?" she warned me as she smacked me again in the ass.

"Ow! No, Mistress Sally Sue," I cried again.

"It certainly looked like you were looking at my crotch. Are you sure you weren't looking at my *crotch*? Are you telling me the truth?" Sally Sue hissed at me.

"No, no, yes, ma'am, I'm telling the truth. I would never lie to you, Mistress Sally Sue," I cried out just in time before getting smacked again.

"Don't you ever look there again if you know what is good for you. Now rub my feet; they hurt," she commanded as she slunk back comfortably into her chair.

I was naked and lying at her feet in a fetal position, rubbing her foot, one toe at a time. I tried to keep my head almost parallel to the floor so I would not look up at her. It sure was hard considering she was wearing crotch-less panties.

Each time I would get caught glancing up at her, she would smack the whip over my backside and demanded, "Boy, you might as well start over. Fuck, you are a slow learnerrrrr." Just then she drove her six-inch spiked heel into my crotch and chortled. "How do you like that? Have I got your attention now?"

"Owwwwwwww. Holy fuck, that hurt. No, I don't." I screamed in agony. As the pain subsided, I went on to say, "I'm so sorry. I'm just a lowlife, Mistress Sally Sue." I tried to agree with her to make her happy.

"That's not good enough," she screamed at me as she grabbed me, threw me over her knee, and started to spank my bare ass with the palm of her hand in a measurable tempo. "Slap … slap … smack … smack."

"Do you know why you are getting spanked?" she mumbled.

I was sure my ass had turned a rosy-pink color by now as I whimpered, "Because I have been bad, Very bad, oh Mistress Sally Sue."

"Yes, you have. You have been very bad. I hope I do not have to do this again. Do you think I like doing this?" she threatened.

"I will be good just for you, Mistress Sally Sue," I said, almost forgetting to end it with Mistress Sally Sue.

She led me up on the bed, handed me a pair of her granny panties, and ordered me, "Now put this on, and never take them off unless I tell you to."

I did not waste any time, as all I wanted to do was please my master. Although they were white cottons, they were very sheer and frilly-like. They felt wonderful. Then she blindfolded me with her scarf and demanded, "This will stop you from looking at my crotch." She scolded me as she whacked me again across the ass for good measure.

"I'm sorry, I'm so sorry. It will never, ever happen again, Mistress Sally Sue," I pleaded as I lay there feeling so helpless. I was just not sure of what was going to happen next. I was scared.

"That's right; it won't happen again. What in fuck is that? Sweet Jesus, is that an erection? Are you getting excited? Are you? That better not be what I think it is. I haven't given you permission yet, have I?" she shrieked at me as she playfully poked me a couple times in the groin area. Then she unmercifully grabbed me in the groin with a powerful grip like she was going to pull it off and commanded, "No, no, this will not do. What are you thinking?"

"No, no, I'm sorry. It's not me. It's these panties; they feel so good. And, and you're so beautiful, Mistress Sally Sue," I cried out as I anticipated what was coming. "Smack … smack."

"Ow, ow, I'm so sorry. I can't stop it, Mistress Sally Sue," I apologized as I heard her reach down into her nightstand for something.

As soon as she clasped it on my right wrist, I knew it was a pair of handcuffs. These were no ordinary sex-play handcuffs; they were heavy stainless steel. They were military-grade. She was about to clasp the other handcuff around the headboard bars when the telephone rang. It only rang about four times, and then the answering machine picked up. All we heard was a very unsettling, shrill voice.

Sally, Sally Sue,
I know you are there; I can hear you.
Pick up, pick up. It's Tomeka.
I just ran into Sammy at the corner-store.
He's home early. Get him out; get him out now.
I hope you get this in time.
Anyways, let's do lunch tomorrow,
Love ya.

"Sweet Jesusssssss. You've got to get out. You've got to get out of here *now*," she cried as she pulled down my blindfold.

"I thought he wasn't coming home till Monday," I quavered, trying to grab all my clothes to put on as I headed for the front door. Just then, we heard a big loud diesel truck pull up into the driveway, and the headlights lit up into the trailer through the front bay window.

"Holy fuck, he's home. No time for that. You've got to get out the back." Sally Sue prompted me back toward the back bedroom.

One thing about windows in trailers: they are not very big. I struggled to get out the back window, landing on my head onto a footstool on the ground beneath the window. "Owww," I cried as I was thinking how much fucking pain I was going to have to endure tonight. Next thing I knew, Sally Sue was throwing out the rest of my clothes. I was standing there with my master's panties on. I stepped up onto the footstool that was under the window to give her a quick kiss goodbye.

She reached out the window to grab me to pull me closer to give me that good-night kiss. The kiss she gave back was no goodbye kiss. It was a this-is-what-you-are-always-going-to-miss kiss. "You will always remember this night, and you will always remember me," she demanded. "And don't you dare tell anybody about this, right?"

"Yes, of course, Mistress Sally Sue," I acknowledged. My heart was racing as I was standing there naked beneath the window, trying to get dressed. I was peering around at the other trailers in the park, and I was noticing something peculiar. They all had some kind of stepstool under the back windows. I was thinking, "Wow, is this some kind of fire escape bylaw because of no back doors, or maybe it's just to wash windows? No, it's trailer trash to the fullest."

As I got dressed, I overheard Sally Sue say from inside, "Hey, honey, is that you? Get in here; I'm ready for you."

"Sally? Oh, or should I say Mistress? How'd you know I was coming home early?" Sammy asked.

I stood up on the step to see how she was going to handle this, and all I heard was a big "smack … smack" as the whip cracked across his backside. Then Sally Sue prompted Sammy with, "Did you forget something? And what the fuck are you looking at? … Sweet-Jesus …" Just then, I heard a crack of the whip again.

"Owwww, owwww, oh, I'm so sorry. I've been bad, Mistress Sally Sue," Sammy cried.

"Yes. Sweet Jesus, you have been bad. You came home early. Now get undressed, you naughty boy. My feet hurt. Get down there and get to work. Smack …" Sally Sue demanded him to obey as she smacked him again.

I could see that they had done this before as he was undressed in no time. Then he went down to her feet, licking each toe as if it was going to be his last. I could see his backside, full of scars from the whippings he so desired or deserved. I was thinking Mistress Sally Sue had everything under control.

As I finished dressing, I came up one shoe short. I peered into the trailer one last time to see if I could see my shoe, and all I saw was Sammy peeking up at Sally Sue's crotch, and all I heard was another "smack" across his ass. "Were you looking at my crotch?"

"Owww. Oh, no, never, Mistress Sally Sue," Sammy cried out.

I could not see my shoe anywhere, but suddenly, I felt like someone was watching me. And of course, the music started to play in my mind, so that confirmed that a female was keeping an eye on me. All I kept hearing was the song "Jump" by Van Halen. It was so fitting. I slowly looked over my shoulder at the trailer next door, and there looking at me was this black girl. I assumed it was Tomeka because all of a sudden, she whispered, "Boy, was that close." Then she gave me a look and asked, "Why don't you come over? I can clean up some of those wounds of yours."

"I've got to get the fuck out of here. I've been a naughty boy tonight once too often," I said as I waved to her, noticing that I still had the one handcuff on.

I was walking back to the hotel. I had the handcuffs tucked up under one sleeve, limping from having only the one shoe and having one tanned sorry ass. My adrenaline of excitement had overcome everything else. My heart was still beating a thousand times a minute. I didn't know if it was because of Mistress Sally Sue or almost getting caught by her husband. Wow, what a night, and I didn't even get fucked.

But then I got to thinking, was this all just a setup? Did Sammy really come home early, or was it all a hoax? Was this all planned out? Was it all planned to make it look like we had gotten caught and that we had not finished? I wanted more, because I just didn't know where it would lead to or where it was going to end. Whatever it was, I took it all in—hook, line, and sinker—and ran with it. All I knew was that I was hooked. How many unsuspecting suckers had they taken advantage of?

I stopped over at the Destination Dreamland Motel for a nightcap. I must have looked pretty stupid walking in with only one shoe on. My excuse? I'm a Canadian. I just hoped that they did not have a "No Shoes, No Service" policy because I needed a drink. I needed a big, strong, fucking drink.

I asked Fanny, my favorite bartender, for a drink and asked, "Have there been any of my crew in earlier?"

"Yep, I think they were all in, and they all left early, something about an early seven thirty-five tee time," Fanny reported as she looked at me somewhat awkwardly.

"I guess it will be an early night for me also," I warned her, as I reached back for my wallet out of my pocket. As my arm came around, the handcuff fell out of my sleeve. Trying to conceal it, I quickly pushed it back up under my sleeve.

"By the looks of things, I would say that you were partying with Mistress Sally Sue tonight, and Sammy came home early," Fanny chimed in, as it was like this had happened once too often.

"No, not me," I tried to lie, but I could see that she was not going to accept that answer. "What gave it away? Was it the no shoe or the handcuffs?" I inquired.

"Neither. It's that stupid white scarf around your neck; that says Mistress Sally Sue's slave. And that you have not sat down since you came in. You must have been a real naughty boy tonight," Fanny observed as she grabbed the end of the scarf and pulled it from around my neck. Then she stated, "I didn't know you were into that."

I grabbed the scarf from her, stuffed it in my pocket, and disclosed to her, "I'm not. Never. And I'm never going back. She can't make me. I think she can't. Can she?"

"You will. Oh, you will. You've been touched. All she has to do is summon you, and you will be there. You are hers. You are spellbound. You are her slave now," Fanny answered.

Although I didn't like her answer, I took it all in and thought about it the rest of the night. Here I was going home early and being a good boy. Well, the one drink turned into ten, and then it was two o'clock, and Fanny was kicking me out again, just like she had done all week long.

I made it back to the room and tried to quietly slip into the room without waking Stewart up. I just got to the edge of the bed to have a seat to get my one shoe off, and the light flicked on as Stewart demanded, "So, how was your date with Sally Sue?"

I came back with, "Oh, better than expected. But you know me, I don't kiss and tell."

"Who are you trying to kid? You brag about everything," Stewart let me know.

"Okay, okay. I think she would prefer you went out with her," I lied.

"What the fuck is that on your wrist? And where is your other fucking shoe?" Stewart asked as he was trying to get all the details from me.

"Holy fuck, I'm missing a shoe?" I joked back as I started to get undressed.

"Tell me what happened and don't leave anything out. Does she not know you do not need to be held down or secured? They don't even have to say please. And besides, it's usually the other way around," Stewart retorted.

So I tried to fill Stewart in on what had transpired earlier. I tried to be as vague as possible and to lie as much as I could, because my master told me not to tell. If I had told him the truth, he would not have believed me anyways. So

I started out by telling him there were the three of us: me, Sally Sue, and her best friend Tomeka. They were having a O'Malley sandwich. I was handcuffed to the headboard, and the two girls were having their way with me until Sammy came home early.

"Sammy? Who's Sammy?" Stewart asked.

"Sammy is Sally Sue's big black husband, and he has guns. Big guns. All I can say is, I was lucky to make it out alive," I cried to him.

"You know, you got to be more careful next time," Stewart chided. "Boy, were you ever lucky."

"I know, I know. I just made it out in the nick of time," I agreed with him. "I was a naughty boy tonight, and that's all I want to say about it. I better go to bed. We have to get up early."

All night long, I tossed and turned; I just could not get Mistress Sally Sue out of my head. I could not get comfortable; I couldn't sleep. I just lay there. Every time I would roll over, I could feel sharp pains from one of her welts that she had skillfully inflicted upon me. She had left her mark. It sure did make me think about her and think about her a lot. And that was making me horny. I couldn't explain it. She was not there, but she had total control of me. Although it was not my cup of tea, it sure was making me want a cup of tea—sweet, sweet Southern tea, if you know what I mean. And I sure didn't want to take those panties off. I couldn't; my master told me to keep them on until she told me to take them off. They sure did feel good, smooth, and silky. All I knew was that I was a naughty-boy and I needed to be punished, whipped silly. Then my mind started to wander. Where did Tomeka fit in all of this? Was she a

Mistress Tomeka also? That sounded like double whippings, double the fun. Could I be that bad? I sure could try. All I wanted to do was please my master or masters. And, and, and then the alarm went off, and Stewart yelled over, "Hey, fuckhead, it's time to get up."

I lay there thinking back on what had transpired the night before as I had awoken with the biggest, hardest hard-on ever. Holy fuck was I horny! Where was my Mistress Sally Sue? I had to find my master.

I waited for Stewart to go to the bathroom before I got out of bed, as I did not want him to see that I was wearing my master's panties because he would just tell everyone. So I got dressed quickly, and I tried to find a long-sleeve golf shirt. Somehow, I needed to hide the handcuffs. Wouldn't you know it? I didn't bring one, so plan B. I guessed I would just have to wear my golf jacket all day. I knew my master wouldn't be in to work today till two o'clock. Hopefully she'd remember to bring the keys. And to give me my soul back or whatever she had of mine. I did not want to be controlled or constrained anymore.

It's funny how some things happen. This morning was the only morning that I didn't take a dump, naked, in Paulie and Buddy's room, only because I didn't want them to see the granny panties. The handcuffs I could explain, but the women's underwear. That would be another story.

I was all set for breakfast. I had my golf shoes on, I had my golf jacket on, I had the handcuffs tucked up under my sleeve; I was all set. We were all sitting around having breakfast. Paulie had ordered his usual pancakes with extra syrup. The crew's brown bag special this morning was vodka. Bloody Marys were our drink of champions. It was a very quiet morning; hardly anybody was talking, and I couldn't pick on anyone because I had more important things on my mind. My master, I could not get her out of my mind. What had she done to me? I didn't like it one bit. But I did. I was confused; I couldn't wait to see her. I wanted, I needed, to get this spell taken off me.

Buddy, all concerned and worried, looked over at me and said, "O'Malley, what's wrong? You don't seem yourself this morning. You're not picking on anybody. What's up?"

"Nothing, nothing at all. I'm fine really. The week of drinking and late nights is finally catching up with me. I think it will be a slow day for me today," I responded as I tried to redirect the crossfire.

"You're full of shit. What's really going on?" Buddy challenged my answer. "I'm starting to worry about you."

Stewart spoke up. "Did you guys not see the handcuffs? He showed up at three o'clock in the morning with one cuff on, and he wouldn't tell me what happened. All he said was that he was a naughty boy. Show them, fuckhead."

"Stewart," I yelled.

"What are you talking about? What handcuffs?" Paulie interrupted as he stopped eating his pancakes for that moment.

"These cuffs," I answered as I lifted the sleeve of my coat up, revealing the cuffs as they fell down, clanking together around my wrist.

"What happened? Hey, these are real," Buddy said as he examined them closely.

"Yeah. You would know. Well, I'm sort of embarrassed about the whole thing, but here goes. I was quite drunk last night, and I was coming home from the Destination

Dreamland Motel. That Fanny had got me drunk again, as usual. The next thing I knew, this Sergeant Joe Friday pulled me over for jaywalking, and I mean jaywalking, not drunk walking but jaywalking. Can you imagine? There are no fucking lights in this town. Of course you have to jaywalk to get to the other side. Anyways, I might have got a little out of hand. The next thing I knew, he had one cuff on me and was about to do the other wrist. And then this big red Dodge-Ram diesel truck screamed by. Then something screeched over the radio, something about a red truck; I didn't catch it all. But the next thing I knew, the copper must have forgotten about me. Because the next thing I knew, he jumped in his car and squealed away, leaving me on the side of the road. I stood there for some time waiting for his return. It seemed forever. So after about forty seconds, I came home," I lied, trying to make it as convincing as possible. I must have done okay, as it seemed everyone believed what I had just said.

"No, really? Wow! Are you ever lucky. I wonder what these initials SSD stamped on the side stand for," Paulie said.

"I would think they stand for Shady's Sheriff Department. What else?" I lied quickly. "Now I just got to figure out how to get this one handcuff off. I'll see if Zackery has bolt cutters."

Buddy piped in, "If they are real, I don't think you can cut them off with ordinary bolt cutters. You might have to cut your hand off or something."

Just then, Paulie leaned forward and said, "Don't look now, but two coppers just walked in. Do you think they are looking for you?"

"You're kidding. Holy fuck. Thank God. It's not the same copper from last night," I said as I quickly looked around to get a glimpse of them, all while rolling down my sleeve to cover up my handcuffs and putting my arm down under the table.

"But they might have a P-B-R out on you," Paulie stated as he rushed to take a puff from his puffer.

"Uhhhh … P-B-R? What the fuck is a P-B-R?" Buddy interrupted.

"P-B-R, Pabst Blue Ribbon? Of course," Johnny answered.

Stewart interrupted, "P-B-R … Professional Bull Riders?"

"I think you mean A-P-B? An All-Points Bulletin. Don't you?" I tried to inform him.

"Whatever. It's one of those. Looks like they've just came in for breakfast anyways," Paulie answered. "Maybe you should get out the back, Jack." Paulie added as he tried not to look guilty.

"I'm done getting out the back …"

"Uhhhhh … Getting out the back?" Paulie questioned. "What do you mean?"

"Ohhhh, nothing," I reasoned as I tried to explain. "It's okay, Paulie. I was drunk last night, and I looked totally different than I do now."

"Yes, I guess you are right," Paulie agreed.

The cuff was on my right wrist, so I made sure that I didn't drink from that hand. I was sure if the cuffs clanked together, the fuzz balls would surely have recognized that sound. Not that I had anything to worry about. It would have just meant that I would have to come up with another convincing story. Everyone at the table was on pins and needles. You should have seen Paulie; he was the most nervous of everyone. He was all fidgety and restless-like. The rest of breakfast, he acted like he was the guilty one. I'm not sure what he was guilty of, but they should have just come over, handcuffed him, and dragged him off to jail.

Now I knew why Buddy said Paulie couldn't keep a secret. Here you had Paulie; he was thinking that he had just had breakfast with a fugitive, an escapee. And he wanted everyone to know it. He wasn't just acting like the cat that ate the canary. He would have been the guy that stood up and pointed his finger at you. "That's the guy, Your Honor. He's the one; come arrest him. Take him away."

He was staring at the fuzz so much, he was starting to make them feel uncomfortable, so I warned him, "Paulie, quit staring at them. You look like you're guilty as shit."

"Shannon, aren't you worried that they will come over here and arrest you?" Paulie whispered as he anxiously took another puff.

"No. But you sure are giving them a reason to come over here, you staring at them and all," I tried to reason with him.

"Don't look now, but here they come," Paulie interrupted me as he nervously dropped his inhaler to the floor.

As they walked over, I was thinking that they were going to ask Paulie, "What are you looking at? Have you never seen a sheriff and his deputy eat breakfast before?"

"Hey, guys. How's the golf been? How's that Sally Sue been treating you?" Sheriff Andy Griprith asked as his right-hand man, Deputy Barney Fife, stood guard behind him as backup. It was funny how he looked and acted like Barney Fife, shaking and trembling with his right hand on top of his holster ready to draw in case someone had to be shot. I'm not sure who was more fidgety, Paulie or Barney Fife. I was thinking someone really might get shot there.

I wondered what he meant by "How's that Sally Sue been treating you?" Did he want me to show him the welts on my ass? So I came back with a safer statement. "Oh, the golf has been great. Nothing but the very best, eh, guys?"

A few of the guys answered with, "Oh, yeah. The best. It's just been great."

Even Theodore piped up with, "I'm having so much fun, and I don't even golf. I'm their designated driver."

"That's great. We're trying to promote our little town into one of the best, affordable golf destinations in the South," Sheriff Griptith stated.

"It's not just the golf. Everyone is so friendly down here. It's that Southern hospitality you have. And the drinking and partying that we have been doing … it's just been unbelievable," I answered.

"Yep, I've been keeping an eye on you guys. I have seen you guys staggering home from the Destination Dreamland Motel every night. How do you guys do it every night?" Deputy Barney Fife said, trembling.

"It was him. It was him, officer. It was him." Paulie accused as he stood up, pointing a finger at me, trying to get the inhaler to sit right in his mouth.

"Paulie, will you fucking sit down?" Buddy interrupted him as he tried to grab him to sit him down.

"It was him? What are you talking about?" Deputy Barney Fife asked for clarification.

"Oh, it's nothing. He just meant that he's the one who keeps coming home drunk all the time," Buddy explained.

"Oh? Yes, I have seen him too. I just do not know how you keep going," Sheriff Andy Griptith stated.

"You know, Andy, it sure does look like him. I'm sure that's the description that Deputy Enos gave me last night. It might be him. It sure does look like him," Deputy Barney Fife tried to clarify his response.

"It's him, I told you. I can't take this anymore. Will you just finish handcuffing him already? I knew it, that they had a P-B-R out on you," Paulie nervously accused me again as he fumbled with his inhaler one more time.

"Paulierrrrrrr," Buddy yelled.

"Andy, Andy, that's him. I tell you; it is him. I'm sure of it," Deputy Barney Fife retorted.

"Hey, are you the one? The one everyone is talking about?" Sheriff Andy Griptith inquired.

"I told you, I told you it was him." Paulie accused me once more as he interrupted the sheriff.

"Will you shut the fuck up, Paulie? Will you let him finish?" Buddy glared at Paulie.

"You're the one, the one that taught Mudcat that lesson the other night, weren't you? It was you, wasn't it?" Sheriff Andy Griptith suggested all official-like.

"Well, you know, it's funny how things worked out. I just got lucky. We had a few drinks, a few laughs, and it was all in good fun. He's a good … no, he's a great pool player and all," I stated, as I was worried now that I was in trouble and or maybe that Mudcat was his best friend or something. "We've got to get back there to try some of those famous topless oysters and, of course, to see that beautiful Latisha," I said as I tried to defuse the situation.

"Ahhhhh, that beautiful Latisha," Stewart agreed as he started to drool.

"Oh, they are the best. You got to go back. I just want to thank you for beating that bottom-feeder. Over the years, he's taken a few dollars off me, and everyone else, for that matter. He needed a good lesson. He has caused more local disturbances and more domestic quarrels than anybody else in the county. He needed a good down-home ass-whooping. And you did just that in a roundabout-way," Sheriff Andy Griptith boldly stated.

"Me too. I know what you mean. I don't even play him anymore," Deputy Barney Fife added.

"And that night that you took him to the cleaners, him and Ethel got into one hell of a fight. She kicked the living-shit out of him. Put the boots right to him. He's still in the hospital. He won't be fishing for a while, if you know what I mean. I just want to shake your hand. He deserved everything he got and more," Sheriff Andy Griptith remarked as he held out his right hand to shake mine.

Now what should I do? I couldn't shake his hand. The handcuff would fall out or clank together. So I reached out with my left hand. I grabbed his right hand and gave it a clumsy, unorthodox, tight shake and apologized, "Sorry. I think I fell down and sprained my wrist last night. I might have drunk too much."

"Maybe you should get that looked at. I think Doc Adams should be in his office this morning. I can take you over if you like. I know, I know he won't charge you because he has lost a few dollars to that fucking fisherman also. Everyone has," Sheriff Andy Griptith suggested.

"No, it's okay. I will be fine. Thanks anyways. I just have to get a few more drinks in me," I said.

"Well, in that case … Miss Vicki, get these guys another brown bagger; whatever they want. Make his a double; he deserves it. It's on me," Sheriff Andy Griptith boasted as he put his hand on my shoulder.

"You don't have to do that," I came back with.

"But I want to. We haven't been called out all week because of that angry angler," Sheriff Andy Griptith claimed. "You sure have made our job a lot easier this week."

As the drinks were delivered, everyone piped up with a "thank you."

So as the sheriff and his deputy went out the door, he added, "Now you guys be safe out there and have a good time. And above all, you do whatever Sally Sue tells you to do. She can be a bit of a control freak. You don't want to be on her bad side, if you know what I mean."

"We will, we sure will," I answered as I was trying to figure out what he meant by the Sally Sue comment. Had he been with her? Was he wearing granny panties? Did he really know the truth about what happened to me last night? Or was he just making small talk?

We finished breakfast and got Paulie out of there without him getting himself arrested. And he wasn't even the guilty one. It was quite ironic or satirical how this all happened. I had made up a story about being handcuffed by the police to hide the truth. Then they showed up for breakfast at our place to eat, and then they bought us all a brown bagger.

As we were loading in the van, Buddy piped up, "Fuck, O'Malley, are you ever lucky! Who would have thought that this town would have three coppers? And we thought you were going to jail there for a minute, and the next thing you know, the fucking copper wants to give you the keys to the town? How do you do this?"

"I don't know. Sometimes I even surprise myself," I responded as I watched Buddy fumbling around in his wallet; he was looking for something.

"There it is," Buddy confirmed as he pulled out a business card and was examining it. "I hope there is more than one Mudcat in this town."

"What do you mean? What's up?" I asked as I tried to examine the business card that Buddy had. On the card, it was advertising everything from boat rentals to fishing charters. There was a picture of a fisherman on a boat holding up a whale of a fish. "Look at the size of that fish." I had recognized Mudcat as the fisherman from the other night, but I didn't want to let Buddy know—not quite yet anyways. "I would think that there would have to be more than one bottom-feeder in this town, seeing that it is the catfish capital of-the world."

"As a surprise, I put a deposit down; on going fishing tomorrow on the lake. It was for all of us," Buddy reported as he got a serious look on his face. "There has to be more than one Mudcat, don't you think?"

I remember hearing a few responses from Paulie that went something like this. "Isn't that nice? … You do love us … I have never gone deep-sea fishing before … Do we have to bait our own hooks? … I'll get seasick; I know I will … Do they have washrooms on board the ship?"

"Paulie, we are going fishing on a lake, not the ocean," Buddy tried to reassure him. "It'll be fun fishing for catfish. You'll be fine."

"I don't want to fish for some kind of slippery, slimy, mudpuppy," Paulie cried as he tried to suppress his gagging. "I'll get sick."

"Paulie, you'll be fine," I assured him. "I'll look after you."

"Count me in if I can drink," Johnny interrupted. "Can you imagine landing one of those three-hundred-pound lunkers?"

"Johnny, you can't catch them that big," I informed him. "What are ya thinking?"

"How do you know? … Have you ever caught one?" Johnny tried to argue. "Do you not remember when I took Mom fishing on the St. Lawrence, and she caught that fifty-pound bullhead? … Now that was huge. It was a log. I think it took her three days to reel it in. It almost dragged her out of the boat a couple of times."

"Johnny, it wasn't fifty pounds. And it sure as hell wasn't a bullhead. And three days?" I tried to reason with him.

"Hey, you weren't there. Do you even know what a bullhead looks like?" Johnny tried to set me straight. "And it's my story, fuckhead."

"Do you guys ever listen to yourselves argue?" Buddy cried as he hurried out to make a phone call. "O'Malley, I hope you haven't fucked this up for us."

"I'm sure it will be okay, Buddy," I tried to reassure him.

A few moments later, Buddy stomped back into the restaurant, pissed. "Way to go, O'Malley … You fucked up another good time."

"What …?"

"It's the same fish guy. He's in the hospital. Not sure when or if he will ever get out, and as she said, I don't give a fuck," Buddy cried as he gave me an unsympathetic look. "She has no knowledge of my fishing trip. Basically, she told me, lots of luck on getting your deposit back and to fuck off."

"Oh well. Easy come, easy go. Let's go golfing," Johnny interrupted. "At least we won't have to hold Paulie's head when he pukes."

"We're not going anywhere until I get my deposit back," Buddy warned as he held his hand out.

"But, Buddy, you just said that you didn't think you were going to get your deposit back." I tried to help. "Come on; I'll buy you lunch."

"Come on? That's not good enough. I need some cold, hard cash. Right here," Buddy demanded as he pointed to his open hand.

I think Johnny was the first to cave; he threw a five-spot into Buddy's hand. "You owe me a beer."

"That's a start. Now, come on, guys; you can all do a lot better." Buddy begged, and everyone started to throw anywhere from a dollar to ten dollars into the palm of his hand.

"Can someone lend me ten so we can get going?" Of course Paulie had to solicit for more funds to help his best Bud out. "What the hell; how about twelve dollars?"

"That's not good enough." Buddy cried for more as he was sort of quickly adding what was in his hand and was coming up short.

"All righty then. Here you go, Paulie. Here's fourteen dollars. Will that help?" I said as I threw the money into Paulie's hand, and he just as quickly pocketed his new riches.

"Paulie," Buddy screamed. "That's not for you."

"Oh, I was just testing to see if you would notice." Paulie laughed, digging out the fourteen dollars from his pocket. Both he and Buddy recounted the entire handful very slowly together to make sure all of the money was accounted for. "Come on; let's go golfing."

On the way to the course, we lined up the teams and made a few bets. Because of Paulie's stupidity at breakfast, I put him on the other team for the first time this week. And the way it all worked out, I negotiated to have Buddy on my team. I was thinking I was not going to be much good to anyone this morning. Having to learn a new swing with a handcuff on, having a raging hard-on, and I still couldn't get my master out of my head. It didn't work out too badly; my right hand gripped through the left cuff and on to the grip of the club. It was like having a thicker-than-normal golf grip. I believe the only downfall was that I acquired a blister from the gripping of the club. I didn't play too badly but ended up losing by a couple of strokes for the first time that week. And you guessed it, Buddy lost too. But the most important thing was that Paulie was on the winning team, so he did not have to eat grits on his pancakes at breakfast. He would be able to enjoy his pancakes and syrup at breakfast tomorrow morning and brag all he wanted.

After golf, I rushed into the lobby to find my Sally Sue. I had to get her back; I had to get her back now. There was Sally Sue, my beautiful Sally Sue; I had found my master. There she stood behind the front counter with another front-desk clerk, and as soon as she saw me, she bellowed over at me, "Sweet Jesus. Mr. O'Malley, get in my office now if you know what is good for you."

"Yes, yes, I'm coming." Her command was like music to my ears. I had waited all day for this. I needed this. I needed for her to bark out more orders toward me. The other thing that was happening all day was her two songs kept playing in my mind: "Mustang Sally" and "Start Me Up." Most times there usually was only one song playing, but when two songs started to alternate, you knew it was going to be good. Then a third song started to play for my Sally Sue: AC/DC's "Thunderstruck." Wow, this was going to be really great.

As I walked across the reception area's ceramic tile in my golf shoes toward her office, my shoes were making a loud "Clickity-clack, clickity-clack" sound. She shouted out, "Sweet Jesus, boy, this is not a golf course. Take those fucking shoes off nowwwww."

I was in heaven; I'd been naughty. And she was ordering me around. She had the same control of me as she had the night before. "Yes, yes, whatever you say," I said as I reached down and kicked my shoes off.

I urgently got back to her office, and she quickly shut and locked the door; then she unsympathetically yelled at me, "You have been naughty. Get the fuck over here *now*, and don't you dare look at me."

I rushed over to her, trying not to look at her, and said, "I have been bad. I've been very bad."

"Andddddd," she scolded me as she swung her hand across my backside, "fuck, you are a slow learner."

"Ummmmm, oh, Mistress Sally Sue." I gasped.

The next thing I knew, she took me in her arms and gave me one of the most long, enjoyable, uncontrollable kisses ever. It lasted forever. As we stood there necking, she put her hands down my pants, like she was looking for something. When she found out that I still was wearing her granny panties, she emphasized, "Sweet Jesus, boy, you still have them on? You have really been a bad boy."

And as soon as those words had been uttered out of her mouth, I shot the moon. That was what I was looking for; that was what I had been waiting for. It was a total weak-at-the-knees moment. Wowwwwwwwww.

She sheepishly looked at me and said, "How was that? Now you can take those panties off. But only if you are ready and want to. Just remember one thing: every time you do put them on ever again, you are mine and only mine. You are my naughty boy. Got it?"

I quickly undressed and took those fucking panties off. She would not have control over me ever again. What liberation; what a relief. She pulled a brown paper bag from her desk drawer, along with a key, and handed it to me. I promptly unlocked the handcuffs from my wrist. In the bag was my missing running shoe. Along with her panties, I handed her her scarf and said, "Thank you. That was great, but I won't need these anymore."

"Are you sure?" Sally Sue questioned me as she took me in her arms once more and gave me the most sensual kiss ever.

"Well, okay, maybe I will take the scarf for a keepsake. Oh, what the hell, I might as well take the panties too. But I'm never putting them on again. Never. Well, maybe I will, just on those special occasions," I tried to convince myself.

"Now get out of here. You're no good to me now," Sally Sue growled.

To be honest, special occasions did occur. But only when I could call my master to make sure it was okay with her. Phone sex was brought to a whole new level. The panties are getting quite holey now, and all the frilly stuff has been worn off. The sheerness of them was translucent to start with, and now they are visibly transparent. Over the years I always thought about mailing the panties back to her after a special occasion. I would get them all packaged up and ready to mail, and then it was like I could hear her voice in the back of my head, which would say, "Oh, Sweet Jesus, boy, just put them on one more time. You've been naughty." She still had control of me. Was I under a spell, was I hypnotized, or what? Fuck, she was good. But till I mail them back to her, they are mine and only mine.

I sure did look at Sally Sue differently the rest of the week. Every time I would run into her, I was hoping, waiting for her to slap me or command me to do something. I wanted her to yell at me; I wanted her to control me. And I defiantly wanted her to kiss me. What a kisser.

I stayed in touch with my master over the years because she wanted me to, or was it because she made me stay in touch? I would phone her for a quick fix whenever possible. I would also make the fifteen-hour trip on more than one occasion. And when we were south, it was always quick in and out. All I can say is that when I was touched, I was touched by the best. I was like a junkie; I could never get enough. And as soon as I came down from my fix, I would be looking for another.

Master Sally Sue had retired long ago from the Happy Holiday Hotel. Fittingly, she had set up her own business … "Sally Sue's Domination." She and Sammy were still together, and he had retired from the military. They both lived very happily off the fruits of Sally Sue's business. They finally did move from the trailer park and found a more suitable place in the country. It was a gated community with one of those cement ponds in the back. She had to move; she needed more space for the business. But in her business, what she really needed was a dungeon, so she had one built in the basement.

So when I got an email from Tomeka that my master had passed away, I was devastated. Then I was ecstatic that I was finally going to be free. Free of the power she had over me, free of the spell she had on me. So I thought. I was devastated. I was confused. I was relieved. I had all these mixed emotions. What would I do now? Would I find someone else? Could I find someone else? How would I find someone else? How could I replace my master was the real question?

I knew that I had to make the trek one last time. I had to pay my last respects, I had to say my goodbyes, but more importantly, I had to find my salvation. I had to do it for me. I made up all my excuses and lies and headed south …

The funeral and wake were not held at the local funeral parlor but at the local sports arena. There were thousands who showed up. Ninety-five percent were men. Was she everyone's master? If she was, I was thinking business must have been very good. The funeral was set up like a dungeon, with all types of paraphernalia hanging from the ceiling and walls. A dominatrix would have a field day there; they had all the things that a master would ever need or use. There was BDSM furniture scattered around the room, like spanking benches, bondage chairs, crosses, slings, and of course, beds with leather restraints. There were things there that I was not even too sure what they were or used for. It was more like a sex show than a funeral. There were a few dominatrices in costumes, walking around snapping their floggers. It looked like they were handing out business cards; they were soliciting for business.

I could see that most of the men were from different walks of life, but they all had one thing in common: Mistress Sally Sue. I was sure they were from every profession. There were a few still in uniform, whether they were from the military, fire department, or the sheriff's office. I even recognized Sheriff Andy Griptith, although I believe he was no longer the sheriff, taking his age into consideration. His trusty Deputy Barney Fife had taken the sheriff's job long ago. I recognized Zackery from the Happy Holiday Hotel. He still had the same NASCAR hat and that old, dirty-green shirt on that he wore the day that we checked in twenty-some years earlier.

Although I never was formally introduced to Tomeka, I knew I recognized her from that night so long ago. All of a sudden, "Jump" started to play, so I knew I had to meet her, up and close. I went right up to her to introduce myself. "Hello, my name is Shannon, and you must be Tomeka; Sally Sue talked about you a lot. You were her best friend for life."

"You're Shannon. Now I recognize you. I know now what Sally Sue meant. We sure could have had fun that night. It sure seems like it was only yesterday," she stated with a little whimper.

"It sure looks like she touched a few lives out there," I sneered as I gestured around the room. "Was she everyone's master?"

"Yes, and then some. This is just the tip of the iceberg. I believe I sent out over five thousand emails," Tomeka claimed.

"Wow! What's with all the other doms here?" I inquired.

"She put it in her will that she wanted all of her submissive-subs looked after. She had a lot of weak subs that would need help finding their way, finding a new master. What better way than to have a bunch of her competition here to help with the transition?" Tomeka declared as she pointed around the room to a bunch of weaklings sobbing in the corner.

"I guess she thought of everything," I observed.

"Do you need me to introduce you to a new mistress?" Tomeka asked.

"No. Oh, no. I'm fine. I just came to pay my last respects," I lied, as I didn't want her to see the pain that I was really in. I really didn't want to look like one of those weaklings over there in the corner. And besides, I had to get one a little closer to home.

I'm sure everyone thought that day that they were coming to pay their last respects to a most beautiful person, to a mistress, to their master. They didn't realize that they were being handpicked by a new master. All the masters there were of power, and they all knew it.

Tomeka gave a beautiful eulogy that day as many a man wept.

CHAPTER 20

Paulie Found Love, Then He Lost It

One of the reasons that Johnny would always join us to go south for golf every year was that they had dentist offices in South Carolina that could replace your whole set of dentures within hours for about half the cost. It was almost as fast as a drive-through. You got there in the morning, they took impressions of your teeth and gums, and you came back after lunch, and they would have a brand-new pair carved out from the finest oak in the Carolinas. As Johnny would say, they had the finest master carvers; they were called master-whittlers in the South. They were worth every penny. So every two or three years, he would get a brand-new pair whittled to perfection. He usually would save so much that it paid for his golf trip down.

The next morning, Theodore and Johnny were going to get his new set of teeth done. They had to head north on Route 95 toward Florence. On the way north, they would drop us golfers at the golf course and then with any luck be back to pick us up on their way home.

We were all up early and down having breakfast with our favorite waitress, Miss Vicki. By the end of the week, she got to know us quite well. It didn't matter what time of the day it was, as we would wander in, she would show up with Bloody Marys like clockwork. I'm not sure why we were up so early; it was pouring rain, and the weather forecast did not look any good at all. We all decided that we were not ducks; well, Buddy decided that he was not a duck, and we all followed suit. I guess everyone concluded that if Buddy was not going golfing, no one was. It just would be no fun if Buddy was not there to pick on. I guess the training of others to pick on Buddy was starting to pay off.

Johnny and Theodore headed off to get Buddy's teeth done. The rest of us stayed behind to have another round of drinks. It looked like the rest of the day would be some TV, poker, and heavy drinking. It was going to be a great day.

By now, we were back in someone's room. We were going to have a high-stakes poker game. The problem was no one wanted to play for money. It seemed that everyone was running out of money. They had either bet too much or drank too much all week. Someone suggested we just play for tees. So we all agreed that tees would be the wagers, with no dollar amount. I think it took over an hour of fighting and arguing before we settled on medium tees being worth twice the value of short tees and that long tees were worth twice the value of medium tees. We had just gotten everything settled when Paulie threw a monkey wrench into the equation. He threw his big bag of short red tees on the table and said that colored ones should be worth more. Then the argument started all over again.

I think Buddy was dealing, and he announced, "To make the first hand simple, we are playing dealer's choice. We are going to play a little five-card stud, and nothing is wild. It's going to cost you ten short ones to get in. Oh, what the hell, you might as well throw one of your longer ones in also."

Paulie tried to interrupt with a question about color. "Uh, does …"

"And, Paulie, I don't give a fuck what color they are. So shut the fuck up." Buddy glared at Paulie as he handed him his last card.

"That's too rich for me; I'm out," Kevin said as he pushed his hand in.

Pudden asked, "If all my tees are the same size, does that make them all long ones or all short ones?"

"What color are …?" Paulie asked.

"Paulie, color doesn't fucking matter. Did you not hear the last conversation?" Buddy interrupted as he was really starting to get irritated with him.

"I know, I know. I just wanted to know if he wanted to trade some of his colored ones," Paulie tried to explain himself.

"Ughhhh, fuck off, Paulie. When we get home, I'm just going to kill you. You will never know when it is going to happen. But just expect it. It will happen," Buddy threatened him.

"Why wait?" I asked.

"Because I'm going to kill you first. And then him. The way I figure it, mercy killings have to be lighter in Canada, even if it is for two," Buddy cried as he pointed at us both.

"You might want to plead insanity. You might be better off," Stewart added.

"There is no insanity here. I know exactly what I am doing and how I am going to do it. I've got it all planned out. It's going to be premeditated." Buddy tried to explain his intentions.

"Buddy, why you always got to be like that? Can you not see we have a poker game going on?" I pleaded with Buddy.

"Hey, Pudden, do you want to buy some long tees? I have lots for sale—ten dollars apiece," Stewart offered as he held up one of his oldest, dirtiest, broken tees for him to examine.

"Oh, that's too rich for me," Pudden answered as he was about to throw his hand in.

I interrupted by saying, "I'll give you ten long ones, and I'll give ten small ones to Kevin for ten dollars if you want."

"That's still a little rich for me," Pudden admitted.

"Take it bro, and I will pay half," Kevin butted in with as he reached around for his wallet.

"Okay, okay. That sounds good to me. But can you make a few of them colored, as you never know when you guys are going to make colored ones worth more," Pudden added as he also reached in for his wallet.

"Will you guys just fuck off? Don't anybody say anything about colored tees," Buddy warned us one more time.

"Buddy, what about big white plastic tees? This one has a stripe on it," Paulie inquired as he held up the red-striped tee. "Are stripes worth more?"

"Paulie, just shove it up your ass. I don't give-a-fuck. Keep it up, and I'm going to go take a nap," Buddy screamed at Paulie.

"But, Buddy, you can't. And besides, this is so much fun," Paulie pleaded.

"Yes, I can. I can do anything I want. I'm on holidays," Buddy warned him.

"But we are in our room. You won't be able to nap with all this noise going on, will you?" Paulie tried to state the obvious.

Looking around, Buddy realized that Paulie was right, so he stated, "Just keep it up, and you guys will have to go somewhere else."

Then it just got stupid. When it got around to Paulie's deal, he stated something like seven different cards were wild. If you thought it was stupid arguing about the value of tees, now we were arguing about our hands. We had so many five of a kind to flushes, it was just stupid. It took a bit of arguing, but we finally did get it all figured out. I was gathering up the cards to deal next.

"Paulie, if you want to play stupid, we will. We are going to play War," I informed him.

"That's a kids' game, isn't it? That sounds stupid. I'm going to bed. Everyone out," Buddy threatened.

"Come on; just one more hand. You will like it. It's called Poker-War or War-Poker, or maybe it's Casino-War; I don't know. It's got to be called something." I pleaded with him to stay.

"Okay. I'm warning you, though. This is going to be my last hand because I'm going to lie down and take a nap," Buddy growled.

I was trying to explain the rules of the game as I was dealing out the cards. I didn't even get everyone dealt before the arguing started all over again. Then there was a knock at the door.

"Come on in," Buddy yelled.

Just then Zackery came in the door with a big cooler of ice and said, "Are you guys not going golfing today?"

"It's pouring rain out. This is drier, and it's more funner," Paulie told him.

"It stopped raining about an hour ago, and the report I got was that the bad weather is happening north of us. It has gone around our little slice of heaven," Zackery reported as he swung open the door farther to reveal that it had indeed stopped raining and that the sun was trying to peek through the clouded sky.

"What are we waiting for?" Buddy asked as he stood up to look out the door.

"Well, for one thing, we don't have any wheels. Remember? Johnny went to get his teeth carved today," I informed everyone as they got up from the table to look outside to make sure that it had indeed stopped raining.

"I can give you a ride if you want," Zackery offered. "You're supposed to be playing at Shady Hills National, aren't you? It's just down the road from here. I can get you there lickety-split."

"Hell, why not? Let's do it," Buddy happily agreed.

"But can we finish our hand first?" Paulie enthusiastically asked.

"No. Go get dressed," Buddy yelled.

"I bet you have a good hand, don't you?" I said.

"I think I do," Paulie maintained as he pushed all of his different-size tees to the center of the table.

"We don't have time for this," Buddy whined.

"But I need the tees," Paulie cried.

"If you are going to be that fucking-stupid, then prepare to lose, bitch." Buddy scolded Paulie as he also saw fit to push all his tees to the center. "You know, poker is a lot like sex; it's always better when you go all-in."

Just then the rest of the guys pushed all their tees to the center. From what I could see, someone was going to be walking out of there with hundreds, if not thousands, of tees. Someone was going to get rich.

Everyone started to stand up around the table, just like the pro poker players do on TV when they are playing their last hand. Suddenly, Paulie pushed himself up from the table. You guessed it. The table collapsed from all the weight. Down went the table, with all the tees hitting the floor. As each beer hit the floor, they detonated, spraying the side of Buddy's freshly made bed.

"What the fuck. Paulie? Watch what you are doing," Buddy screamed as he tried to jump out of the way of the exploding beer. "You are going to clean this up."

"I didn't mean it. It wasn't my fault," Paulie tried to apologize as he also tried to get out of the range of the beer spray.

"Now you guys are going to smell like Pabst all day, and that's not a Blue-Ribbon smell," I stated as I hurried to the bathroom to grab Buddy's freshly laundered towels to soak up the mess.

Just as I threw his towels on the beer-drenched floor, Buddy screamed again. "Nooo, don't fucking do that."

"Too late," I answered as I stomped on the towel to absorb the lagered ale. "If you can't get rid of the smell, Buddy, want me to exchange another tile?"

"Noooooooooo. Speaking of which, where is my fucking tile?" Buddy cried out. "You leave my tiles alone."

"It's no trouble at all. I can get that changed," I tried to reason.

"Everyone, out now," Buddy interrupted as Paulie went down on all fours, trying to fill up his pockets with all the tees that were on the floor. Once his pockets were full, he started to gather the rest up with the newly formed pouch that he made with the bottom of his golf shirt. It was sort of funny watching him, as he would come across a broken or dirty tee, and he would just throw them away over his shoulder.

So the rest of the week, every time someone went into Buddy's room, they would spill a little more beer onto that carpet tile. And the funny thing is, I didn't have anything to do with that. It seemed everyone else liked to watch Buddy explode also. By the end of the week, that tile started to smell a little ripe, just like skunky beer. Occasionally, Buddy would step there; it would soak his socks, and he would just scream, "Fuck, Paulie. See what you have done. I can't believe that it is still wet, and the smell … it stinks like stale beer in here."

The six of us got out front with our coolers and golf bags, and around the corner came Zackery in his black S-10 pickup truck. It had a big NASCAR #3 painted on the door. The rest of the truck was covered in decals. I guess it was made to look like DALE EARNHARDT'S racing Dodge. He must have been a bigger fan than we thought. One thing about S-10s; they are really not that big. I believe Pudden, because he was the biggest, got in the front seat with Zackery. That left five of us in the back, with our clubs and coolers. Zackery was a good old boy; he had a black leather couch up against the rear window. We were all pretty crammed in there. But it did not matter; we were going golfing, and besides, it was not far to the golf course.

Pulling out from the Happy Holiday Hotel, Zackery gunned it. The little S-10 must have had a little extra power under the hood, as it laid a little stretch of rubber down the highway. I don't think we were a mile from the inn, and the next thing we knew, the sheriff had come up behind us fast, with his flashing lights and siren on. I don't think Zackery was speeding, but who knows? He did lay down a little rubber leaving the hotel. Or maybe it was because it was not safe in the back of a pickup truck. We should have been all right because this was South Carolina; you don't even need a helmet to ride a motorcycle there. That's just stupid …

The sheriff pulled us over. What had Zackery done wrong?

"Keep your beers down and hidden," I told everyone.

"Uh-oh, we are all going to jail," Paulie cried.

"No, we're not," I tried to console Paulie.

"Oh, shut up, Paulie. We're not going to jail," Buddy yelled.

Sheriff Andy Griptith climbed out of his squad car and walked up alongside our NASCAR knockoff. "Did one of you guys lose a hat as you squealed out back there?" he asked as he approached our truck, holding on to a black hat.

"Hey, Paulie, it's your pesky wyboo hat," Stewart said as he recognized the logo on the front.

"Oh, it is. It must have blown off when we took off back there," Paulie acknowledged as he felt around the top of his head, looking for his hat, which was not there.

"I tell you, you would just lose your head if it wasn't attached," Buddy retorted.

"Thank you. That's my new lucky hat," Paulie thanked the sheriff as he handed him his hat.

"Oh, it's you, Shannon. You guys sure lucked out with the weather today," The SHERIFF commented. "How's that wrist of yours?"

"Wrist? What? Oh, yeah, it's much better today. Thanks. The guys won't have to give me any strokes today," I said as I raised it above my head, shaking it, to show him that I was good as new.

"Strokes? What strokes?" Paulie worried.

"Paulie, will you just shut the fuck up? I'm going to give you a couple good strokes to your fucking head," Buddy threatened him.

"You guys be good, and Zackery, you get them there safe. And please keep it under a hundred, you hear?" Sheriff Andy Griptith warned Zackery as he banged the side of the truck bed.

We got to the golf course all in one piece, and we all tipped Zackery well for saving the day. To make a long story short, it did not rain the rest of the day. When Johnny and Theodore got back to the Happy Holiday Hotel and found out that we were not there, they drove to the course and picked us up.

When they arrived at the course, we were just finishing up on hole eighteen, so I asked, "What took you so long? How did Patricia like your new teeth?"

"Patricia? She sure … Oh, we didn't go back that far," Johnny said with a silly smirk on his face.

"Are you sure you …"

"I told you, we went to get my new carvings," he said as he gritted his teeth to show off his new yellow-stained dentures.

"Should they have not used some brand-new white oak instead of that secondhand driftwood?" Paulie said as he tried to grit his teeth with a smile to match Johnny's pearly whites.

"Are you sure you didn't go have something to eat?" I asked again as I was still unsure if he was lying or not.

Paulie piped up, "Did you go motorboating without me? I knew I should have gone with you guys this morning."

"No, Paulie, we didn't. Really," Theodore maintained.

To this day, I'm not sure if they went back to motorboat or not. Pretty stupid if they hadn't …

That evening we were relaxing back in the bar at the Happy Holiday Hotel. We were all drinking quite heavily. When did we not? There were a few locals in there. We were all having a great time. Especially Paulie. He had taken a hankering to one of the local ladies. Her name was Eleanor and was she ever drunk. She was older, a lot older. Maybe she was in her sixties. Paulie would have been an old forty, a very old forty. She was a chamberbabe from another local hotel. I think Paulie said something to the effect of, "Can you imagine if you had booked us at that hotel? Wow. That would have been the best trip ever. Just imagine."

I came back with, "I would have never called it that."

"Just imagine. That sure would have been some ugly fucking," Buddy stated.

Paulie was still thinking that he was going to get lucky that night. If he could only feed her enough booze. He had spent all his money and everyone else's money that he had borrowed. There was no stopping him. He just kept buying her drinks. She was old enough to be his mother and ugly enough to be his sister. But he was drunk, and she was beautiful in his eyes. There was no way to convince him otherwise. She just kept flirting enough or gave him enough attention to receive another drink.

I think Johnny spoke up and said, "Paulie, you keep this up and nobody will be able to afford to buy chicken in Pennsylvania on the way home."

"Look at her. She is worth every dime," Paulie stated with glistening eyes. "She is so beautiful."

"I hope you guys don't have any kids." Buddy stated the obvious. "Fuck, they'd be ugly."

"That's never going to happen. Do you not see how old she is?" I said.

Buddy came back with, "Thank God. There's enough ugly in the world."

"I'm right here," Paulie slurred.

"Hey, Paulie, if you are going to make this work, maybe you should go upstairs and freshen up or something," I tried to encourage him.

"What do you mean?" Paulie asked.

"Go upstairs and, I don't know; change your underwear or something. Maybe wash your undercarriage. Get rid of that yeast infection, at least. You know, freshen up. Do something," I advised him.

"No, I'm fine. Everything will be fine," Paulie claimed.

"Well, at least go upstairs and put some of Buddy's whooer-looer on. Hell, put some of mine on. It's right beside my TV. You don't need much; it's strong. She just won't have a chance," I boasted.

"Okay, okay. I'll be right back," Paulie finally agreed. "Now don't let her leave," Paulie added as he scurried out of the bar. He was going to get ready for a night of passion or maybe just some good ole ugly fucking or maybe just some fucking ugly.

Anyways, Paulie had been gone for some time, maybe a half hour or so. Eleanor was getting restless, and rejection might even be setting in as she worried. "Where did my little stud muffin go? Do you think he is okay? Is he coming back?"

"I think I'm going to puke," Buddy stated.

"I don't know; maybe he got cold feet, or maybe he is waiting for you upstairs. He's in room number …" I tried to console her.

"Fuck off, O'Malley. That's my room. Don't you dare give her that room number," Buddy cried.

"Come on, Buddy. Why would you stand between true love?" I inquired.

"Why do you encourage him so? Will you just leave the poor bastard alone?" Buddy whined.

"I'm only trying to help him get laid," I retorted.

"He's not going to get laid. You know that. And he has spent all his money again. Someone will have to lend him some money again," Buddy cried.

Paulie still had not come back, and the bartender was kicking us out. Eleanor had just left with someone else. Now our concern had turned to worry about Paulie and where he was. "So before we go out for our usual nightcap, we better find Paulie and make sure he is alive and well."

We got upstairs, and Buddy went into his room; I did likewise into my room. We both yelled, "Paulie, Paulie, are you all right?"

There was no answer. As I opened my adjoining door, there was Paulie passed out. He was leaning up against his door, and I said, "Found him. Here he is, Buddy."

Just then Buddy opened up his door, and Paulie fell back into his room. Trying to wake him up, Buddy wondered, "Paulie, what in the fuck are you doing?"

"Paulie, where have you been?" I asked. "We were worried about you."

"Oh, what's going on? I must have accidentally locked myself between the two doors," Paulie retorted as he tried to pick himself off the carpet.

"Where's your key, Paulie?" Buddy demanded to know.

"I must have left it in the room. Because I came through Shannon's room to get some of that smelly stuff on," Paulie tried to explain.

I interrupted, "How much did you use? I told you that you didn't need much."

"Paulie, did you bathe in it? It sure stinks in here," Buddy cried. "But it sure does smell better than that stinky-beer smell."

"I only used seven splashes. That should be enough, right?" Paulie reported. "Anyways, I thought I could just sneak into our room. I went to push on our door, realizing that it was locked."

"Like it is supposed to be, right?" Buddy added.

Paulie, trying to explain, said, "Right. Somehow, I pulled your door closed on me, which locked, trapping me here."

"The most important thing is you are okay now," I tried to comfort him.

"More importantly, where's my Eleanor? Is she waiting for me downstairs?" Paulie cried.

"Sorry, Buddy, she waited as long as she could for you. The two old guys, Johnny and Theodore, took that beautiful lucky lady home," I teased him.

"Oh, no, say it ain't so," Paulie cried as he thought for a moment that they did in fact take Eleanor home for an Eleanor Sandwich.

"Oh, well, easy come, easy go," I tried to console him.

"That fucking slut, that fucking crack whore. She doesn't know what she is going to miss," Paulie cried as he fumbled around looking for his inhaler. "But I loved her; we were going to have a life together. And I could have had children with her. We would have named our son Urian, you know, after my father and his papi. I could have kept our legacy ongoing. You know, it would have made them all so proud. It would have been so magical."

"Paulie, shut the fuck up and go to bed," Buddy yelled.

"Okay," Paulie agreed.

Me and Scott went out for our nightly nightcap over at Double-D's. Our day would not be complete if we did not go and see Fanny. There was nothing better than Fanny putting us to bed in a nightly fashion.

CHAPTER 21

Buddy Finally Finds His Tile

We were all up early. We had an early tee time as usual. Just a quick three S's: shit, shower, and shave. Then it would be down to meet our wonderful breakfast person, Miss Vicki.

I was sitting there enjoying one of my S's. You know which one; no one sits down to shower or shave. And you guessed it, I was enjoying the solitude in Buddy's bathroom. I was isolated and secluded, so I thought—until Buddy barged in and started to scream, "What in the fuck are you doing? How did you get in here?"

"What does it look like I'm doing? I'm having a shit, you idiot," I informed him as I threw the-end-of-the-roll tube at him. "Oh, by the way, you are out of toilet paper."

Buddy disgustedly backed out of the bathroom from the smell; then I heard him phone the front desk. "Do all the guest rooms in your hotel have their very own bathroom?" Then there was a short pause. "Then why in fuck is this ugly fucker, having a shit in my room?" I heard another short pause, and then I heard the receiver slam down. "They are on the way, to throw you out."

"Come on, Buddy, I'm just about done here. I've got this big turtle, and it is just starting to peek its head out. It's almost there."

"Will you just fuck off? Why do you have to talk about your shit that way?"

"You wanted to know," I answered with a grunt and a groan. "Hey, what do you use to knock the head off it with?"

"I don't use anything. What are you talking about now?" Buddy yelled from the other room.

"It'll never go down if you don't knock the head off it first," I tried to warn him.

"Oh, will you just fuck off?"

Just then Paulie stuck his head in the doorway, so I asked him, "Hey, Paulie, come on in. Do you want to see something huge and neat?"

"Yeaaaaaaaaaaah. What is it?"

"Look; have you ever seen anything so gigantic in your life?" I asked as I stood there in amazement.

"Wow, I have never …"

Just then Theodore stuck his head around the doorway and said, "What's going on? What's all the ruckus about?"

"Come on in. You got to see this. Look at the size of this." Paulie marveled at the length of the unit. "I guess you really are the biggest O'Malley."

"Oh, my God. Is it always that big in the morning? How does a guy your size have such a huge thingamajig?" Flabbergasted by the size, Theodore went on to say, "That thing has to be over a foot long."

There we all were standing around the toilet admiring this log when I realized that they were not looking at the log but something else. "Not that, you stupid fuckers. In the bowl, you dummies."

Someone spoke up and said, "Wow, that's even bigger. How do you get such a huge thing out of your ass in one piece? It will never go down, I tell you."

"Look at the way it has curled around the bowl." Paulie was still astonished by the way it had already started to curl for the spiraling descent down.

"How come you use Buddy's toilet every morning?" Theodore asked as he backed himself out of the washroom from the stench.

"Why? Do you feel left out or something? Do you want me to start using your bathroom?" I asked as Johnny walked in to join the gathering. "I can; you know I can."

"Like fuck you will. That's my room," Johnny cried out.

"It makes me so mad," Buddy stated.

"It's, it's just a ritual. Oh, it's more than a ritual. It's, uh, I'm just reaching out to him. I love him so," I said as I tried to get someone to believe me … anyone.

"I think you should find some other way to show that you love him," Theodore warned. "One of these days, he's going to snap."

"I know. I just want to be there to see it," both me and Johnny said in unison.

"Don't worry about that. I'm sure one of you fucking O'Malleys is going to be there," Buddy threatened us.

Just then there was a knock on the door. It was Zackery. He had come up to see what all the commotion was. Or maybe he had come up to see Buddy explode, or just maybe he had come up to see this anaconda lurking in the bowl. "Buddy, what seems to be the problem? Sally Sue sent me up to make sure Shannon was okay. Where is he?"

"I'm in here."

"I'm the one that called. I'm the one that needs the help. I don't give a flying fuck about Shannon." Buddy interjected. "You just get him the fuck out. I got to have a shit."

"Zackery, don't worry about him. I'm the one with the problem." I tried to get him to come into the bathroom to take a look.

"What's wrong?" Zackery asked as he came around the corner.

"You should see it. You won't believe the size of it," Paulie piped up.

"I hope you brought something with you to knock the head off it," Johnny added. "You probably don't know that he is the biggest O'Malley."

"You are going to need a plunger," Theodore warned him. "A big one."

"Wooooowwwww. Holy fuck, that's gigantic," Zackery marveled at the spectacle all curled up in the bottom of the bowl. "Have you tried flushing it down yet?"

"No, I didn't want to flood Buddy's bathroom," I said as I stepped aside to let Zackery flush. "I don't want Buddy to be mad at me."

"You are such a good friend. I don't know why Buddy says such bad things about you all the time," Zackery responded.

"I wouldn't do that …" I warned as I headed for the door. "Everybody out. She's going to blow."

I heard someone say, "Blow. It will go down, won't it?"

"Oh, it will go down. We have these newfangled toilets that no matter what you have in there, it's going down. Just as long as there is nothing plugging or stopping it, it's going down," Zackery informed us as he reached over and turned the handle down. "These new toilets use a little more water but have a much bigger bowl, so there is less clogging, less mess. I don't have to play in the shit anymore."

"I don't know; that's a pretty big turd," Paulie cried out as he watched the flush go around and around. The bowl started to slowly fill up, and the next thing you saw was it started to spill over the sides. "I told you it wouldn't go down."

"I don't understand," Zackery puzzled as he danced around in the puddle that was forming. He grabbed for towels to soak up the mess.

"I told you, you had to knock the head off it first," I advised them as they all were dancing around trying not to get their feet wet.

"There has to be something else that is blocking the flow," Zackery cautioned as he flushed it one more time; with the same results. He grabbed for more towels to help soak up the second mess. "Are you sure that there is nothing else down there?"

"No, it's taken it down all week. I don't know what the problem is," Buddy stated as he looked around for some sympathy from everyone. "O'Malley has crapped in here all week."

"How's your toilet next door?" Zackery asked. "It hasn't given you any problems all week, has it, Shannon?"

"No, not at all. Well, I don't know. Come to think of it, I don't think I have used it. Because I have used …"

"You have used this one all week," Buddy interrupted me as he echoed my statement. "Seeeeeeee."

"Well, I got to go and get a snake," Zackery stated as he headed out the door. "Don't touch anything."

"Are you fucking nuts? We're not touching anything," Paulie agreed. "I think we are all going down for some breakfast anyways." We all started to head toward the door, so Zackery could clean up and maybe fix the problem.

We got downstairs and had all gathered together at the doorway to the restaurant. Buddy had forgotten his golf shoes again and gone back upstairs to get them.

Miss Vicki came up and said, "Good morning, guys. Just give me a minute, and I will throw a table together for you all." As she walked away, she added, "Shannon, can you see if you can close that door for me? It seems to have been stuck open all week."

Knowing full well why it was stuck, I answered, "Yeah, No problem." I tried to close the door. "It's really stuck on something."

At the entrance, there were these two French doors, both propped open. I still went through all the motions of trying to pry the one door from its open position. I started to let everyone in on the secret—that Buddy's ripped tile was wedged in under the door. We were going to try to set Buddy up one more time. I had arranged to have every one of us take our turn to try to close the door. I said, "Buddy will come up and try to help. He always wants to be part of everything. He won't want to be left out. He is like that."

Buddy walked up and said, "Has anybody seen my brand-new Nike socks? I can't seem to find them." Before anybody had a chance to answer him; Buddy's attention was diverted toward Paulie and what he was doing. He had one foot on the wall and both hands on the handle trying to pry the door from its stuck position. Paulie was giving his best academy performance. "Paulie, what in the fuck are you doing? No, what in the fuck is O'Malley having you do?"

"No, it wasn't Shannon. It was Miss Vicki, with-an-eye. She said the door was stuck and wanted to see if we could close it for her," Paulie added as he pulled his foot down from the wall. "I can't get it; it's stuck on something."

"Shouldn't Zackery be fixing this?" Buddy said as he was taking a good look at the problem door.

"He probably should, but I think he is unplugging your toilet, isn't he? Or maybe he is getting you more ice," I said.

"Holy fuck, guys, I don't need any more ice," Buddy cried as he gave the stuck door a little pull.

"But we do. So shut the fuck up," Johnny urged. "I'm tired of drinking all your rotten skunky warm beer.

Always trying to help, Buddy said, "See? It's catching on this doorstop on the bottom here." He gave it one big yank that almost pulled it off the hinges, and all you heard was a big "Wwwwaaarrrrrrrriiiiipppppppp."

And then all you heard was, "Sweet Jesus, Mr. Parker," Sally Sue screamed as she walked up behind us. Looking down at the ripped tile, she added, "What have you done now?"

"Nothing, nothing at all. The door was stuck, Miss Vicki. Uh, I should say that fucking O'Malley made me do it," Buddy cried.

"O'Malley? You're not blaming poor Shannon again?" Sally Sue tried to protect me as a good master would. "I don't even see him."

"O'Malley, tell her," Buddy urged as he looked around for me. "Where have you gone now?"

"Buddy, what have you done?" I charged as I walked out of the restaurant. Picking up the torn tile to examine it, I added, "This looks like we have seen it before."

"Whatttttt?" Sally Sue wanted to know more.

"Nothing, nothing at all," Buddy cried as he finally clued in that this might indeed be his missing ripped tile.

"Mr. Parker, how come I always am catching you doing something wrong, and you are always blaming your poor friends?" Sally Sue accused him as she shook her head in disapproval. "Sweet Jesus, what am I to do with you?"

"He'll be all right. I'll look after him for you. I will make sure he is good the rest of the stay, Mistress, uh, Sally Sue," I answered as I almost let the cat out of the bag. "Hey, Buddy, why don't you go upstairs and get that tile out of your room that smells like skunky, old beer? I think they are about the same color."

"Sweet Jesus, you have what?" Sally Sue stood there with her arms folded, trying to understand. "Let me get this straight. Buddy has just torn a tile in my lobby, and he has a matching tile in his room that he wants to exchange it with that smells like warm, pissy beer."

"Yeah, I think you nailed it," Johnny agreed as he had heard enough and started to head in for a morning pick-me-up. "Can we go now? I'm thirsty. Who wants some grits?"

"Nobody is leaving nowhere until I get some answers." My beautiful Sally Sue was taking control.

"Butttttt," Johnny cried.

"But nothing. Who is going to pay for this?" Sally Sue charged as we all glared over toward Buddy.

"Don't look at me. I haven't done anything wrong," Buddy tried to answer defensively as he picked the ripped tile up from underneath the door.

"Oh, I'm sure Buddy will pay for this. Won't you? Just put it on his bill," I stated as I tried to get the situation under control.

"I'm not paying for ..." Buddy cried out as he threw the ripped tile at me.

"We will take a collection up. It can't be that expensive to replace a couple of tiles, can it?" I interrupted as I put my arm around him to lead him away to breakfast. "Come on; I will buy you breakfast."

"How stupid do you think I am? Breakfast is included in our package," Buddy claimed as he tried to wrestle my arm off his shoulders.

"Okay, then. How about I get Johnny to buy us lunch today, and I'm sure he will include a couple of beers with that," I said as I looked over toward Johnny. "Won't you?"

"I sure will. Just as long as we get going soon. I'm getting pretty thirsty," Johnny agreed as he again headed into the restaurant.

"Okay then. But I'm still going to keep an eye on you, Mr. Parker. You only have a couple of days left here. I wouldn't want to have to throw you out," my Sally Sue threatened him one more time.

"I'll make sure he behaves. We all will. Right, guys?" I promised as I turned toward her and winked.

"Sweet Jesus, I think you will all have your hands full," Sally Sue said as she started to head toward her office.

Just then Zackery came around the corner, and he was holding his plunger upright; from it dangled two, stinky, stained Nike golf socks. "Buddy, are you looking for these? See what I found in your toilet? No wonder it was plugged." Zackery laughed as he tried to balance the socks from falling. "What a mess it made. I haven't seen anything that bad since last month, when I found a hair blower in the shitter."

"How the fuck did they get in the toilet?" Buddy cried as he tried to rub the tears from his watering eyes. "O'Malley …"

"Don't look at me. Well, I did tell you, you were out of ass-wipe," I came back with. "I had to wipe up with something, didn't I?"

"Oh, I'm going to kill you. They were brand-new," Buddy warned me.

"Buddy, they will clean up. You can still wear them today," Paulie said as he tried to defuse the situation.

"But, Buddy, they were too short for you. They were. They made you look really short, and …" I argued.

"They were golf socks. They are supposed to be short." Extremely upset, Buddy demanded, "Is it ever going to end?"

"Noooooo."

"Well, it is, because I'm going to kill you. Not once but twice. Hell, I might even kill you the third time," Buddy boasted. "It all depends how much I'm going to enjoy it. I might even have Paulie piss on you a couple of times."

"Oh, I could never pee on Shannon. That's not right," Paulie claimed. "How do I always get mixed up in all this?"

"You'll piss on him if I tell you to," Buddy informed him.

"Shannoneeeeee, he's starting to scare me." Paulie looked for help.

"I'm going to cut you up into some very small pieces, stuff you down the toilet, and have Paulie piss on you," Buddy threatened. "Then if you are not careful, I will do the same to you, Paulie."

"It's okay, Paulie. He's starting to scare me, too." I tried to calm Paulie down. "You know, Buddy, they have programs geared for this. You should think about enrolling."

"I don't need no fucking program. I just need for you to die," Buddy argued.

CHAPTER 22

It's Time to Head Home

Today was the day; our vacation was coming to an end, and we had to head home. So it was a sad day for everyone, but in a way it was a little bit of a relief to finally have to go. That morning we were all up early, while some of us never went to bed. We still had to pack, check out, play some golf, and if that wasn't enough, drive sixteen hours home, a piece of cake. I'd done it before with less sleep and was sure I would do it again.

First, we had to get everyone packed up and ready to leave. I knew we were going to have problems, as everyone dragged all of their belongings toward the van; and besides that, we still had to all check out.

Buddy spoke out. "O'Malley, will you go check out for me? I think that Sally Sue, that slave driver, doesn't like me very much. I'd rather not see her again if I don't have to." And in my mind, I was thinking that was all I wanted—to see her again and again.

"Yeah, no problem, Buddy. You get us all loaded up, and we will go in and get checked out," I stated as the rest of us headed inside. "She has your credit-card on file, right?" Not that I needed it because I had memorized it long ago, and I was pretty sure I could match his signature to a T.

"Yep, she does," Buddy agreed, as I was sure he felt relief that he did not have to go and confront the old battle-ax. "Here's my key. Make sure she gives me my key deposit back. Take Paulie with you and make sure he pays his fair share."

"Okay, guys, let's go pay the piper," I proposed. "You get everyone loaded up, and we will go say our goodbyes."

We all took our turn on checking out, paying whatever extra charges we had incurred for the week. As Sally Sue got to Buddy and Paulie's room, she spoke up. "And where is that Mr. Parker anyways?"

"Oh, he is helping Zac load up." I handed over Buddy's key as I added, "Here is Buddy's key."

"Sweet Jesus, where is the other key?" Sally Sue asked.

"I seem to have misplaced it," Sweating profusely from his forehead, Paulie spoke up. "Shannoneeeeee."

"Sweet Jesus, young man, what were you thinking? I would have thought it would have been Mr. Parker who would have lost his key, not you," Sally Sue addressed us as she scribbled something down on the statement.

"I know, right?" I added as I knew exactly where Paulie's key was; it was in my back pocket.

"Well, it is going to cost you that deposit," Sally Sue sternly stated as she scribbled some more stuff down on the bill.

"Why is it so expensive?" I questioned as I confronted my master. "It's only a key."

"You have to understand. Our national policy here at the Happy Holiday Hotel is when someone loses a key to a room, we have to change the lock to the door. No matter what," Sally Sue tried to explain. "We don't want someone finding a key and then barging in on some unsuspecting hotel guest."

"I guess you are right. I have never thought about it like that," Paulie reasoned as he fumbled around looking for money that he knew he did not have.

"Don't worry, Paulie. It's only twenty dollars; we will just add it to Buddy's bill," I said as I tried to comfort him. "You can just owe him."

"Okay, but I would hate to see Buddy lose his deposit on something I did," Paulie worried out loud. "He'll just yell at me again. Oh well."

"So, Sally, I know you have to pay Zackery to change the lock. That's what the twenty-dollar deposit is for, but what if when we get home and Paulie finds his key in his luggage and he mails it back to you, will you give Buddy his twenty dollars back?" I asked as I tried to get all the information possible from her.

"Sweet Jesus, Shannon, I couldn't do that. I would have to charge him another twenty dollars to change it back to the original lock," Sally Sue reassured me with a smile.

"You would do that?"

"I sure would, I have to," Sally Sue answered quickly.

"I guess I better not look too hard for it then," Paulie stated as he was worried that Buddy would have to spend more money on his stupidity.

"Paulie, for some reason, I'm pretty sure you will probably find it," I confirmed as I grabbed a business card of the hotel and handed it to him. "You will need the address if you find the key."

"I hope not," Paulie cried as he folded the card up and put it in his pocket. "Promise me you won't tell Buddy that I cost him that key deposit."

"Don't you worry, Paulie. I would never tell Buddy; it would just upset him more, right?" I said as I tried to ease Paulie's mind. "I better take a card just in case you lose yours. And when we get home, me and your mummy will help you look for that fucking key."

"Come on, guys. Let's get going," someone said.

"Yeah, we should get going," I approved as I took Buddy's new itemized bill from Sally Sue. "Does it have …"

"Yes, it's all there," Sally Sue interrupted me.

"What about …"

"Sweet Jesus, boy, I got it all." She quickly interrupted me again with a smile.

"Good," I agreed as I hastily looked at the bill. "I just wanted to make sure it was well itemized before I give it to him." I folded it up all neatly and tightly and put it in my pocket for safekeeping. I wanted to give it to him at the most opportune time.

Let's see, from what I could see on the bill, we had a new flower bed, four times he was charged for faxing golf vouchers to the golf courses, quite a few rounds of drinks, a key deposit, and it looked like he bought a few carpet tiles for his room. I thought he was getting off pretty lucky, though. Considering he didn't have to buy a new toilet for his room or buy that shitter that he ruined, and how about not getting charged for that flower bed that he let me drive through at the entrance to the golf course? But the best would come later. A couple of months from now, he will have gotten over the initial shock of that large VISA bill and have just started to talk to me again. When all of a sudden, he'll gets his new VISA bill, and it would have another twenty-dollar key deposit from the key that Paulie will find and mail back to the Happy Holiday Hotel. I couldn't wait …

Just then Sally Sue came around the counter to give everyone a hug. "Y'all come back, hear?"

"We sure will," I agreed as we gave all the rest of the staff hugs goodbye. "Come on, guys, we still have to say our goodbyes to Miss Vicki."

"Sweet Jesus, I'm going to miss you guys." As she gave me a tighter hug than everyone else, Sally Sue whispered in my ear, "You will remember me. You will …"

As I unwrapped myself from her tight grasp, I mouthed, "I love you. I will miss you, my Mistress-Sally Sue." Oh, I wanted to kiss her so but knew I couldn't right then and there.

We stepped into the restaurant to say our goodbyes to my favorite schoolteacher, Miss Vicki. There she was, standing at the entrance in her best teacher's outfit. It was her only teacher's uniform because she had dressed in it all week. Her arms were folded, her foot was tapping the floor, and she was giving me a look, over her round glass frames. "Where have you been? Were you not going to come by and say goodbye?"

"Oh, Miss Vicki, I was saving the best for last," I lied as I headed over toward her to plant a big one on her beautiful puffy lips.

"Get over here and give me that big kiss goodbye before I have to punish you," she scolded me again as she took me in her grasp and wouldn't let me go. What is it with all these women down here in the South? They all want to be in control, and all they want to do is punish you. How much arousal can one person take so early in the morning? Lots, I say. Lots."

We all finished our goodbyes so we could get out to the van to help Buddy with all the loading. Finding room for all that extra stuff that we were bringing home would be a challenge. Although we did not need the roof rack for the trip down, it surely would be loaded fully for the trip home.

There we were in the parking lot of the hotel, and Zackery was up on the van's roof stowing whatever he could. As fast as he secured one bag, we would throw up another. I think even Zackery was going to be sad to see us leave, or at least sad to see Buddy leave. 'Cause Buddy was always the one who had to tip Zackery for the ice for the day or for anything else that we needed for our stay.

"Zackery, I don't remember having this much stuff when we arrived," I yelled up to him.

"You're right. I don't remember unloading this much stuff," Zackery agreed as he caught another bag from below.

"I don't remember buying any souvenirs." I tried to find the answer. "Zac, did you pack Buddy extra ice or something?"

"Noooo. That would be just stupid," Zackery came back with. "Well, I did pack a little extra ice for Paulie. He said something about stopping in Pennsylvania for some cheap chicken and tree sauce?"

"Paulieeeeee," Buddy screamed. "We are not stopping for chicken."

"Pleaseeeee. Come on, Buddy," Paulie whined. "Then can we at least stop for some maple syrup?"

"Nooooo. We are not stopping for anything," Buddy warned Paulie. "We are going to be late for our tee time."

"Okay then, next time I invite you over for breakfast, I'm not going to give you any syrup for your pancakes," Paulie tried to threaten him.

"Paulie, you have never invited me for breakfast before," Buddy stated. "Why would you now?"

"Because Mum has told me that I should start inviting friends over more often," Paulie informed him. "She is a pretty good …"

"Are you sure your mother isn't looking for a date? Maybe even a father figure for you," I interrupted him. "Hey, Paulie, do you think you could call me Daddy?"

"Noooooo, Shannon, that's my mummy you're talking about," Paulie claimed. "I'm sure all she is looking for is a hot breakfast."

"I'll give her a hot breakfast!" I joked. "No matter how old she is, even if I don't eat breakfast."

"Paulie, it doesn't matter, because I'm not stopping," Buddy maintained. "And besides, I'm pretty sure you don't have any money left."

"Money left? Did he ever have any money?" I laughed as we all knew Paulie was out of money the day we left Canada a week ago.

"Oh, don't be like that. I'm sure someone will lend me some money," Paulie claimed. "And they will be the first to be invited over to have breakfast with me and Mummy."

Like clockwork, everyone took their turn on answering poor Paulie on lending him money or dating his mummy. "Noooo … I'm broke … I got no money. I don't like to lend money to friends … Johnny, why don't you lend Paulie

some money; she's about your age. I don't eat breakfast …
Is that how Mummy gets dates? … How old is she again?"

"Guys, that's my mum," Paulie cried.

"Paulie, here is another twenty dollars for … for … for
maple syrup. Yeah, that's it, for maple syrup," I quietly said
as I slipped him the money.

We were all packed up and almost out the driveway
when I decided that I had to say goodbye one last time to
my Sally Sue. I knew it wouldn't take long. "Shit, I forgot
something back in the room. I'll be right back."

"Leave it; we still have eighteen holes of golf to play,"
Buddy countered.

"I'll be right back. I forgot to say goodbye to my Mast …
Sally Sue, I mean."

"Whattttttt?" Buddy wondered out loud what I was
up to.

"Nothing. I think I left your seven-iron in your
bathroom."

"My seven-iron? Why would you have my seven-iron
in my bath … Oh, never mind. Don't answer that," Buddy
grumbled.

"Well, I didn't want to get mine all shitty-like," I
interrupted before he finished.

"Shitty-like? What are you talking about?" Buddy cried.

"Well, you know, when you have just laid that perfect
log and it won't flush down in the toilet right … You know
what I …"

"You better the fuck not have done what I think you did."

"How else would you get it down the hole? You know
you have to knock the head off it first, and if that doesn't

work, you have to poke and prod it down into the bowl." I laughed as everyone else joined in.

"I'm going to kill him if there is so much of a ... if I even smell shit, I'm going to kill you." Buddy screamed bloody murder as I started to hurry inside.

As I got almost to the door, I could see that everyone else climbed out of the van to check their clubs to make sure that they were all there and that they weren't used for shit prodding. I thought to myself, this will give me a little extra time to say goodbye to my master. It's funny how things worked out. The rest of the day when we were golfing, if someone saw a mark or blemish on one of their clubs, they would bring it up to their nose for a smell.

For the last couple of days of our trip, I tried to stay away from my master as much as possible. I was trying to get accustomed to not having her around. You know, not having her control me the way she did. It was a losing battle; no matter how hard I tried, every day it seemed that I would end up right beside her. I was like a little puppy dog, with my tail a-wagging; I was waiting for approval. No, that's not right; I was waiting for her to command me, to order me. What was the control she had over me anyways? How did she do it? How was I ever going to survive without her when I got home? How was I ever going to get rid of this; or for that matter, did I even want to get rid of this feeling? Was I hypnotized? It was like, as soon as she gave me that look, I was drawn over right beside her side.

I had no control, and as soon as I heard the words from her commanding voice, "Sweet Jesus, what are you looking at? Get your sweet little ass over here right now," I was there right beside her side, waiting for her to give me approval. But each time, I was cast aside, rejected and dejected.

That fateful morning, she only kissed me goodbye and ordered, "You will always remember me."

It was like I blacked out, because I had no known memory of what went on after the kiss goodbye. One minute, I was giving her a passionate kiss goodbye listening to "Start Me Up" in my head, and the next thing I knew, I awoke to having a dump on Buddy's toilet with his seven-iron in hand.

Oh well, it was like one good thing led to another …

CHAPTER 23

No Motorboating Today

After a quick round of golf, we were finally headed home. I was sure we would all be hungry by the time we got to the motorboat store. Although it was the middle of the afternoon, I was sure we could force ourselves to eat some breakfast. We just had to convince the rest of the crew that they were hungry also.

"Paulie, do you think you could eat some more pancakes and syrup?" I tried to convince him as I pulled off the thruway.

"You had me at syrup." Paulie perked up, thinking he was going to get another needed fix of sugar.

"I know the perfect spot."

"We're not stopping ... No one is hungry ... Are you crazy? ... We just got on the road ... What are you thinking? ... I would rather have a nap ..." Almost everyone put in their two cents until they found out where I was stopping.

"Yeah, I'm not really hungry either. Okay, I will just pull back onto the thruway. Soooo, no one wants to go boating today?" I said as I drove past the marina.

"Where are you going?" someone screamed as I looked back and saw that everybody's head was on a swivel following the BOOBIES-R-US sign.

"Boating, you idiot. Of course, we want to go motorboating," everyone screamed in agreement.

"Too late. I just drove past it," I reported. "And you know we are not allowed to do back-me-ups, turnarounds, or do-overs on this trip. And I'm not paying the twenty dollars to do it."

It seemed to be quiet in the van for some time, as no one wanted to step forward and agree to the new expenditure. I even started to slow down the van to get someone to speak up. I was about to turn back onto the thruway when Paulie finally spoke up. "Okay, okay, I'll pay the twenty dollars. Can someone lend me some money?"

"No, I can't lend you any more ... I got none ... I'm never going to get it back, am I?" a few answered as it seemed everyone wanted to go for a boat ride, but no one wanted to pay for it.

So there we sat at the entrance to the ramp for the thruway, waiting for some time for someone to get off their wallet. Buddy finally spoke up. "Okay, Paulie, here is another twenty dollars. Your total now is three hundred eighty-three dollars. I can't believe that I have lent you that much. I'm going to have to put you on a payment plan or something."

"Good luck with that. He has already promised me his first, second, and thirdborn. But we all know that that's not going to happen because his swimmers are always swimming solo," I said.

"Are you sure it's that much? I'm thinking it was closer to forty-three dollars, wasn't it?" Paulie disagreed with the total. "And Shannon, what are you talking about? Are we going swimming now?"

Buddy had no sooner handed me the twenty than I had the van turned around and headed back toward a beautiful afternoon boat ride.

We needed to say goodbye to Patricia and the rest of the girls. As we walked in, we received the friendliest greeting. "Shannon and Johnny, I was hoping you guys would stop in on your way home. I was thinking I'm ready for that little twin action you so promised me." As she greeted us at the door, giving Johnny the longest hug, she said, "I can see you brought in a few extra friends with you."

"Oh, these guys … they decided that they all wanted to come in to see what they missed out on the first trip," Johnny responded as he gave her a tight hug back.

"You know, now that I take a closer look at you two, you must be twins. It really is hard to tell you apart," Patricia jokingly said.

"Only our mother can tell us apart, you know. But I will let you in on a little secret. I'm the biggest O'Malley. You want to see?" I joked as I gave her a much bigger and tighter hug than Johnny.

"I don't know. I think you told me that the last time. I don't think that you are that much bigger?" Patricia added as she stepped back to take an overall look at us.

"That's not what I meant," I bragged as I pretended to start to remove my pants.

"Shannon, you are such a kidder," Patricia teased back as her face turned a little red. "That's my job, don't you know?"

"Hey, Kid, I think you are embarrassing her; look at her," Johnny added. "I know you are embarrassing me."

"Sorry, Patricia, but we had such a great time last time, we had to come back for more of your Southern hospitality."

"Enough of that Southern shit," Stewart argued. "I came back for those luscious boughten boobies."

"That's enough of the small talk. I'm hungry," someone said. "What's on special today?"

"I hope we are boat racing today?" Paulie enthusiastically cried out. "I've been practicing all week."

"Practicing?"

"Yes, it's a great, great day for motorboat racing," Stewart piped up with his best Jackie Stewart impersonation.

"Sorry, guys, there is no motorboating racing today," Patricia informed us. "This afternoon, we have waffles and fruit …"

"That's my favorite," Paulie interrupted. "And what does it come with?"

"Paulie, give her a chance to finish," Johnny scolded him as he himself could not wait for the answer. "And what does it come with … eh … eh?"

"Well, it comes with two thick fluffy waffles imported from Belgium, freshly frozen fruit, maple syrup, and of course …"

"And … and …" someone butted in.

"Whipped cream, of course."

"I'll take two," Paulie ordered. "This has to be the best trip ever."

"I thought you said that it came with something, something extra special?" Buddy piped up as he seemed dejected. But I could see that he still had not taken his eyes off any of the boobies of the girls who were working over in the distance.

"Did you not hear her? It's waffles from Belgium; they are the best. What else do you need besides maple syrup?" Paulie argued. "Maybe ice cream …"

"Oh, did I forget to tell you that it comes with your very own thirty-second lap dance?"

"Well, that doesn't sound very long?" Buddy, though skeptical, still seemed very intrigued by the whole idea. Was this really going to happen?

"Thirty seconds … I'm sure that's all I could take after eating all that syrup," Paulie enlightened everyone. "I'm sure going to try my damnedest not to be an early preemie this time."

"Paulie don't even try. You won't make it, I tell ya," I warned him.

"Yes, I know. But I got to try, don't I?" Paulie reassured us all.

Patricia, blushing again, spoke up. "So, who are your friends?"

As I went around the table introducing everyone to the girls, Paulie piped up, "How do you remember their names?"

"First, Paulie, they are not just pieces of meat." I tried to educate him. "And second of all, you have to learn to look only into their eyes."

"I don't know if I can do that. I can't get past …"

"Patricia, why don't you bring us eight of those specials of yours?" I quickly interrupted Paulie and ordered for the group.

"Coming right up," Patricia answered.

Johnny said, "You are going to have one of us fall in love all over again."

"What do you mean?" Patricia questioned. "Because it comes with a lap dance?"

"No, well, okay, that too. No, it's just that Paulie is the connoisseur of maple syrup. He can probably tell you when and where it was tapped from. Right down to if it is real or that knockoff shit that they are making from corn from Chineee ... Imagine ..." Johnny informed her.

"Look at his shirt. See those spots? Anybody else would think that they had an explosion of ecstasy. Not Paulie. That's just maple syrup from breakfast all week," I added.

"Wow, that's a lot of syrup." Amazed at all the spots, Patricia started to walk away to place our order. "I need eight specials. Make one with the real maple syrup; we have a connoisseur."

"Look at all the booooo ... girls, Buddy. Don't you just love them?" Paulie said.

"This is amazing; they are all different sizes, colors, and shapes. I can't believe you guys let me sleep through this the last time," Buddy whined, as it seemed his head was on a swivel and he could not stop staring at all the girls.

"Can you imagine if this was back home? What a way to start the day," I enlightened everyone.

"Pinch me," Buddy said as he thought he was in a dream.

"But that's not the best part. This is," I said as I pinched Buddy's cheek. Then I pulled beers out for everyone from the inside of my coat.

Just as I pulled out the last of the beer, without hesitation Patricia showed up at the table with takeout cups. As she set them down, she said, "Shannon, I figured you would need these."

"I think I am in love," Buddy said in admiration. "This is just getting better and better. You keep this up, and I might take you home."

"Do you want to phone Marilyn to see if you can?" Johnny laughed.

"I told you she was good," I added. "You haven't seen nothing yet. Wait till you taste the food. And then don't forget about that special somethin somethin."

Just then, over in the corner, one of the girls was sending another trucker off. She was gyrating those hips like there was no tomorrow. Boy, if anything ever got caught up in that gyration, she would have snapped it right off.

"We call that twerk heaven," Patricia bragged.

"I think I want to have a franchise," Buddy stated.

"I don't know, Buddy; I have seen you twerk before. I'm afraid you would scare most men away."

"Women too …" Pudden chuckled.

"Fuck off. You know what I mean."

We ate quickly so we could get to our special surprise at the end. It was like eating Cracker Jacks just so you could get to the prize. We paid the bill and were ready to go; just one last thing to do. One by one everyone took their turn for their special something.

Just as we got to the end for our anticipated dance, there were only Johnny and I left, and Patricia piped up, "I got something special for you two." The next thing I knew, she had us sit side by side. "Get closer …"

She started by giving us the best lap dance. As one would say, she was the best twerker ever. But that wasn't the best part. The next thing I knew, the other four girls were climbing all over us. They were climbing a mountain that wasn't there. Well, maybe it was.

We said our goodbyes, and out the door we went, promising that we would all be back soon. It became a must, that special stop every time we went south. As the years went by, Patricia became a little older and a little bigger. Johnny fell more in love with her with each year that passed. Or should I say with each pound that she gained. I think finally some trucker made an honest woman of her. When she left or finally retired, the service was never quite the same. The young'uns never really were able to fill her shoes, or I should say bra. But it didn't matter how bad the service was, you had to stop for the food. It was unbelievably good; it didn't matter about the service or the girls, right? … Of course it was about the girls and the service.

CHAPTER 24

Sir, Do You Know Where Your Keys Are?

One annoying thing that Paulie did continually throughout the trip was ask questions. There was no question too stupid for him to ask. He asked over and over again. One question always led to the next. If it could be asked, he would ask it. Although we all put up with it for the week, it was really starting to annoy Buddy to the fullest. On the way home, Paulie got so bad that Buddy pulled over, not once but twice. Each time he threatened that he was going to duct-tape Paulie to the roof rack, but only after he had stuffed his mouth full of Johnny's underwear. That only shut him up for about five miles. All I can say is for Paulie's sake, it's a good thing that the roof rack was packed full with ice …

Paulie was getting closer to his allotted time to pull over and have his much-needed piss break. Buddy was driving; Paulie was in the back seat with Johnny, and Paulie was getting more fidgety with each passing mile. We had just gotten into six lanes of rush-hour traffic in Richmond,

Virginia. Buddy had his foot to the floor as he was trying to keep up with all the evening commuter traffic. Although Buddy was not doing badly, it was becoming apparent that it would be a losing battle. This three-quarter-ton van was loaded up with the eight of us, with all of our clubs and luggage; I was sure we were overweight. Not to mention the weight of the twenty cases of cheap beer that we were going to try to smuggle across the border. Buddy was preoccupied with all the traffic. We were going seventy-five miles per hour, and we were just not keeping up. Occasionally, you would hear Buddy cry out, "Scotty, I need more power."

And Stewart, with the worst Scottish accent ever, would come back with, "Captain, I'm givin' her all she's got. She caun't take much more. She is gonna blow."

"Captain, captain, I gotta pee, I gotta pee," Paulie cried out in his best Scottish accent as he tried to fit in with the rest of the gang.

"Shut the fuck up. Can you not see that I'm busy up here?" Buddy cautioned him. "I'm trying to keep everyone alive here."

"I can see that, but it sounded like you guys were watching a movie or something." Paulie cackled. "But seriously, I really, really have to go."

"I don't fucking …" Buddy screamed back at Paulie just as the van did a little swerve to miss the transport that had just cut us off. "Holy fuck, that was close."

"Great job … I didn't even spill a drop," Johnny thanked him as he took another gulp of beer. One thing about Johnny: when he took a mouthful of beer, he was always missing his mouth. He always had a wet stream of beer sliding down his chin onto his shirt.

"Are you sure you are all right? You look like you are turning red right before my eyes," I suggested as I looked back toward Paulie.

"I knew it. I feel I'm going into septic shock here," Paulie said. "I'm going to die if you don't pull this bucket of bolts over soon."

"Pull over? Where in fuck am I going to pull over?" Buddy countered as we could see that the traffic was racing by on either side of us. "And Paulie, do you even know what septic shock is?"

"No, but I'm sure I will get it," Paulie pleaded hypochondriacally. "I'm starting to feel full and puffy. Look how swollen I look."

"It's too bad that you don't have that harmonica of yours. I'm sure if you blew into it, he would find a spot to pull over." Johnny laughed.

"You fuckhead. Oh, I'm so sorry, Paulie, that i called you a fuckhead. I hope I didn't hurt your feelings. Will you ever forgive me?" Buddy sarcastically apologized.

"Oh, it's okay. I know you …"

"Well, you stupid fucker, I meant to call you a stupid fuckhead. Where do you think I'm able to pull over?" Buddy glared back at him through the mirror. "I'm in the middle lane going a hundred miles per hour. Maybe I should just stop right here?"

"Would you?"

"No, you stupid fucker. Where in fuck are you going to piss?" Buddy insisted.

"Right here. I could hang it out the door and just let it go," Paulie pleaded. "I really, really have to go."

"No, you won't. If I stop, I will just push you out on your fucking head. See how long you would survive in all this traffic." Buddy laughed.

Someone suggested, "We should start up a pool on how long Paulie would survive out in all this traffic."

Just as that was said, everyone started to speak up to get in the pool, and me being me decided that I should pass Paulie's hat around to put the money in. "I've got five dollars ... I have a fiver ... I think he would be killed before we pulled away ... Would he be able to piss before he got hit? ... Buddy, I'll give you five dollars if you stop and let Paulie out in this traffic ... I think he would be killed before he got his unit even out."

"After you die, would you still be able to piss yourself?" Paulie asked another stupid question.

"Okay, let's find out." Buddy snickered as he started to slow down to let Paulie out. "Knowing you, you would still be able to piss yourself, but the problem being you wouldn't be able to feel it 'cause you would be fucking dead."

"What are you doing?" Paulie worried.

"Oh, I'm stopping to let you out to piss," Buddy described as the van was coming to an imminent stop. "Isn't that what you wanted? And besides, we have a pool going on. You want in?"

"No. You know I have no money. And I'm not getting out here. I need you to pull over to the side." Paulie kept arguing with Buddy for quite a while about stopping, not stopping, pissing, or not pissing.

Would they just make up their minds? I think everyone was getting tired of all the bickering that they were doing.

Paulie was about to piss his pants and screamed, "Look, I got piss up to here. I can feel it up to here." Paulie took his hand up to his throat to show how far his piss had risen. "I can taste it."

"Jesus, will someone give him something to piss in?" Buddy begged.

"Like what?" I asked.

"I don't fucking care. Someone give him a juice box," Buddy urged.

"A juice box? I'll need something bigger than that," Paulie protested. "I can't take much more."

"Someone must have a beer bottle, don't they?" Buddy added. "Give it to him already, will ya?"

"Here, Paulie," someone said as they had passed back a half-empty bottle of beer. "You will have to finish it first."

Paulie hurriedly took the bottle and downed the remaining drink. "Fuck, that was stupid. I really have to piss now. That's not going to be big enough either. I've got gallons to piss out."

"Fuckhead, you don't have gallons," Buddy retorted.

"But I do. I think I'm going to drown … gurgle … gurgle …" Even his speech seemed to sound underwater, or should I say toxic piss? "Anybody got a gallon jug?"

"Oh, ohhhh, I got one … No, I don't, you stupid fucker. I always carry one when I go on vacation, you stupid fucker," Buddy joked. "Does anybody have an empty liquor bottle that he can piss in?"

"It's not empty yet, but I have a vodka bottle that is close to being empty," I told him as I took a large swig of that Russki concoction; then I passed it on to Johnny.

"No, thanks," Johnny declined as he tried to pass it back. "I have had my fill of vodka today."

"There's no thanks, nothing," I asserted as I passed it back to him. "Do it for Paulie."

"Okay," Johnny finally agreed as he guzzled down his portion and passed the bottle on to someone else. Everyone drank their fair share to help poor Paulie out.

It finally got back to me to take the very last mouthful so I could hand the empty bottle over to Paulie. "Here you go."

"Thanks. I didn't think I was going to make it there for a while," shy Paulie claimed as he grabbed the bottle in a hurry. All of a sudden, it got awfully quiet in the back seat. You could hear a pin drop—or I should say you actually could hear the warm piss splashing up against the inside of the bottle. "Will you guys make some noise? I can't piss like this, if everyone is listening to me."

"Pssssss … pssssss … drip … drip … drip … psssss." You could hear it so clearly that someone suggested, "Is your flow always like that? You should see your doctor and get some Flomax. Or is it Flonase? I keep getting those two mixed up. You know, to help with your pressure."

"Flonase? I think that's for nasal flow, isn't it?" Johnny tried to help.

"Oh, I think you are right," someone agreed. "But it wouldn't hurt, would it?"

"How would you administer it? Would you still spray it up your nose?" Paulie asked.

"Noooo. I'm thinking that you would have to be very careful. But with a little practice, you would just stick that nozzle right up into the end of your …" Dr. Johnny alleged.

"And then you would give it a good squirt. You should try it."

"Oh, nooooo. I would think that it would sting a lot," Paulie cried. "Wouldn't it?"

"A little, but I'm sure it would fix your problem." Dr. Johnny tried to emphasize his prescription plan. "And I think with pressure like that … Do you find you piss on your feet a lot?"

"Noooooo. Now how would I piss on my feet?" Paulie chimed in, confused.

"Guys. He probably sits down to piss," I added.

"Sit down to piss? Doesn't everybody?" Paulie begged.

"Yes, Paulie, especially if you are a little ole lady," I stressed.

"Sit down to piss?" Dr. Johnny laughed. "I just use that little blue pill called VIAGRA … You will never have to worry about pissing on your feet ever again. You are always ready and willing and standing at attention. You are always pissing straight up like the Fountain of Youth. And they think that li'l blue slice of heaven is only for sexual pleasures?"

Every once in a while, you would hear from the back seat; psssss, then nothing for a while, then psssss. Paulie cried out, "It's going to overflow."

"No, it's not. Will you just fuck off?" Buddy warned from up front.

"It has to be. I'm getting wet back here. I'm going to make a mess. I can just tell," Paulie whimpered, with his hands full, balancing between holding on and getting the head of his pisser stuck in the bottle's neck. "Will someone turn a light on so I can see what I am doing?"

"Paulie, no one is turning a light on. It's bad enough that we can smell it, and we can hear it spray. We sure as hell don't want to see it," Buddy growled as he was still maneuvering between all the traffic.

"I'm going to make a mess," Paulie warned.

"Paulie, for the last time, that bottle you have will not overflow. I'm sure you just have your knob stuck in the end of it. That's why it's splashing up on you," Buddy maintained. "Pull it out. Let some air in, and you will be able to fit more in."

Suddenly we heard a suction pop, and then heard Paulie go, "Ahhhhhhhh. Pssssss. Oh, that's better."

As Paulie finished, he tried to hand the bottle over toward Johnny, who was sitting right beside him. "Don't even think about it. I'm not touching that piss warm bottle of yours."

"But I need help. I can't get it away and hold the bottle. I'm going to drop and spill it," Paulie cried. "I know I will."

I tried to help Paulie out; I took the bottle from him, so he didn't make a mess. "Holy fuck, your piss is warm. Now put that thing away. Where'd the cap go?"

"What cap?"

"The cap for the bottle, you idiot."

"I don't think it came with one." Confused, Paulie fumbled around in his pockets, looking for the screw-on cap.

"Paulieeeeee, you better find it, or you will be holding on to this open bottle for the rest of the trip home," I scolded him as I handed the bottle back over to him.

Not finding the cap, Paulie sat there quietly and motionless for the next couple hundred miles. He was focused on not spilling a drop, as he knew that if he spilled anything, it would not only upset Buddy but everyone else in the van. I was thinking that if Paulie traveled with us again, all we had to do was give him an open bottle of warm piss to hold on to. He sure was awfully quiet and a whole lot less fidgety.

So we finally had made it about halfway home. It was dark, snowing, and just plain miserable out and Buddy had decided that we were going to stop for the night. For some reason he had pulled the van into a skanky motel along the way. It was painted up brighter than a two-bit whore.

"Buddy pull right up front. They might have valet parking," I suggested.

"Are you nuts? Look at this place," Buddy barked. "This sure is no Happy Holiday Hotel, and I'm sure there is no Zackery."

"So why did you stop here?" Johnny asked.

"Oh, me an' Marilyn happened to stop here a couple years ago. It's clean and cheap. It not only is in the middle of all the good food places, but look: it's right next door to a truck stop. And we all know that food has to be the best there is," Buddy informed us. "But the best thing is …"

"Wow, it sure does look like a diamond in the rough," I interrupted him. "Look how brightly it is lit up."

"You can rent your room out for … by the hour." Buddy bragged. "That's perfect, because that's all we need is a couple hours sleep."

"Buddy, by the hour? There is more than sleep going on here." I tried to enlighten his way of thinking. "With that truck stop next door and all those lot lizards running around, it's perfect."

"Do you think?" Buddy asked with a smile.

"Lot lizard? What in the fuck is a lot lizard?" Paulie raised the question as he started to look down at the pavement, looking for any and all creepy crawlers that might be about.

"Paulie, you are in for a treat. Just be careful where you are walking." Johnny laughed. "You don't want to crush one of those lot lizards."

"Leave him alone," Buddy demanded.

As we all climbed out of the van to go check in, Paulie was taking his time, as he still had that open bottle of warm piss in his hand. As he was stepping out of the van, he was looking around for any of those daddy long-legged critters scurrying about. But not paying attention, he tripped and fell out of the van, dropping the bottle of piss, which smashed to the pavement, covering him with piss.

"I guess you don't need this anymore," Johnny spoke up, pulling the cap from his pocket.

"Ughhhhhhhh. Johnny, have you had that the whole time? I had to hold on to that piss for how long?" Paulie cried as he quickly jumped up and tried to shake the piss from his clothing.

"Of course I did. It got your mind off of having to piss every minute, didn't it?" Dr. Johnny countered.

"Yeah, it did, but now I smell like piss," Paulie cautioned as he tried not to step on the broken glass. He was still trying to dab his piss-stained pant leg dry, all while trying to spot some of those creepy crawlers that we had warned him about.

One thing about being close to a truck stop, especially during the wintertime, all you smell is burned diesel fuel that lingers in the air. And the sounds … continually, all you hear are big diesel engines running, air horns, and brake retarders. It can be very noisy at times twenty-four hours a day.

It probably was the only time that week that every one of us was not falling-down drunk. We all had just started to stumble into the lobby when everyone came to a complete stop. They could not believe their eyes. Looking around at the other guys, I saw they were all in different states of shock; they all could not believe what they were looking at. I knew we were in the right place when the song "Mustang Sally" started to play, which brought a big old smile to my face. Did my master follow me? No such luck, but this might work out even better, as I came upon the night clerk. I thought Buddy was going to puke, as his nightmare had followed him home.

There she was—a petite Sally Sue. You would swear she was a mini Sally Sue. She had to be twenty years her junior. Maybe Sally Sue had a daughter? Yes, she had to be. She was the spitting image of her. This girl had the same beautiful, beautiful blue eyes. Yes, that's what they were, beautiful blue eyes. It couldn't be. They couldn't be related; there were way too many states between them. And besides that, she was white. But who knows? Maybe they were mother and daughter. I was not going to ask, but maybe I could get Buddy to; or Paulie for that matter.

Her name was Bobby-Joe, and she was beautiful. Those big blue eyes were the biggest, roundest, you would ever come across. They were mesmerizing. She wore her uniform a little tight, but she wore it well. When I first laid eyes on her, I was going to fantasize about her being a dominatrix, just like that look-alike Sally Sue. I was still not sure that I liked being a slave, but I knew I had mixed emotions that I had to look after. We would just see how well she handled me or all of my drunken friends.

"Sweet Jesus, what are all yous looking at?" Bobby-Joe demanded; sounding a whole lot like Sally Sue.

"Nothing, nothing at all," Buddy cried as he peered up from his hiding spot in the back row.

"And you, short stuff, what are you fucking hiding from?" She commanded an answer from Buddy, who was still in his safe place, crouched down behind Pudden.

"He thought he was seeing a ghost," Johnny answered.

"Sweet Jesus, boy, you can see I'm no ghost," Bobby-Joe retorted as Buddy tried to make his way up to the front of the line. "Well, get up here and sign in."

"We need four rooms for the night," Pudden piped up. "The whole night."

Bobby-Joe did some quick calculations as she gave us all a good look up and down. "I don't think you guys could last that long."

"No, no, we are just here to sleep," I answered, but I'm sure she was wondering what the chances of eight queer truckers were coming in for a good night's sleep.

"Sure you are." Bobby-Joe winked as she laughed out loud.

"No, really, we are," Pudden argued.

"Okay, whatever you say," Bobby-Joe joked, as if she still did not believe us. "I don't want you guys to make too much of a mess. I don't want to have to change the bedding again this week …"

"What?" a bunch of us interrupted her.

"Sweet Jesus, I'm kidding," she teased us. "That will be one hundred dollars a night then, but you all need to be out by eight o'clock."

"Eight o'clock?" I asked.

"Yes, eight o'clock. I don't need you interfering with my morning rush hour," she pleaded as she was still examining her registry. "I call it our lickety-split-rate, so those truckers can get on the road quicker."

"How much if I'm out by six o'clock?" I tried to dicker with her to get the best rate, as her song abruptly changed to "Highway to Hell." "God, you are beautiful."

"Well, in that case, just for you, honey, how's seventy-five dollars?" Bobby-Joe looked up, blushing.

"We'll take them," Pudden agreed.

"No, no. Sweet Jesus, you are not getting all the rooms for that price," Bobby-Joe said as she pointed over at me. "Just him. The rest of you will get the ninety-five-dollar rate."

"Even if we are out by six o'clock?" Buddy cried.

"Sweet Jesus, boy. Fuck, I hope you are not the quick one of the bunch."

"No, I am," Pudden argued as he pushed Buddy to the side. "In that case, I guess we will only need three rooms, and we will be out by six."

"I guess I'm bunking with you, Kid, Miss Congeniality of the group," Johnny said. "Here's thirty dollars. That's got to be close."

Bobby-Joe went to hand me my key, but she didn't let go; instead, she winked and whispered, "I hope you sleep well tonight."

"Oh, I will," I said as I tried to pull the key from her clenched grasp. "Will you be here in the morning to check us out, beautiful?"

"Oh hell, yes. I got to make sure you guys are out by six," Bobby-Joe advised as she finally let the key go from her grip.

After we all got settled in our rooms, we all went our separate ways to get something to eat. Everyone had their own safe place to get their daily allowance of grease. It could be the Clown, the King, the Little Red-Headed Orphan, or my favorite, Taco Bell. Not really a good choice for some, because after a week of heavy drinking, I was sure everyone's innards were starting to rumble. Or as I called it, "getting emotional."

Me and Johnny were sitting around our room, just finishing our drinks before we went out for the evening. There we sat, praising and congratulating each other for all the fun that we'd had all week.

We finally headed out toward all the food joints to get a bite to eat. Suddenly we saw someone running toward us, and Johnny said, "That looks like Buddy. I didn't know Buddy could run with those little short legs of his. Look at that troll run."

"It is Buddy. And that's not running; he calls it scampering," I agreed as I was amazed at how fast he could run. "Buddy, what's going on?"

"I can't talk right now." Buddy hurried by us. "I'm gonna, I'm going to shit my pants."

"You are not going to make it," I yelled as both me and Johnny started to laugh. "Run, Buddy, run."

A week of heavy drinking had finally caught up with all the lightweights. The next thing we saw, there were two more trolls and an ogre that raced by, back toward the motel. Johnny spoke up. "Has anybody seen Paulie or Theodore?"

"I think they said something about going to IHOP for some much-needed pancakes and syrup," Pudden yelled back as he tumbled by.

"I thought Buddy looked funny running clenching his ass," I said to Johnny as I watched in dismay. "But you put that heavyweight rolling down the road holding his ass; sure is funnier."

"Yup, he's pretty funny to watch, isn't he?" Johnny chuckled. "How do you think he wipes his ass? I don't see how his short little arms can get around to his butt."

"Well, it's a proven fact that when a fat person sits on a toilet, it compresses their spine somewhat, almost like they are a hundred and fifty pounds or more, lighter. This makes it easier for them to reach around and wipe," I informed Johnny.

"No, I can't see it."

"That's good because I sure as hell don't want to see it either," I agreed.

"That's not what I mean," Johnny argued. "I mean there is no way in hell he can wipe his own ass."

"Well, it's like this; at home, he moved his umbrella stand into his bathroom, right beside the toilet. There he has this newfangled three-foot grabber. It has a soft-grip, ergonomic handle," I lied.

"A what?" Johnny asked.

"You heard me. It's a reach-a-rounder-for-the-big-pounder."

"That's better. Has Mom not told you about using big words?"

"No."

"She will. Remember, you are still in training."

We had a wonderful meal at the King; just the right amount of protein and our daily allotted amount of grease.

We started to head back toward the rooms, and Johnny said, "Do you think we should stop and pick up more beer and pork rinds?"

"No, I think we are good. Remember, someone suggested a long time ago that we always had to finish off all the extra booze that we had left over on the final night," I reminded him.

"Who was that?" Johnny worried.

"I wonder … It was you, you stupid fucker. I can't believe you sometimes. Don't you remember anything?" I tried to reason with him.

"Why would I do that?" Johnny worried.

"Remember? A couple of years ago, you wanted to see how much tequila Buddy could drink, even after he had passed out," I tried to explain.

"That was different. He was the one who wanted to see how much tequila he could drink. I think he was the one that made us promise to pour it down his throat after he had passed out," Johnny chimed in. "Remember, he even went out to the van to get those bungee cords to strap himself in the chair when he passed out."

"No, that's not what happened. It was the three of us. We all made a pact that night that the first one that passed out, we could pour it down their throat." I tried to set him straight.

"Are you sure? I don't even like tequila," Johnny argued. "I would never agree to something that stupid."

"You were there," I reasoned. "You drank your fair share."

"I know I was. But I think tequila obliterates any kind of memory that you may have." Johnny babbled on, "I truly believe that it destroys brain cells."

"I'm sure it does. All you got to do is look at Buddy," I informed him. "Yeah, we almost killed him that night. No one should have alcoholic poisoning for a week."

"I'm sure glad it was Buddy and not me. It really doesn't agree with me, 'cause I think I'm allergic to tequila. I tried to get my doctor to give me one of those poison-sucker-outers."

"A what?"

"You know. One of those needles that you poke yourself in the groin with that lets all your bad-swelling air out of your body," Johnny explained. "You know, so you don't swell up and die. That's the last thing I need is for my tongue to swell up more than it is. It's hard enough for me to talk as it is. And when your tongue swells up like that, it's really hard to puke."

"Don't you mean an epinephrine autoinjector, so you don't get anaphylactic shock?"

"Uhhhh, yup, that's exactly what I mean," Johnny agreed. Now you have to understand that from about that time period forward, anytime Johnny used that line, "Yup, that's exactly what I mean" or "Yup, whatever he said," basically what that meant was he didn't know anything about the subject but was just trying to look extremely intelligent and not stupid.

"Johnny, you're not allergic; you drink enough of anything, it will make you puke," I tried to inform him. "I'm the one that is allergic to tequila. After I drink tequila, it's like uncontrollable heaving, and I black out for days …"

"Maybe we should make a pact not to drink tequila ever again?" Johnny cautioned as he carefully examined the contents of the bottle of Jose Cuervo. I'm not sure what he was looking at. Whether it was that complimentary, round, little, slimy serpent, or maybe he was just looking at how much he was going to have to drink of this toxic stuff.

"Like fuck we will. Then we would lose Buddy on all of these entertaining times. That's his national drink, you know?" I warned him. "Yeah, the last time I ate Mexico's national animal, that fucking worm bit me back. I woke up on a train in Montreal with someone else's clothes on. And the worst thing was I was married …"

"Now that's a lie. You were already married," Johnny interrupted.

"Hey, I'm sure you have been married on more than one occasion. And it's my story; I will tell it the way I want. Or the way I remember it, at least," I tried to set him straight.

"All I can say is you can't blame your marriage on some little defensive preserved worm," Johnny argued.

"Okay, can I at least blame my divorce on that li'l fucking pickled worm?"

"Yes, you can. Yes, you can …"

We were sitting around trying to finish off as much booze as we could; we knew the crew would eventually show up for their fair share of booze that was left. Johnny's pork rinds had run out long ago, and Johnny piped up, "I knew we should have stopped and got more pork rinds. I don't know how you talked me out of it."

"Johnny, if you are having withdrawal pains, just lick anything you have been in touch with. I'm sure you will get the fix you need," I declared as I took my finger and swiped the TV remote.

"It's not the same. You need to be able to crunch on some of those pork membranes that are in there," Johnny informed me as he licked the pork dust off my fingers.

As some of the guys started to feel better, they started to come over to help with the drinking of all the booze. We talked or rehashed about everything that had happened the week before. Most said they wanted to stay here and play some more golf; they all had just found their game. Whereas, I thought that they were all perfecting their flaws.

Buddy came in, got himself a drink, and wondered, "Does anybody have any extra underwear that I could have? And, O'Malley, I don't want your slightly used shit."

"Why, Buddy?" I worried. "What happened? The last time we saw you, you were like a racehorse. Guys, you should have seen him. Who would have thought Buddy could run so fast while clenching his asshole? Or should I say stumbled down the road? How many times did you fall?"

"I almost made it. I just got back to the door and was fumbling around, looking for my keys. It seemed like forever. When …" Buddy reported.

"You should have just left your keys in the door's lock, like we do," Johnny interrupted him. "The O'Malley way. That way you always know where they are. You might have made it."

"Yep, I might have. Just as I slid the key into the lock, it was like an explosion went off in my anal regions. Just be very careful walking by my door. Where's Zackery when you need him?" Buddy confided. "I should have brought him home with me. It sure was handy to have him around."

"What? You are not starting to appreciate Zackery, are you? And everything he did for you all week?" I asked.

"I don't know. I don't think any amount of ice money would clean up that fucking mess in front of my door." Buddy laughed. "They might have to bring in a pressure washer to clean it up."

"Pressure washer? Knowing you, I'm sure they would need a sandblaster to clean up that mess off the concrete," I joked. "Just think, you have left a special welcome mat for their next guests."

"I don't think I would want to stay there. Was it something you ate?" Johnny asked as he went over to his golf bag and pulled out his freshest pair of holey underwear. "Here, I think I only used these for a couple of days."

"A couple of days? I don't want them. Do you have anything fresher?" Buddy whined as he took a drink of his national drink. "I don't want to put anything on that you have had next to your hairy gonads."

"Buddy come on. I'm only kidding. They are fresh." Johnny laughed as he put them up to Buddy's nose to smell. "Here, smell. Tide-fresh, I tell ya."

"I'm not smelling them," Buddy cried as he pushed them away from his face. "Johnny, why do you have underwear in your golf bag?"

"Why? Don't you?" Johnny claimed.

"I always carry a couple pair." I laughed. "You never know when the time will come, and you have to replace a lipstick-laced pair.

"Noooooooooo, I don't." Buddy cackled.

"Well, look at it like this. If you did, you would not need underwear now, would you?" Johnny scolded him as he handed the tighty-whities toward Buddy once more. I hate to call them tighty-whities because they looked more like stretched-out-holey-shitty-brownies.

"Thanks." Buddy picked them up on the seam between his fingernails. It was like he did not want to touch them. "Maybe this was a bad idea."

"Don't look at me. I have already shit in my drawers a couple times this week. I have been going commando for the last three days now. Look." I tried to reassure Buddy that I did not have any underwear to spare as I tried to undo my pants to show that I was indeed going commando.

"What's wrong?" Johnny added as he grabbed his underwear back from Buddy to smell. "They're clean, I assure you—I think. I don't think I got them from the dirty hamper. Here, give them a real good whiff."

"I told you, I'm not smelling them."

"Buddy, they are clean," I tried to convince him.

"How can you tell?" Buddy asked as he shook his head in disbelief.

"Look, there is no pork dust," I tried to explain.

"No pork dust?"

"Yeaah, look at this pair." I went over to Johnny and pulled down his pants to reveal a pork-dusted nutsack. "See? See how the pork dust accumulates around his jewels? Every time he scratches his nuts, it's like he leaves a trail behind of crop-dusting."

"Are you sure that's piggy shit?" Buddy questioned.

"Of course it is. You want to taste?" Johnny assured as he reached down and swabbed his private area and brought it up to his mouth to taste. "That's not bad. There's still some life in these briefs. I think I can get another week out of these."

Reluctantly Buddy took the stretched-out-holey-shitty-brownies into the washroom to put on. A couple of minutes later, out he walked showing off his new stained underwear. He was like he was on a catwalk. The only difference was he was not a skinny, anorexic model, but a fat little troll.

"You want us all to throw up? They don't look any better on you," I told him as I mixed him another drink. "Will you go and put your fucking pants back on? We have some business to take care of."

"What's that?"

"We have quite the mixture of booze to get rid of," Johnny said. "I can't believe we have a whole bottle of Jack left. That's usually the first to go."

"I think you bought it for Theodore. But it turned out that he was allergic to it," Buddy reported. "Something about blacking out for days."

"I don't think it was the Jack. I think he got into some bad ice," I argued.

"Yep, I know what you mean. Bad ice, it sure can get you into trouble. I remember one time …" Johnny laughed.

"What else do we have?" Buddy interrupted him as he did not want to hear for the umpteenth time of the many occasions that Johnny puked. We had heard it all before and then some.

"Well, there is a little vodka, half a bottle of rum … And what is this? Ginnnnnn! Who the fuck bought gin?" I shouted as I tried to account for all the remaining alcohol. "Nobody drinks gin."

344

"You did. You wanted to see if it would help Theodore's upset stomach, remember?" Buddy claimed.

"That's just an old wives' tale. That can't be true. Because I'm sure it made him puke more," I said as I started to line up all the partial bottles of fun. "Oh, there might be a couple dozen bottles of beer in the cooler."

"That's not much. We should have that all gone in a couple of hours. I knew we should have stopped and got more," Johnny said as he took his first swig of gin, followed quickly by a beer chaser. He downed the beer all in one gulp. "Next."

"Jeezzzzzzzzzzzza, you must have been thirsty?" I told him.

"No, not really. I'm just trying to cover up the taste of that upset-stomach remedy of yours," Johnny said. "Ughhhhh. Never buy that shit again."

"You're right." As I took my first swig of that shit, I almost puked myself. "Ughhh, this stuff is god-awful … Oh, I need a chaser."

"Oh, it's not that bad," Buddy said as he jumped in, trying to keep up with us O'Malleys. "Oh, it is." He looked around, trying to figure out where he could spit the leftover taste from his mouth.

"Don't you dare waste that. That is alcoholic abuse to the fullest. Swallow it, Buddy," Johnny warned him as he tried to put his hand out to catch whatever was going to appear to come out of his mouth.

I started in. "I know what you mean. I remember one time … I used to put a bottle of water in the freezer after a night of drinking. So when I got up in the morning, I would have a somewhat frozen drink of water to help with the oncoming hangover that was going to happen," I remembered. "It was great for a while. Anyways, one-time Sandy had poured the water out and replaced it with gin sometime in the middle of the night. It was like she was paying me back for something I didn't do, or maybe it was for something I did. Imagine, me doing something wrong, right? … Anyways, the next morning I needed something to drink quick. Besides being drier than a popcorn fart, I had this explosion of pain going off in my head. Any second I believed my head was going to explode or pop off."

"I have had headaches like that."

"Me too. You just want to die."

"It hurt so much; I was just wishing my head would pop off. I grabbed a handful of Extra-Strength TYLENOL, some B-12s, and grabbed for that cold, wet, half-frozen bottle of water out of the freezer. I opened it and took the biggest gulp I could muster, hoping for a brain freeze. Or at least some kind of pain relief …"

"You didn't …" Buddy fretted, but he knew the answer before I had finished.

"Yeah, I did, and all I got was gin, gin, and more gin. The next thing I knew, total projectile. I didn't even get the TYLENOL down. They spewed all over the inside of the freezer. I remember puking and puking some more. I even brought up corn niblets, and I knew I hadn't had corn for at least a week. Sandy, was she ever pissed! She cut me off for a week and made me sleep on the fucking couch. But the worst thing was, she made me clean it up. Magine … me, cleaning?"

"She didn't! Gin will sneak up on you like that." Buddy pitied my misfortune as he examined his gin drink to make sure there weren't any hallucinogenic stimulants floating around.

"Yeah, so from that day forward, I always smell before I drink," I answered as the three of us were sitting around trying to inhale all of the leftover booze we had. Some of it went down well, whereas some of it went down really harsh. A few of our golfing holidayers came in to help, while some of the lightweights had a quick drink and off to bed they would go. I could see that the majority of this work would have to be done by us three, the Three-Amigos. As each bottle was finished, we would throw it over to the vacant bed in the corner. If someone would have walked in, they would have thought we had a drinking contest going on. It was more than a drinking contest. It was us three heavyweight combatants going toe to toe to see who could last the longest. We were playing chicken with booze. We were waiting to see who would tap out or say when. The problem was, sometimes you were so drunk that you could not tap out or even talk for that matter. You just didn't want to lose. Besides being labeled a loser, you'd lose all kinds of bragging rights. But the worstest was the stuff that would happen to you while you were passed out. I'm not talking about the little stuff, like drawing cocks or boobies on their forehead. I'm talking about actually doing something to them, like duct-taping them naked to a tabletop covered in booze bottles or putting them on a bus or train with a one-way ticket with no money.

Probably one of the greatest; was when we put a plaster cast on someone's arm while they were passed out. Considering how drunk we were, we must have done a pretty good job fabricating that cast, because the next morning he really thought he had broken his arm. We had even drawn on his cast and, of course, signed it. So it had to be real. Originally the thought was after he woke up the next morning, we would tell him it was all a hoax. But we had him believing that he had climbed a tree drunk and could not get down. We talked him into jumping down; I think we had promised him more tequila if he came down. This was where he had broken his arm in his drunken stupor. We had him believing that he was the luckiest guy alive, as he could have easily broken his leg or his neck for that matter. And when he started looking for some painkillers to ease all of his pain, we had to keep the deception going. I came up with the hospital not prescribing any pain erasers because he had too much alcohol in his system. I told him that they had advised him to see his family doctor when he got home. And us being in the States, he wondered how he had paid for the ER. Of course, I stepped in and told him that I had paid for it and that he owed me $683.92. That was US money, so that was pretty close to a $1,000 Canadian. He finally did pay me when we got home, but that was not the best. The best was when he had to go out on the streets to find painkillers to ease the pain of his nonbroken arm. This went on for weeks, him whining about not being able to stand the pain. I think we almost got him addicted to Quaaludes. I think he missed about a month of the golf season, which he was just livid about.

His whining got so bad that we decided to take Buddy out—I mean the lightweight out drinking one night. You guessed it; he passed out again. So we cut that fucking cast off his arm; we'd had enough of his whining, but more importantly, we were losing out on a bunch of golf bets.

We were so drunk that night, we almost cut his arm off doing it. We started with a SAWZALL but ended up using my high-speed Dremel tool. Remember that when you are trying to cut safely, you should not be drunk. Or as they say, "I'm a trained professional; do not try this at home." The next day he woke up and wanted to know where his cast had gone. So we had to come up with something clever, like he made us cut the cast off. He was tired of his broken arm. A couple days later, he went to his own doctor to see if his arm would be all right without a cast. They did x-rays. And wouldn't you know it? His arm was completely healed. Well, except for a couple deep cuts from the power tool … Praise the Lord, he was healed … So we had to go out and celebrate once again.

We only had a couple of hours left before we would have to get up to start our last leg of the trip home. It looked like we would not have a winner tonight. We stood up with our last drink in hand and toasted each other on what a great trip we had.

"Buddy, go the fuck home. I've got to go to bed," Johnny ordered as he stumbled back toward the bathroom. "All the booze is gone, so you have to go."

Deciding that it was time for him to go home to his own room, Buddy piped up, "See you fuckheads in a couple of hours."

I got into bed just as Johnny came back from the washroom naked and said, "I guess I'm sleeping with you."

"Like fuck you are," I screamed.

"Look at the other bed; you covered it with all of your empties," Johnny came back with as he pointed over toward the covered bedspread.

"My empties?" I looked around as he tried to get into my bed. "I think you did some of that."

"Do you like to be spooned? Or are you the type that likes to spoon?" Johnny laughed as he snuggled up against me. "Now just relaxxxxx and breathe …"

"Fuck off," I cried as I climbed out of bed, went over to the other one, and threw the blankets back, throwing most of the empties to the floor.

It wasn't long before we fell asleep, and out of the blue, the phone rang. "Ringgggg … ringg … ringggggggggg."

"This better be important," I screamed as I picked up the receiver. I was not very happy to be woken up at five in the morning; but then it was okay as the song "Highway to Hell" started to play.

On the other end of the phone came the most cheerful and sexy voice that you would ever want to hear in the morning. "Good morning, sir, and how are we this fine morning? Mr. O'Malley, do you know where your keys are?"

"Of course I do … Well, I think I do," I answered, and then my attention went to trying to wake Johnny up. "Hey, Johnny. Johnny, wake up … Hey, fuckhead." Johnny did not flinch; he did not move an inch. I guess there was no waking the dead. "Where'd you put the keys?"

"Sir, can you check for me?" she kindly asked over the phone.

To get up to look for the keys, I swung the blankets off me; knocking more broken bottles to the floor. Just as my feet hit the floor to look, I was hit with massive amounts of sharp pain in my feet. "Ughhh … Oh, awww … Jesus Christ, that hurts." I was stepping on shards of glass as I tried to find the light switch. "Johnny, why in the fuck is there broken glass all over the floor?"

"Sir? Sir, are you all right?" I heard over the receiver as I walked over toward the door.

I swung the door inward to reveal the keys were indeed in the outside lock, just as I thought. "Yes, they are in the lock just where I left them." I stated this back over the receiver, and then I realized that there I was, standing naked in the doorway in front of the night manager, Bobby-Joe.

There she was standing there, talking on her phone to someone. "Yes, sirrrrrrrrrrrrrrr … Sweet Jesus, I can see that …"

I finally realized that she was talking to me on the phone. I took my handheld phone and embarrassingly tried to cover my piss-hard-on with it. There was no comparison; I conceitedly had that phone beat by half an inch or so.

Blushing, she turned her head a little, but her big blue eyes never left my unit. Even though she stood right in front of me and didn't need to talk to me over the phone anymore, there she stood, still speaking over the receiver, trying to trick me. She sincerely said, "Sir, I just wanted to make sure you were all right and that you knew where your keys were."

Being tricked a little more, I raised the phone up to my ear and shyly said, "Well, thank you." Then I quickly moved the phone back down to cover up my privates.

Still talking to me over the phone, she sexily said, "Can I get you anything else? Or can I help you out with …" It was like she didn't want to leave the conversation or go back to her boring desk job. Not realizing what I was doing, I brought the phone back up to my ear and said, "No, I better not." And just as quickly as the phone went up to my ear,

I quickly put it back down for coverage. I was thinking, if she keeps this up, she will keep me talking on the phone for a while.

Knowing full well what she was offering, I glanced over at Johnny to see if he was still sleeping. "Hey, Johnny, wake up." No movement or sound came from him, but I was sure he was faking that he was asleep. I was sure he lay there with one eye open and knew exactly what was going on. And he knew what was going to happen next. So I thought, *Fuck him. I'm not going to give him a free show. Not again ...* I glanced back over at her as I rejected her advances. "No, I better not; I better go." As I shut the door, I hung up the phone.

The phone rang again, and I quickly answered, "Helloooooo."

"Sweet Jesus, sir. You do know your keys are still in the door?" she responded sexily.

"Yes, I know."

"It's your loss. I'm taking them for safekeeping." Before she hung up the phone, she suggested, "If you want them back, I'll be in my office."

Maybe it was a change of heart, or maybe it was I just wanted to give her one more look. As I opened the door, I noticed the keys were gone; and sadly, so was she. I stepped out to see her sexily parade her stuff down the walkway, twirling the keys between her fingers above her head.

I had forgotten all about my glass-laden feet as I shut the door once again. I just wanted to go back to bed as I was sure I had only about twenty minutes of sleep left. I was thinking I would need that sleep; it would either make the day or ruin it. Just as my head hit the pillow, the alarm went off. That had to be the fastest twenty minutes ever. My head still hurt, I was still tired, and I started to think about the dream I had about the night clerk. It must have been a dream, because if it was real, I surely would have asked her in. Then I started to feel the many cuts on the bottoms of my feet. Maybe it wasn't a dream. But then I talked myself around in a circle. Am I losing my touch? No, it had to be a dream. I pulled the blanket off, and more of the bottles hit the floor.

Johnny woke up all refreshed. As he stretched, he said, "Will you keep from breaking any more bottles over there? All night long, you just kept kicking more bottles to the floor. You kept me up most of the night."

"I'm not sure how I got all this broken glass in my feet," I said as I sat on the edge of the bed examining my feet. "Did we go out in the middle of the night? Is there any kind of alcohol left that I can pour on my feet?"

"I don't know; I don't think so," Johnny answered. "I slept like a baby." Maybe Johnny was asleep all along, because he did not mention anything about the night-clerk.

We were all packed up and loaded in the van when I said, "Oh, I forgot to check out. I will be right back. This won't take long."

"You don't need to check …" Buddy informed me.

"No, I do. There might be extra charges or something."

"There won't be unless you watched porn all night." Buddy argued.

"No, I really do have to go in."

"No, you don't. Stay in the fucking van," Buddy warned.

"This won't take long. I forgot to hand in my key. Yes, that's what I've got to do. Hand in the key," I reported as I climbed out of the van. "Go get some breakfast or something. Pick me back up in twenty minutes."

I overheard Johnny ask Buddy, "How's the underwear? Pretty comfy, eh? Don't get too used to them. I want them back."

"Want them back? I don't think you want these back," Buddy answered as he adjusted his bottom around on his seat.

So I jumped out of the van and rushed in to … to … hand in the key; yeah, hand in the key. I think I must have set a new world record for handing a key in. I was sitting on the curb waiting for them when the van pulled up alongside and Johnny yelled out the window, "Hey, Kid, did you get the keys back?"

"Yes, sweet Jesus, I did."

"Good. I was afraid that I was going to have to pay for them again," Johnny agreed. "If you would just leave them in the door like MOM has told us to, you wouldn't lose them as often as you do."

"Johnny, you know, I left them in the door. That's how I lost them," I tried to explain.

CHAPTER 25

No Chicken Tonight

As we were traveling through Pennsylvania, Paulie piped up, "Don't forget we have to stop and pick up some legs of chicken."

"Paulie, we are not stopping for chicken," Buddy screamed. "That was last week. It would not still be on sale."

"Do you think?" Paulie cried. "Shannon said we could pick some up on the way home. He promised."

"I don't give a fuck what he promised. I'm driving, and I'm not stopping," Buddy warned as he gave a stern look back in the rearview mirror.

"Buddy, it might even be cheaper this week. Especially if they weren't able to sell it all before it went bad." I argued. "And who knows? Maybe that tree sauce is even cheaper than it was last week."

"I don't fucking care. I'm driving, and I am not stopping," Buddy said. "And besides, Paulie does not have any money left, and I am not lending him anymore."

And just as quickly as Buddy had threatened; it seemed everyone else took their turn around the van and answered. "Money? I'm not lending him anymore … What does he need money for now? … What the fuck is tree sauce? … How cheap was the chicken again? … How much chicken can we smuggle back into Canada?"

"Guys, we are not stopping. And we are sure as hell are not going to smuggle," Buddy cried.

"What about all that extra beer you have us loaded down with?" Paulie cautioned. "Is that not smuggling?"

"Paulie, fuck off. That's only beer. That's not smuggling. That's our national drink; you can't get into trouble for that," Buddy informed him.

"We will see what smuggling is when we get to the border," Paulie threatened.

"Paulie, aren't two of those cases of beer yours?" Buddy cautioned him.

"Well, I would rather have chicken and maple syrup." Paulie tried to make a deal. "Then beer."

"How much do you want for your beer?" Johnny tried to negotiate. "You never can have enough beer."

"What kind is it?" someone asked.

"Old Milwaukee, I think," Paulie answered.

"That's my brand." Johnny's enthusiasm for beer bubbled through. "I'll give you a dollar."

"A dollar? A beer?" Paulie bargained as he tried to calculate how much chicken he could buy. "I'll take that."

"Nooooooooo. A dollar for both cases?" Johnny bartered as he put his hand out to shake.

"Nooooo. They cost me more than that," Paulie argued. "That won't buy me any …"

"Paulie, it did not cost you anything. I'm the one that lent you the money for the beer," I interrupted him. "Those two cases cost me almost thirty bucks."

"I know, I know; but I will pay you back," Paulie promised.

"So let me get this straight. I lent you thirty bucks for two cases of beer to take home to your mummy. And you probably are never going to pay me back. And Johnny lives in the States, so he can buy his Old Milwaukee anytime for that price. And you want to sell them to Johnny?" I tried to reason. "So you can buy some fucking American chicken that is pumped full of antibiotic steroids and whatever else they can get into that pump."

"Yes, I think you have just about got it," Paulie agreed. "What do you think that pump looks like? That they pump up the chicken with?"

"Well, I've seen pictures of them. The funny thing is they hire these people to run around the chicken coop trying to catch the birds." I tried to convince them. "I think they call them chicken wranglers or chicken hawks for short. And, Johnny, you will like this. They have found pork skin in some of the lesser-quality chicken brands. I think this is where they get 'pork is the other white meat.'"

"I guess we should stop and get some of that juiced-up chicken, then," Johnny added. "Who wants to stop and get some porky chicken?"

"No, let's just get home," someone reasoned.

"So, these chicken-hawks race around the coop trying to catch these birds. And when they catch one, they drag it over to this conveyor belt, where they will sit down with this chicken on their lap. Keeping a firm grip around the chicken's throat, so they don't get away. Some of the better chicken hawks will sit down with two chickens, one in each hand," I lied as I tried to confuse Paulie a little more.

"I wonder what they make an hour," Paulie asked.

Buddy interrupted. "It doesn't matter, Johnny. He is not selling you the two cases of beer for a dollar. That's just stupid."

"Buddy, will you shut the fuck up?" Johnny scolded. "Can you not see that we are in negotiations?"

"Yeah, can you not see that we are in nego ... negot ... negotiat ..." Paulie cried, as he was having a tuff time pronouncing the word. "We are trying to make a deal here."

We were on our last leg homeward as we dropped Johnny off in Syracuse on the edge of Interstate #81 and Thruway #90, the exact same spot where we had picked him up. I believe his wife Patty or one of his kids was picking him up later. He would survive as the sun was shining, and it was only about zero degrees Celsius. We left him secured with a six-pack of Old Milwaukee and a couple of bags of his much-loved pork rinds. We still had about another three hours on the road to Canada. I just wanted to get home; we all just wanted to get home. We were all hungover from a week of drinking, and I'm sure we all needed a lot of sleep. Most people went on their vacations to rest; not us—we went on vacation to party. We came home and went to work to rest.

After dropping the others off, I had only one person left in the van to drop off, and that was Paulie. We had to get Pookie home to his mummy. Just as I pulled into the driveway, I saw Mrs. Groper pacing back and forth on the veranda. And you guessed it: the soundtrack from "Three's Company" started to play. You could tell that she was eager for her little fella to be delivered home safely. She looked like she had been waiting by the door since we left. Her housecoat and slippers were the same. What didn't make sense was her whole outfit looked like she was lounging around and ready for bed. But her makeup said something completely different. Her Mary Kay looked like it was professionally done. It was on thick for maximum coverage. Her lipstick was glistening bright red. She looked like she had just stepped out of the salon, as if her hair had been done up for a night out on the town. We climbed down out of the van to get Paulie unpacked; and I noticed that she had discarded her robe to reveal that she was indeed dressed up for a night out on the town. Did she have a date, or was she just all dressed up to welcome her Li'l-Pookie home? She ran over to the van in her slutty red dress to greet us.

"Am I ever glad you are home. I sure did miss you." When I saw her open her mouth to speak, I could see that her Revlon lipstick had streaked her teeth. As she spoke, she was looking at me and not at her Little Pookie Man.

"Hey, Mrs. G, you are looking mighty fine today. Going out tonight?" I asked.

"This old thing? I just thought I would dress up a little to greet my little man home," she anxiously insinuated as she gave me a tight welcoming hug home.

"I'm over here, Mum." Paulie eagerly tried to get his mummy's attention.

"Oh, hi, Pookie. Did you have a good time?" Gertie asked him.

"It was just magical. It was the best trip ever. I wish I could have stayed down there," Paulie answered as he tried to get in between me and his mother for a hug.

"That's nice." Gertie, not interested in her son's answer, asked me, "How about you? Did you have a good time, Shannon?"

"Oh yes, I, we all had such a great time. But some of us looked forward to coming home more than others. I spent most of my week making sure that everyone was safe and looked after. I sure was busy," I answered as she gave me another hug and kissy on the cheek, I'm sure leaving a big red Revlon smear.

"I bet you were really busy."

"I sure was," I answered. "Enough about me. How was your week?"

Pookie, trying to get everything out of the van, kept looking over at his mum with disgust and finally interrupted her. "I'm right here. Can you guys give me a hand?"

"You'll be fine. You get it all in the house, and I will put it away for you." Mummy answered him, all the while still looking at me. "I was awfully lonely this week without a man in the house." Winking at me, she gave me another passionate hug. "If you know what I mean." As Paulie took each piece of luggage into the house, Gertie would sneak a big passionate kiss from me, trying not to get caught by her little man.

"That was so much fun. When are we going again?" After Paulie had everything finally into the house, he looked back at me and said, "Shannon, are you bleeding? Your lip looks like it is bleeding."

"No, I don't think so," I reported as I licked my lips, knowing full well it was lipstick. But I was not sure, as Mrs.

G. bit down on my lip real hard on our last embrace. She bit down so hard on my lip, I could tell that she had all of her own teeth, or she sure was using a lot of Polygrip. I might have been a little disappointed, as I had started to think that maybe I was going to miss out on a gummer or two.

"You are just bleeding a little." As Mrs. G quickly took her thumb and wiped all the evidence from my lips, she said, "You will be just fine. Shannon, you sure you don't want to come in for a drink? Or how about a bite to eat?"

"I knew we should have stopped and got some of that chicken," Paulie spoke up.

"Sorry, Paulie. There's no chicken tonight."

"Chicken? Does that mean you had enough money left?" a concerned Mrs. G asked.

"Oh, he had lots of money," I confirmed. "Didn't you, Paulie?"

"Yes, I had lots left," Paulie tried to explain as he pulled his wallet out to show his mummy that he, in fact, had very little left.

"Well, just as long as you didn't run out," Mrs. G answered.

"How about some pancakes or French toast? It won't take me long to turn the waffle maker on." Paulie tried to entice me to stay for supper or overnight so I could help him with all of his manly chores that he had to do, all the while looking over at his mummy to get her approval.

"I've really got to go. I've got to work early in the morning," I apologized as I looked over at the dejected-looking Mrs. G. I was not sure where this situation was headed or even if I wanted it to develop. It was just I was tired and just wanted to get to bed as quickly as possible—alone.

"Sorry, Mrs. G. Maybe next time. Bye, Pookie." I apologized once more as I gave her a little pat on the bottom as she headed up toward the house. "Paulie, don't forget about your mother's two cases of beer."

"Oh, I almost forgot. Thanks, Shannon."

"Oh, and I almost forgot," I said as I gave her a flirting wink. "This is for you. Paulie said you could always use more."

"Huhhhhh?" Mrs. G questioned as she pulled the bottle of Tarn-X out of the brown paper bag. She started to blush as soon as she finally clued in. "Maybe you should come over sometime, and we will polish up some silverware."

"Okay, it's a date."

CHAPTER 26

I Swear to God

I no sooner got in the door than the phone was ringing. It was either Mom or Mrs. G. It was Mom; I sort of knew it would be her. I was sure she was just checking in to see if everything was okay and probably wanted to know about the trip. I was thinking that Johnny must have phoned her already and probably let her know about some of the shenanigans that we had pulled off that week. Boy, was I wrong …

"You got me," I answered the phone.

"Hello, Shannon. It's your mom. It's about time you got home. I've been calling you it seems forever. Were you ever going to call me?"

"Hi, Mom. Yes, I just walked in the door. It took a little longer than I expected to get everyone home safely."

"Safely? What about your poor brother?"

"Yeah, I dropped him off about three hours ago. He should be home."

"I know. He just called me. He just got home himself."

"Just got home?"

"Yup. He was crying."

"Crying?"

"Yes, crying. He was so upset that you dropped him off in the middle of nowhere."

"Dropped him off in the middle of nowhere?" I thought back … *That's not right … What's he trying to pull now? … This all doesn't make sense.* "Mom, that's not right. I dropped him off in exactly the same spot that I picked him up from." I fumbled with words to try to appease her concerns. Thinking back, I should have just licked my wounds and said, "Yes, Mom. Johnny is the best. Johnny is right. I must have been mistaken. How could I have ever disagreed with you? I stand corrected. I love you. Bye." Because I knew he had loaded her mind full of all his lies and untruths.

"He said you dropped him off in a snowstorm, on the side of the thruway, in the middle of the night with only a six-pack and a bag of pork rinds. One bag? What were you thinking? It was a very busy intersection. It was dangerous. He could have gotten hurt."

"But, Mom …"

"But, Mom, nothing. One bag; what were you thinking? Sometimes *I swear to God.*"

"I don't know what he has told you, but that's not what happened."

"Are you calling your brother a liar? *I swear to God.*"

"Oh no, I would never call him a liar."

"Well?"

"But, Mom, I'm not remembering this. I'm sure I dropped him in the same spot as usual. I'm sure I put him in Pat's car. I even gave Pat a kiss and hug. I'm sure I did.

And, Mom, it wasn't in the middle of the night. Look, it was only about three hours ago."

"Shannon Paddy, that's nothing like what he told me …" I knew she was getting upset with me when she used her line "I swear to God" more than once. And when she called me Shannon Paddy. She only called me Shannon Paddy when she was fully pissed with me or when she was taking Johnny's side. "He said he had to take a taxi home. It cost him one hundred thirty-eight dollars. He would like you to reimburse him. And, oh yes, he wanted me to remind you that it was US money."

"But, Mom …"

"But, Mom, nothing," Mom scolded me. "And what's this about you making him drink Old Lady's Gin? You know that doesn't go with pork rinds."

"Well …"

"And what about all this cheap chicken that was on sale somewhere in Pennsylvania? And you wouldn't let him buy any. Or for that matter, you wouldn't let him buy any for me."

"Mom, you wouldn't have liked it. That chicken was so pumped up with stuff that it shone; it actually glistened."

"Glistened? And what is wrong with something that shimmers?"

"I was totally wrong, and Johnny was totally right; I should have let Johnny buy … No, Mom, I should have bought you the chicken. What was I thinking?" Knowing that I could not win this argument, I tried to make things right by making it sound like her favorite was right as usual.

"You have to start listening to your brother. He is older and much wiser," Mom pompously scolded me. "And what was this about you going motorboating? You know you can't swim. You wouldn't even let your poor brother drive the boat. You only let him rev the engines once or twice. *I swear to God.* Sometimes ..."

"He told you about that?"

"Yes, he told me about everything."

"Everything?"

"Yes, everything."

"Okay, Mom, I'm so sorry. Next time I will let him drive the boat. Hell, I will even buy him a captain's hat."

"That's more like it," Mom reprimanded me. "And who was this designated driver you hired? Don't you think you should have hired someone who didn't drink or at least someone who could have handled his liquor?"

"Mom, his name was Theodore. He is a great guy. He didn't even know he was allergic to alcohol until he spent a week with us O'Malleys. He spent most of the trip either in bed or the bathroom."

"Poor fella. I can't imagine being allergic to booze. Can you?" Mom added. "He probably will never go with you guys again, will he?"

"Oh, he might. He had the one good day, the day that he and Johnny went to get his new teeth carved."

"So what are you saying? Maybe you are the bad influence."

"Well, maybe, but ... noooo ..."

"Can you tell me again why all of you went golfing that day instead of going with your poor brother to get his teeth? He was disappointed that you all didn't go with him," Mom scolded me again.

"I didn't think it was a big deal." As soon as the words came out of my mouth, I realized that it was the wrong thing to say, and I was going to get an earful.

"No big deal? … *I swear to God,*" Mom cried, as she was getting annoyed with me. "Sometimes I don't think you use your brain that God so generously gave you."

"Well …"

"You know he needed your support that day. Getting new teeth is a very big deal," Mom answered. "You don't know, you just don't realize, you don't have dentures; one of these days when you need them, I'm sure he'll be there for you."

"I know he will," I approved, as I was trying to divert some of the pain that she was going to inflict on me.

"It can be quite devastating, you know, to get new teeth. It changes your looks. It changes your whole outlook," Mom informed me. "It's a good thing he is the best-looking O'Malley and is so confident in whatever he does."

"Yes, Mom …"

"It's just … it would have been nice if you all would have gone with him to give him a little moral support. I can see him now, just sitting in that cold, drafty waiting room all by himself. And with all those toothless people there, just eyeing him up and down, trying to count what teeth he has left. You know, most people would have just walked out. I just can't imagine; what he went through. I can feel his pain."

"I know. I screwed up. Mom, I'm so sorry. It will never ever happen again." I asked for forgiveness.

"Okay, I forgive you, but it's not me. It's your brother who needs the apology. He was the one who was all upset with you. He was devastated. I think he was crying a little."

"I will call him tomorrow and apologize. I promise."

"That's nice. But maybe you should call him right now," Mom pleaded. "You know, so he can ease his mind and get a good night's sleep."

"No, I will do it tomorrow. He probably has gone to bed by now. I don't want to wake him."

"Good idea," Mom agreed. "And make sure you compliment his new carvings. He said you didn't even notice."

"I didn't? Oh, I will when I get him on the phone. Boy, will I ever."

"Johnny was talking about some Paulie fellow on the trip? I hope it wasn't that Paulie Groper, was it?"

"Yeah, it was him. Why?"

"Because is he still sleeping on his mother's couch? Gertrude, isn't it? I haven't seen her in years."

"Yeah, that's him. God, he is an old woman. His nickname is Pookie."

"Tell me, is she still wearing too much Mary Kay?"

"Yeah, she's still layering it on thick." I agreed as I took the back of my hand and tried to wipe some more evidence from my swollen lip; even if she couldn't see it over the phone.

"I can see it. I think she must have shares in the company. Johnny also was telling me about all the maple syrup he eats. He puts that stuff on everything. You know you will get blamed when he becomes a diabetic?"

"Why?" I was trying to think what Johnny had filled her mind with now.

"Buying him pancakes and syrup every morning and having extra syrup come at every meal," Mom answered. "Nobody should eat that much syrup, especially on everything. And putting him on the winning golf team every day just so he didn't have to eat grits."

"But, Mom, Pookie was like a little kid. I don't know how we put up with him all week."

"Okay, okay. And he also mentioned you guys shared a room last night. You lost the keys to the motel room. What's that all about?"

"Oh, I misplaced the keys for a while, but it all ended up real good in the end. Everything worked out."

"Have I not taught you guys anything? What is it with you? Do you not listen when I speak? Do I just flap my gums to hear myself speak?"

"No, Mom, I hear everything you say and some. I really do."

"Well, then how did you lose the keys then? Have I not taught you to leave the keys in the door? That way, you won't lose them. And you will always know where they are at all times."

"It's a long story ..."

"I've got time. Well, I'm an old lady, so just give me the short version, okay?"

"Well, I did leave them in the door, just like you have showed us over the years."

"Then how did the night manager get hold of them? And how did she lose them?"

"Lose them? She didn't lose them ..."

"That's not what Johnny told me."

"Uhhhh, so what did Johnny tell you?"

"Nothing much, nothing at all. All he said was you guys had a great supper and went back to the room to have a quick nightcap before you guys went to bed for a good night's sleep. And somewhere between supper and getting up in the morning, you lost the keys."

"That sounds about right, but the main thing was I was able to get them back."

"Oh, I almost forgot. He said something about almost being trampled by a pack of trolls."

"A pack of trolls? Oh, that's right. I almost forgot about all the lightweights in the group; they were running back to their rooms before they shit their pants."

"What about you shitting your pants?"

"Shitting my pants? He told you I shit my pants. I didn't shit my pants. That was all the lightweights."

"Okay, maybe it was all the lightweights that he was making fun of. But you made fun of his shitty-colored shorts."

"Yeah, I did."

"Well, you shouldn't. You know your brother is very sensitive about things like that. You know he has feelings."

"Mom …"

"Well, he does. And he wanted me to tell you that the brown color is the natural color of those Fruit of the Looms of his."

"Okay, I'm sorry, Mom. I will buy him a new pair of shorts."

"Good, seeing you ripped his best pair. You might want to buy him two pairs."

"Two pairs? Why two pairs?"

"Because you should replace the pair, he lent Buddy. He really doesn't think Buddy will give them back."

"Why?"

"Something about Buddy probably will not want to give them back."

"And why?"

"Well, as Johnny put it, besides the color, Buddy is going to find out that they are going to be the most comfortable pair that he has ever put on. These prize possessions are over forty years old, and they are stretched and worked in so perfectly, they won't pinch or creep up on you or gather at the waist. They have that perfect bacon-type waistband. And talking about bacon, they have the perfect balance of pork-rind flavor and cotton-ball texture. His balls are fully cupped for maximum comfort."

"Thinking about it, I guess you are right. But I'm thinking that maybe Johnny wouldn't want them back. You know, something about Buddy's nutsack touching something that would touch his ... And it's Buddy. We just don't know where Buddy has been half the time ..."

"*I swear to God*, will you quit saying all those bad words in front of your mother? Jack, you really have to get over this phobia of yours. It will get you in the end."

"But, Mom, it's Buddy ..."

"Buddy nothing," Mom scolded me for the umpteenth time. "And what's this about you guys not letting poor Johnny play that harmonica? You know he has all the musical talent in the family."

"Talent? What talent?"

"Now, don't be like that. Just because that musical train blew right by you and all of your brothers and sisters, you don't need to be bitter. He has the gift."

"But, Mom ..."

"But, Mom, nothing. You just know who has all the musical ability growing up. All you had to do was watch him in the bathtub farting. Besides a good rhythm, it was a sight to be seen; all those bubbles, bubbling to the ceiling, bouncing off the ceiling fan. You know, if they would have had *'America's Got Talent'* way back then, I would have signed him up. I'm sure he would have won."

"It was more like the *'Gong-Show,'*" I answered under my breath.

"Whattttttt did you say?"

"Oh nothing, nothing at all." *I swear to God*; she has the bestest hearing out there. "Well, Mom, it was not like we wouldn't let him play it. He only blew on it once, and then Buddy threw it away."

"Buddy threw it away? Why would he do that?" Then Mom informed me, "All I know is that you guys probably missed out on one hell of a musical performance. I'm sure it would have brought many tears to your eyes. Listening to him would have just made you want more."

"Uhhhh … Oh, it was just Buddy being Buddy; he just gets all caught up in the moment, and sometimes he forgets where he is or what he is doing."

"That doesn't sound like Buddy at all. He has always acted like a gentleman when he has been around me."

"We are talking about Buddy, Buddy Parker, right?"

"Yes. Maybe you and your brothers pick on him too much? There is a limit to how much someone can take, you know. I know Wilhemina would never raise him to be like that. How is Wilma? I haven't seen her and Hank for years. They are such a sweet old couple."

"Pick on Buddy too much? This doesn't sound like you. What have you done with Mom?"

"Shannon, I'm right here. I'm only kidding. I guess if you are going to pick on someone, you should pick on Buddy and not your brother. How is Buddy anyways? How is he still alive? You should bring him over for a visit."

"How long did you talk to Johnny on the phone for?"

"Oh, not long enough. I know it was not long enough. I had phoned over to see if he had got home safely, and he was all upset about the taxi ride home. As he said, he was wondering if he had done something wrong to deserve such a bad ordeal."

"Mom, I thought we had discussed this … that he didn't take a taxi home."

"Shannon Paddy, are you calling your brother a liar again?"

"No, Mom, I would never, ever call …"

"Then …"

"It's just sometimes he forgets when he drinks."

"Drinks? Are you saying what I think you are saying?"

"I don't know what I am saying."

"Well, it sounds like you are saying he has a drinking problem."

"Oh no, Mom. What I'm saying is the only problem I can see he has is when he runs out of beer."

"Runs out of beer? Are you calling him an alcoholic? *I swear to God* I should just come over there and wash your mouth out with soap. *I swear to God*, I should."

"Oh no, Mom. You know the way he is when he drinks. He can't stop. You know …" I rethought what I was about to say. So I changed my thought process because I was about to get in trouble with her for calling her favorite a drunk and for arguing with her. "When he drinks, he can't stop eating pork rinds. He is forever picking pork crystals off everything he comes in contact with …"

"I don't see the problem here."

"But, Mom, he is like … he just finishes off one of those bags of artery-clogging shit, and he wants more. He is like a druggie clamoring for his next fix."

"Those are pretty harsh words there …"

"But I'm just worried about him."

"So what are you calling him? An alcoholic? Some cracked-up whore? Or a pork-alcoholic …"

"A pork-rind aficionado. Yes, that's what he is," I tried to explain. "And heaven forbid you buy him the wrong brand."

"Aficionado? You are using pretty big words in front of your mother …"

"No, that just means he is a connoisseur …"

"A what? *I swear to God.* Don't be calling your brother names behind his back, especially big names. What have I told you about using big words? If you can't spell it and you don't know what it means, then don't use them."

"Uhhhhh, all that is … is a … one that is a … you know … he loves pork rinds. That's it." I stumbled with the words as I tried to compliment my brother. "And his favorite brand has those chewy, crunchy membranes in it. You know, the ones that get stuck in your throat or back teeth. It's like chewing on shrimp shells. I think they are the cheapest kind. I believe that when they clean out that smoker once a year, that's what's leftover."

"I see you are changing the subject here. Can you spell it?"

"Yes, I can spell it," I bragged. "P-O-R-K …"

"Not pork rind. Everybody can spell that. Try commiesewer."

"Yeah, I can spell it. C-O-N-N-A-S-E-W-O-R … Yeah, that's got to be close … connasewor."

"Okay, I guess you can spell it," she answered. Was I ever relieved that she knew how to spell it and that I didn't make her look stupid. "And what was this about you making him sit in the back—in the trunk, I think he said?"

"Mom, we drove down in a van. There was no trunk."

"Even so, why would you make him sit in the back? You know he gets nausea back there. You are just lucky he didn't throw up."

"It was the only place where we could fit him with all of his beer and bags of pork rinds. It made him very happy to have all of his prize possessions close by."

"You seem to have all the answers here."

"No … no, I wouldn't say that. I just want to make sure I have all the right answers."

"And you finally got to stop by Buddy's hometown? Did you meet some relatives?"

"Yeah, we finally did get there. It's quite the place. You can't miss it. They have signs everywhere."

"Signs everywhere?"

"I think they have them every mile or so."

"What? Just so Buddy doesn't get lost?" I'm sure, in her mind, she was picturing every sign with Buddy on it.

"Yeah, you don't want him to get lost, do you? Remember the last time? He wandered around for weeks."

"We never did figure out where he was, did we?" Just when I thought, or I was hoping that, we had got her off her favorite subject, Johnny, she came back with, "Tell me about all that money you took off Paulie the first night? Did Johnny get his fair share?"

"Oh yes, he got his share and some."

"Are you sure? Was it not his idea?"

"I guess you are right. I guess he should have got a little more."

"A little more? By his calculations, you ripped him off and yourself for that matter."

"Mom, did Johnny ever go to school? Because I have to think that numbers isn't one of his strong suits."

"*I swear to God.* Are you calling your brother stupid again?"

"Oh no, I wouldn't …"

"Okay, I know he is no Rainman," Mom interrupted. You have to understand that we already had a Rainman in our family. Our brother Randy was the numbers guy. He could rattle numbers off with the best. Problem was, no one knew if they were right or not. "He is no Randy, but he tries. When he starts to spit all those numbers out, you should pay more attention."

"I know, Mom, but the only numbers Johnny seems to get right are his daily consumption of six bags of pork rinds to twenty-four cans of beer."

"That seems to be about right. But I start to worry when his bags of pork rinds start to grow."

"You don't worry about twenty-four cans of beer?"

"Are you calling your brother an alcoholic again? *I swear to God …*"

"No, not at all. But if that ratio of beer cans goes up, the bags of pork rinds go up, and as I said before, no one should have that much piggy shit in their veins. One of these days, his arteries will just give up and close."

"Well, if you put it that way, now I see where you are coming from. You do love your brother."

"Oh yeaah, I wish I could love him to death …"

"And what do you mean by that?"

Trying to figure out what to say next, I came out with an answer that I thought would save me from being reprimanded again. "I love him. I wish I could be just like him. I will try harder."

"Okay, but you will never, ever be able to fill his shoes." Mom shut me right up as I tried to save myself. "And what was this about you tipping one of those Johnny-on-the-spot washrooms over? He said he almost got some of that green slime all over his brand-new golf shoes."

"Nothing really. We were pulling a prank on Buddy, and suddenly out of nowhere, one of these microbursts hit. It was awful; there was thunder and lightning everywhere."

"And you almost let your brother get struck by lightning? He said it was close. *I swear to God*. What were you thinking? I don't know what I would have ever done if he got hurt."

"Mom, it wasn't that close … Well, maybe. Lightning struck a tree nearby, and a limb came crashing down on the shitter, knocking it over."

"Am I ever glad he didn't get hurt!"

"Why does he have to be so dramatic?"

"Dramatic? He's not dramatic. He's … you know … he's the sensitive one of the family. He can be very emotional at times. And what was that all about being attacked by a possum of boos? That sounds incredibly dangerous."

"A possum of boos? Oh, oh, not possums; it was wyboos. You know wyboos."

"That's worse. There wasn't a posse, was there?"

"Yeah, this course was loaded with them. There had to be hundreds, if not thousands, of them. Not to worry; they weren't after Johnny; they were after Paulie in his yellow shirt."

"They didn't get him down into their hole, into their lair, did they?"

"Oh no … How do you know about posses or wyboos?"

"Have I not told you about your father, when he ran into a bunch of wyboos? It was ages ago."

"No, I don't think you ever did … Well, maybe you have … I don't know … I think I have heard about this. Maybe Johnny has mentioned it before? … I don't think I was even born, was I?" I responded so I could get more information.

"You know your father; he was such a straight shooter … Well, one time he was missing for a whole weekend."

"A whole weekend?"

"Yes, he went missing from Friday night to Monday morning … Nobody saw him that whole weekend. I was so worried. But come to find out, he had been attacked by a posse of wyboos … Thank God he was able to escape and make it back home safe. Or you guys could have all been fatherless."

"Are you sure that's what happened?" I questioned her, as she really had no reason not to believe his story. Other than it was all made up.

"What, are you calling your father a liar now? … God rest his soul."

"No, Mom, I would never do that."

"I'm just glad that you and your brother are okay."

"So what else did Johnny tell you?"

"What else? Well, let me see, there was something about you guys arguing about the size of that catfish I caught a number of years ago …"

"Yes, that's right … I hope you set him straight on how big it was."

"Fifty-three and a half pounds. Don't you remember?"

"Mom …"

"Jack … It was that big. Are you calling me a liar now?"

"Oh no, I would never …"

"Good. Don't you remember when we made a live well out of the bathtub? That big lunker hung over the ends … Remember?"

"Vaguely. I think I was two … But I'm sure you are right."

"Well, it did. It was a big brute. It was a monster," Mom tried to inform me. "You were so scrawny, I'm sure it could have swallowed you whole."

"Mom, I wasn't scrawny. I was just a little small for my age. Thank God I grew out of the phase to become the biggest O'Malley."

"Biggest O'Malley? I'm not too sure about that. Have you not seen the size of Bubbles lately? *I swear to God*; I've got to put her on a diet soon."

"Mom, that's not what I meant. Mom, Bubbles is in her fifties; can't she put herself on a diet?"

"Yeah, she should know better. But if I don't help her, she's not going to do it herself. She will just burst like a big fat bubble, you know."

"Mom, you're not calling her fat, are ya?"

"Nooooo, she's just a little on the big-boned size … Now don't say anything about her weight. You know she can be a little on the touchy side. Poor Russel."

"Poor Russel?"

"Yaaaaaa. Besides Johnny, I don't know how any one of you has stayed married. Patricia, even though she was an island girl, she sure is the lucky one."

"Mommmmmm … island girl … lucky one …" Thinking that the conversation was going nowhere, I tried to end it early. "I've got to get going. I've got to work early in the morning."

"What? You don't have any time for your mother? Maybe I will just call Johnny back."

Not wanting that, I decided to stay on the line a little longer. "All righty, I can talk a little longer … How was your week?"

"Oh, that's more like it. It was just great, but I sure did worry about Johnny a lot."

"But Mom, I told you I would look after him."

"But did you really?"

"Yes, I did."

"Then why was he crying about you being on your last legs or something? I think he said something about you dying. All I know is that he was really upset."

"Dying?"

"Were you planning your death?"

"Noooo … Now I remember. I was talking about how I would like to have an Irish wake."

"Irishhhhhh! … How many times do I have to tell you guys? … We're not fucking Irishhhhh." I could tell that all she wanted to do was spit. See, Mom wasn't sure what we were; it all really depended on what type of mood she was in. Because the next time you brought up our heritage, she would say we were French or Native, or she might even go back to being Irish. See, back then, we didn't need no stinking ANCESTRY.COM to tell us what we were because we knew what we were. Mom was our 23andMe …

"Mom …"

"Well, that's good, just as long as you are not going to die. Johnny will be so relieved to hear that. He also said something about you calling him an effing farmer. What was that all about?"

"I didn't. He was trying to tell everyone about how smart he got once he joined the local horticultural club down in Penn Yan. You wouldn't believe some of the big words he was using."

"Could he spell them?"

"Yes, he could," I lied so I didn't make him look stupid or get me into trouble.

"So I don't see a problem, then. Do you?"

"Oh, no …"

"So, who was this Sally Sue? He thought she didn't like him very well."

"She was the manager at the hotel we stayed at. She was a little bossy at times, but other than that, she just liked to be in control all the time."

"So she didn't have it in for your poor brother?"

"Oh, no. If anything, I'm sure she liked Johnny a lot. It was Buddy she had a problem with."

Two things that I was hoping that Johnny had not brought up were about Sally Sue and those handcuffs. And just as I was thinking this, she came out with, "What was with the handcuffs? Was someone trying to play a practical joke or something?" Am I ever glad that she didn't know the real truth about my master!

"Yesssssss, that's what it was. It was all a joke. Everything worked out in the end."

"That's good. I really wouldn't want your brother to go through the rest of his life thinking he was related to a criminal in jail."

"Mommmmm."

"Well, it's true. He also mentioned something about yellow golf balls. How come you didn't buy any for your brother?"

"Yellow golf balls? I didn't buy ..."

"He said something about you buying balls for Paulie."

"I bought yellow golf balls for Paulie?"

"He said something about WGC. Yes, it was Watertown Golf Course that was selling them or going under? Does that ring a bell?"

"Oh, now I remember. Mom, he wouldn't have wanted them. They were yellow. They were range balls."

"He thought it might make him a better putter."

"Better putter?"

"Yes. Don't range balls have two black putting lines on them for practicing?"

"But, Mom, he is already the best putter in the family."

"I know he is. But what, you don't want him to get better? *I swear to God.* Sometimes I just don't understand you. I should just come over there and wash your mouth out with soap," Mom scolded me. "I didn't raise you or your brothers and sisters like that."

"But, Mom …"

"But, Mom, nothing. I know you think I love your brother more than you. Well, maybe I do, but that is beside the point," she interrupted me to set me straight. "And when you phone him, don't forget to compliment his new teeth that you forgot too. And I mean don't just say, 'Your chompers done look gooder than before.'"

"*I swear to God*, Mom …"

I finally got off the phone with Mom because I couldn't take it anymore. And I had to phone Johnny to set him straight. I dialed his number. Mom's sweetheart, Mom's cannot-do-anything-wrong, Mom's favorite. That swine … that … that beer-swilling, pork-rind-cannibalistic, that lying piece of shit; I had to get that so-and-so on the phone now.

He answered right before the first ring even ended, like he was waiting for my call. That pork-swine commiesewer answered, "I've still got it."

"Like fuck you do," I screamed at him over the receiver. "Don't you dare think I'm giving you any money whatsoever."

"Do you want me to call Mom again?"

"No, I just spent forty-five minutes on the phone with her, and all she talked about was how sensitive, considerate, and thoughtful you are, and how I was a piece of shit," I tried to explain. "How do you do it?"

"Like I said, I've still got it. I done good. I done real good," Johnny bragged.

"Yes, you did. You got me this time …" Not giving him a chance to answer, I hung up saying, "The check is in the mail … Oh, by the way, fuckhead, your teeth look darn well good, considering they are full of termite fissurettes. I love you, you fucker. Bye."

So from that day forward, every time Johnny and me got together and were out terrorizing the rest of the world, he would always phone Mom and complain about me. And in the end, I would always owe him something, whether it was monetary or a compliment. But more importantly to Johnny, it was just to prove to me that he was still her favorite …

The End

Wrapping Up This Adventure

So, as I said earlier, when I first started to write these lies, I just wanted to let readers know how extremely gullible some can be. But I also wanted them to know that with some trickery and a little manipulation, how others can get drawn in further until it is too late.

When I first started to write the book, I was set on the title to be:

The Names and Places
Have Not Been Changed
to Protect the Innocent,
Because I Don't Give a Fuck

But as I wrote more and more, I was finding that I had to keep changing the names and the stories to protect the innocent. See? I do care. Just so you know, everything that I wrote about did, in fact, happen. It's just I had to write it, to make it sound like it all happened to me, when in actual fact; it all happened to all my so-called friends. Your job as the reader; all you have to do is, figure out who it actually did happen to.

I think I had let Buddy read the first couple of chapters, and all he came back with was, "You know, I wasn't that bad, was I? And you can't say all that; that's not the way it happened.... *It's all but lies....*" So, we changed the title to appease and protect Buddy.

The other thing that became apparent as each story was written; was that we were all somewhat racists back then. Not full-blown bigots by any means, but racists, nonetheless. And you will ask, how can you be somewhat racist? It's not that I'm a racist or prejudiced against any minorities. Hell, as Mom would say, "You and your brothers were never raised to pick on those people that way." It's not that we were bigots; it's just that twenty to thirty years ago, we weren't really all that politically correct. Thank God, we have all become somewhat sensitive and edgamacated toward things like that.

Printed in the United States
By Bookmasters